MEMOIRS OF WORLD WAR I

MEMOIRS OF WORLD WAR I

"From Start to Finish of Our Greatest War"

BY BRIGADIER-GENERAL

WILLIAM MITCHELL

RANDOM HOUSE · NEW YORK

PUBLISHER'S NOTE

On March 22, 1926, only a few months after the famous court-martial which forced him to resign from the Army, Brigadier-General William Mitchell wrote a letter to Harvey Deuell, then editor of *Liberty* magazine:

Dear Mr. Deuell,

I have just finished re-writing and adding explanatory notes to my diary of war-time experiences, which I started keeping when I left the United States on March 17, 1917, en route to Spain to look into the possibility of that country's entering the war against France. I was in Spain when war was declared by the United States against Germany. Then I went to Paris and reported at the Embassy, at which time I laid the ground work for our aviation and participation in the war, then joined the French Armies and participated in active operations and attacks, both with the infantry and in the air. It is a record of the first American Officer to actually serve in the Allied armies against the Germans. . . .

I wonder if your magazine would like to handle it in a series of articles when it is finally completed. . . .

Liberty was indeed interested, and on April 7th, Mitchell sent Deuell a 45,000-word manuscript entitled "Before Pershing in Europe," which covered the first months of his adventure in the

v

Great War. It was a good story, filled with observations and technical details about a conflict few Americans had understood at the time—perhaps too many details for the general public. *Liberty* was still interested, but only, it turned out, in what was to come. After all, there was almost a year to cover before pilots of our fledgling air service actually got into combat.

The manuscript grew to a considerable length as Mitchell continued to work on it through 1926. *Liberty* finally agreed to serialize the last part of the book, and these chapters were published in the March, April, and May issues of 1928 under the title "Leaves from My War Diary."

The present book, *Memoirs of World War I,* marks the first time Billy Mitchell's whole story, "From Start to Finish of Our Greatest War" (his own title), appears in print as he intended.

The original diary Mitchell mentioned in his letter to Deuell has unfortunately been lost or destroyed—at least only one small section of it is known to exist—and it is quite possible that it might have made a more interesting document to us today than his expanded version of it. Yet the new version probably represents the diary to a remarkable degree. In many cases Mitchell didn't even bother to change the "present-tense" character of the original document or add transitions or explanations which might have made a smoother and more complete narrative.

He doesn't say, for instance, that while a Captain in the Army he not only learned to fly on his own time but that he had to pay for his lessons himself. About certain individuals he gives odd sidelights, yet forgets things more important about them: he writes that Roland Garros was the first man to loop-the-loop, but neglects to mention that he was also the first pilot to engage the enemy with a machine gun firing through his propeller blades, which were protected by metal plates, thus beginning the deadly war in the air. His comments about General Benjamin Foulois seem unfair to say the least; at one time Foulois was the most active flier in the Aeronautical Division of the Army Signal Corps—and this was long before Mitchell even thought of becoming a pilot. The rivalry between Mitchell and the "old guard" was obviously a bitter one. The full story is not told here and never has been told.

The exploits of Frank Luke, the Arizona cowboy who became the famous Balloon Buster, also receive a somewhat unusual telling here: When General Mitchell recommended to Harold Hartney, Commanding Officer of the First Pursuit Group, a plan to destroy dangerous enemy observation balloons in the early evening he was unaware that Luke, under Hartney's command, had already shot down several balloons in this manner. (A humorous possibility presents itself: that Hartney was in a ready-made position to impress Mitchell with his ability to carry out a superior's suggestion speedily the same way Mitchell himself later was able to impress General Bullard after a similar request.)

This book is not an official or formal history. Rather it is a unique picture of our first great war and the birth of American air power. It is also an unsurpassed portrait of one of the most colorful and controversial figures in our military history. Mitchell was not right in all his many opinions, but at least he always tried to base them on personal observation and not on second-hand information. It is a rare general officer who devotes as much time and energy describing all that he sees and accomplishes as Mitchell did. The details of every gun, plane, wireless set, shell, camera—in short, almost everything—he recorded with meticulous care. He kept his camera with him constantly.

Time-honored theories and customary ways of doing things had little appeal for him. He saw immediately, for instance, that land planes were much better for military use over water because of their superior performance, even though they would necessarily sink if forced down. He believed that airplanes, tanks, submarines and gas—all new to practical warfare and his own experience—would be decisive in the future. He even conceived and almost carried out a daring attack using paratroopers.

Mitchell's flamboyance and energy are in evidence everywhere. His strong sense of history is clearly revealed in the way he constantly related the present to the past. Only a man with a vision of the future role of air power clearer than many and with an ambition greater than most could have accomplished what Billy Mitchell did—and failed in the special way he did.

The original manuscript of this book resides in the Library of Congress. It runs over 560 typed pages. Mitchell himself admitted that some parts of it were "rather technical"—at times the story has the flavor of an official military report on equipment and tactics; it also contains many lengthy official orders, commendation, recommendations and appointments. These have been cut or omitted when it was felt that they would not interest the reader of today. Repetitions, which occur often, were also eliminated, and passages which still inadvertently retain the "present-tense" quality of the original diary were changed to the viewpoint of the rest of the manuscript. Only rarely was a phrase or a transition added for clarity, although occasionally it was necessary to alter the structure of a chapter because Mitchell, again following his diary's lead, would perhaps say "I forgot to mention . . ." and then tell of something interesting which had happened earlier. First names of important people have been added when they could be found, but no attempt has been made to change a date when it seemed to conflict with other records of the period.

Several people deserve thanks for help in publishing this manuscript. Among them are Mrs. Elizabeth M. Byrd, Mitchell's widow; and his daughter, Mrs. Kenneth N. Gilpin; Major James F. Sunderman, Chief of the USAF Book Program; Miss Elizabeth Brown of the Institute of Aeronautical Sciences, Inc.; and especially Marvin McFarland, Head of the Aeronautic Section, the Library of Congress.

Table of Contents

ix

gate aeronautical matters—Aviation Mission under Major Bolling—Recommendation of liaison officer—Lack of cooperation in U. S.—A.E.F. Headquarters—Arrival of 1st Division, St. Nazaire—Visit to Lafayette Squadron with Dr. Gros—Hospitals at Compiègne—Visit to Napoleon's Tomb with General Pershing.

ference with General Degoutte—To Paris—Beginning of the great battle—Discussion with Major Gerard—Flying over battle lines—La Ferté-sous-Jouarre—Up the Marne—I find the German crossing at Dormans—Report to Liggett—1st and 2nd Division and Moroccan Division move to Soissons—The counterattack.

MEMOIRS OF WORLD WAR I

Preface

Much of war history is written to bolster up damaged military reputations or to support views engendered by a jealousy which seeks to minimize the work of others and to show to especial advantage the work done by the authors. Usually it is the generals and superior officers who write and are heard from. They have the records with which to support their views. Seldom do they ever enter into intimate details of execution and combat in the great wars such as the last one.

No nations ever want war; they do not resort to war unless all other means of attaining their ends have been exhausted. War itself is a continuance by physical means of an altercation between nations, and its object is to impress one's will upon the enemy. This can only be done by seizing, controlling or paralyzing his vital centers, that is, his great cities and the sources of raw materials, his manufactories, his food, his products, his means of transportation and his railway and steamship lines.

The old theory, which has been followed for centuries, has been to protect these vital centers against the enemy by covering them with the flesh and blood of the people, putting out in

3

front of them what we call armies. So it was supposed heretofore that in order to obtain victory, this hostile army had to be destroyed, so as to open an avenue to the vital centers. In times past, when the only avenue of approach was over the land, the axiom that the object of war was the destruction of the hostile army in the field was sound.

For an army to obtain victory, according to the methods employed in the European war, it was necessary to kill off the opposing army slowly, and in doing so, to destroy all the resources, material and personal, of the other country. In accomplishing it, the attacker suffered even more greatly than the one attacked. The result of the European war was a more or less lasting exhaustion for all those that participated in it, except the United States which came in at the very end and used up very little of its vital force.

Should a war take place on the ground between two industrial nations in the future, it can only end in absolute ruin, if the same methods that the ground armies have followed before should be resorted to. Fortunately, an entirely new element has come into being, that of air power. Air power can attack the vital centers of the opposing country directly, completely destroying and paralyzing them. Very little of a great nation's strength has to be expended in conducting air operations. A few men and comparatively few dollars can be used for bringing about the most terrific effect ever known against opposing vital centers.

The power of airplane bombs, fire of various kinds from the air, and the use of chemical weapons will unquestionably decide a future war. On the sea, the battleship no longer has the power to decide the destinies of sea communication; that has passed to the submarine. As a result of these changes, we have an entirely new arrangement of the combat forces of a nation. Instead of having merely land and sea forces, we now have three: land, sea and air. It is no longer necessary to pierce first the battle fleet, then the line of armies on land; aircraft, flying over both sea and land, can go directly to the vital centers and reduce them to ruins.

We must now bring together all our defensive forces under one general head. National defense is a thing which applies to the whole country; it is one concrete proposition. It is not a monopoly exercised by what we denominate as an army and a navy. It is no longer a thing removed from the people. National-defense forces and the people must be synonymous. The bodies and organizations which the people created for the purpose of protecting them are merely agencies to carry their will into execution. Armies and navies, or any defense forces, must not become a means of misleading the people and making them think that they are secure, with the object of giving special privileges to these organizations.

Today, armies and navies are entirely incapable of insuring a nation's defense. Air power is the great determining influence in the world's development, both as concerns national defense and economic development. An army's value today lies only in holding the ground, it cannot conquer it. A navy's value lies only in undersea operations, away from the attack of aircraft, because aircraft can destroy any kind of a surface ship that has ever been built or that can be built. Air power, therefore, conquers the opposing state in war by paralyzing its nerve centers; the army occupies the ground so conquered; while the navy, by submarines, attempts to destroy hostile commerce and acts as a means of supply for air forces operating from islands or possessions contiguous to the sea, which require transportation over and above what they can effect through the air. If the total value of national-defense elements be placed at one hundred, air power is worth as much as both army and navy combined; air power is worth fifty, an army thirty and a navy twenty.

It was my privilege to lay the foundations for the participation of our country in the air operations of the last war. This foundation, well laid, was torn to pieces by scheming politicians, both in the army and out of it, which delayed the creation of our air force by many months, causing the wasting of hundreds of millions of dollars and the lives of great numbers of our brave men. If it had not been for the arrangements we made with foreign powers to arm, equip and instruct our men, we would have been perfectly helpless in the last contest. It was not Congress that was to blame for this, nor was it the people; it was the regular army and navy. The attempt by the personnel of these organizations to run them as closed corporations and to furnish misleading information to Congress and the people about the actual condition of our defense is what rendered us helpless in this war and in the wars that have preceded it. To continue to entrust our national defense to these organizations, composed of men trained only as a national police, for duty in time of peace instead of for duty in time of international war, is to jeopardize the existence of our country. What we need is to organize a single department of national defense, and in this organization to give to the citizens of this great country a controlling voice in the development and organization of our national-defense system.

As to the actual fighting, I had the great honor of participating with every branch of the land service in actual combat and of commanding the aviation of the United States and the Allied aviation, composed of American, French, British and Italian forces, against the enemy in the greatest air operations ever known. We could see the utter helplessness of the armies on the ground. They were merely thousands of men led to the shambles, as the result of a faulty system which was entirely oblivious to the meaning of modern war.

Those of us in the air have had a vision of the future which we believe to be unquestionably correct. We do not wish to see our country rendered helpless. Now is the time for us to weigh carefully the evidence of the last war and prepare for any contests that may come in the future. As long as trade endures, and persons or peoples have the desire for obtaining something which they do not possess, wars will result.

In the following pages, I have laid down an imperfect account of my observations and deductions, based on actual experience in the greatest of all wars that have ever taken place on this planet.

1

Before Pershing in Europe

The closing days of 1916 indicated plainly that the United States would have to enter the world war. Notwithstanding the fact that the Wilson administration had been elected on the platform "He kept us out of the war," every move made by it had been directed toward preparing the public mind for what was inevitable. The sinking of the *Lusitania* by German submarines had had a great effect, but still greater was the influence of the foreign loans which were being taken up throughout the United States, in subscriptions as small as one hundred dollars each. It was a clever way of enlisting the interest and sympathy of the people.

The United States, in a military way, was absolutely helpless. The American regular army and navy knew nothing of up-to-date war and refused to be taught, so great was the valor of ignorance in the majority of the directing minds of these services.

In 1914, I had made a report that if the Allies were allowed to float loans in this country, it assuredly meant war for the United States, and I suggested that we should immediately start preparations to meet that eventuality. Had this been done at that time, it would have saved thousands of men and millions of dollars.

9

I was on the General Staff of the United States Army at the beginning of the war in 1914, and handled the information that came in from our attachés in Europe. I kept up the war maps for the War Department, the White House and Congress, that portrayed the progress of the various armies from day to day. I made an intense and accurate study of the strategy and tactics of the warring nations. At first it was the general opinion of the ordinary American individual, contributed to by Allied propaganda in the newspapers, that the Allies would win a hasty victory. This, I was firmly convinced, would be an impossibility without the entrance of the United States into the conflict.

Progress on the ground by the armies had come to a practical stalemate as early as 1916; neither side could advance or retreat. The Russian menace had been removed from the German rear by the destruction of the Czar's armies, and the war had settled down to a gruesome competition to see who could kill the greatest number of men on the other side. The art of war had departed. Attrition, or the gradual killing off of the enemy, was all the ground armies were capable of. The high command of neither army could bring about a decision, and the alarming conviction was beginning to dawn on the world that it must stand by and witness European civilization being destroyed and ruined for many years, if not for all time.

Air operations, however, in contrast to ground activities, were constantly increasing in importance and effectiveness, and it was quite apparent to me that if the war lasted until 1919 or 1920, air power would be the deciding element. Since the Spanish War I had been in the Signal Corps of the army, which was the branch of the service charged with the handling of aircraft at that time. I had known the Wrights, had followed intently all aeronautical development, and while in Washington on the General Staff, I learned to fly airplanes. This I had to do outside of office hours. The only time I could get away was on Sunday; so I used to take a boat down the Potomac River from Washington to Newport News, Virginia, on Saturday night, fly all day Sunday, and be back in the office on Monday.

It was almost impossible to awaken the slow-working minds of our regular army officers to any action. A few took a passing interest, but there was practically no effort made to revise the old military system we had been using since the Civil War. In spite of the fact that the foreigners were ordering a great number of aircraft in this country and taking many of our best young men into their services, we still sat by and did practically nothing. I therefore decided to seek service in Europe and learn as much as possible about the trend of affairs before this country entered the war. I was sure in my own mind that we would enter, and equally as sure that when we did, we would have to be controlled, taught and armed by the Europeans as we knew nothing about that kind of warfare ourselves.

I obtained permission to go to Europe as a military observer for aviation, and left Washington on the 17th of March, 1917, booking passage at Havana on a Spanish ship, the *Alfonso XIII,* for Corunna, Spain.

I wondered if Spain was still capable of playing a decisive role in the world's development. It was feared by the Allies that she might attempt to do that very thing. Situated at France's back door, and hating the French with an old hatred born of the excesses of the Napoleonic campaigns when the French troops invaded Spanish soil, pillaging and sacking the towns, she was in a good position to make her power felt.

Entering the harbor of Corunna between the massive cliffs, we saw several ship's-boats being towed in. Later we found these belonged to a Portuguese gunboat that had been sunk in a surface fight with a German submarine, which, after sinking the boat with gunfire, had towed the crew in the ship's-boats to the mouth of Corunna Harbor and turned them loose. The Germans then bought fish from the itinerant Spanish fishermen off the coast, borrowed lines and fished for a little while themselves, then proceeded to sea.

The whole of Spain was in rather a nervous state. It was flooded with spies from all countries. The subsidized newspapers were filled with propaganda put out by the agents of every belligerent country in Europe, in an effort to influence the people's minds. The English were afraid the Germans might induce the Spanish government to attack France, and the Germans likewise feared the English might prevail on it to declare against the Central Empires. A peculiar situation existed in the royal family. The Spanish queen, Victoria, was an English princess and of course wielded a great deal of influence, not only with the King, but with the whole country. King Alfonso was a Hapsburg and was related to the Emperor of Austria. Incidentally, Spain and Austria were the only two entirely Catholic countries remaining, as such, in the world. These conditions created a balance in the royal family and made for neutrality.

I found that economic conditions in Spain were not good, especially in the agricultural regions, which on account of transportation difficulties could not dispose of their products to the warring nations. In the province of Valencia the great orange crop lay almost untouched. The people complained a great deal. In Barcelona, however, with its great manufactories, considerable money was being made. The wonderful new Hispano-Suiza airplane engine had been invented there.

In Catalonia considerable unrest existed. The Catalans, feeling that they were carrying the major portion of Spain's debts, wanted to secede from the rest of the country, setting themselves up as an independent state. Only the force of the King's character and the love the people had for their sovereign prevented it. Most of the Catalans openly sympathized with Germany, and were said to have offered aid and assistance to German submarines that came and went outside the harbor of Barcelona.

Wherever I went, I was watched by one side or the other, or both of them together.

A commission of Spanish officers had recently returned from a visit to the German army. I talked with one of them. He maintained a very distant and suspicious attitude, as he thought, and rightly, that we would soon be fighting against Germany. The Spanish army, as a whole, undoubtedly sympathized with the

Germans. The King, however, with his usual sagacity, perceived it was much better for Spain to stay out of the war, not only because the outcome was in doubt but because if Spain entered the war, serious internal disturbances undoubtedly would arise which might bring the reign of his house to an end.

My estimate of the military value of Spain, in case she sided with Germany and attacked France, was not high. Her railways and roads were so bad near the French frontier that only with great difficulty could she concentrate her troops there. The troops themselves were poorly armed and poorly instructed. There were no adequate industrial plants for rapidly turning out great quantities of munitions of war and the navies of the Allies dominated the surface of the sea around her coast.

2

War Declared by U. S.

April 6, 1917

Even though I had expected it for some time, I was startled by the actual declaration of war on April 6, 1917, by the United States against Germany. Setting out at once, I reached the frontier at Santander and passed into war-ridden France. The change was astounding. The people looked tired, strained, haggard; no young men were to be seen in the streets. The guards consisted of men over forty years of age. Few horses and mules were to be seen, as all serviceable animals had been sent north to the armies.

Conversations on the train pivoted about the great attack which the French and British were about to make. General Joffre had been relieved of command because he had refused to advise an attack against the German position, knowing full well that the cost in lives would be entirely out of proportion to the results obtained. The French politicians in the Chamber of Deputies had forced a change, and now General Nivelle had superseded the man who had saved France at the Battle of the Marne. General Nivelle was committed to an offensive campaign, and the people, knowing the conditions, were anxious and troubled concerning their fate. France was strained to the breaking point, and she could not hold out many more months without serious consequences.

The work imposed on the French armies had been accomplished at the cost of terrific effort. At the outset, the British army had amounted to almost nothing and the French had borne the brunt of the German onslaught. Each time the Britons were pounced upon by the German army, it was the French who not only had to come to their assistance, but hold their own front as well. As the British army increased in numbers, it naturally became stronger, but the French army, having already passed the crest of available man power, steadily became weaker and less able to resist the crushing impact of the blows directed against it. Yet at this time they were holding more than two-thirds of the Allied front.

I reached Paris on the 10th of April, amid the gloom that pervaded the whole country at that time. The scheme for the spring offensive was for the British and French armies to attack the Germans simultaneously from two sides, but the Germans, knowing this full well, had retired from the front of the British army, destroying absolutely everything for a space of about thirty miles: towns, factories, roads, farms, fruit trees, forests; damming up rivers and canals so as to flood the country, and mining crossroads and all bridges and culverts. It left the British army high and dry for at least two months, as they could not cross this area with all their heavy guns, ammunition and supplies in time to attack the German army before the spring was over.

What a foolish kind of war this seemed, where an army could not advance twenty or thirty miles for months, even with nobody opposing them! How could such an army ever possibly end a war, except by indirect pressure? It seemed to me that the utility of ground armies was rapidly falling to about zero, due to the great defensive power of modern firearms.

I reported to Ambassador Sharp and made the acquaintance of Captain Boyd, our military attaché, later General Pershing's senior aide, and Majors James A. Logan and Marlborough

Churchill, in charge of the military observers. These two men merit more than passing notice, as few officers in our history have rendered as valuable service to their country and received so little credit for it. Long before our actual declaration of war, they had laid out in remarkable detail plans which included the designation of ports at which American troops should be debarked, the railroads they should use, the areas to which they should be assigned for training, what their organization should consist of, their points of supply, locations for hospitals, military schools, parks for motor vehicles, horses and mules. They thoroughly realized that our regular army, bound by red tape and obsolete traditions, would be unequal to the task of organizing, training and handling the vast hordes we were about to throw into the contest. French and British officers of experience had to direct that.

I began the arrangement of an office for handling aviation. No funds were available from Washington, nor would they allot any, even after repeated cables. The French army loaned me two officers, Captains Raulin and Benedict. A French adjutant, Boyreven, who had been badly wounded during the early part of the war, volunteered his services.

After consultation with the French Aeronautic Headquarters, a scheme of organization for the prospective American aviation was prepared. We made up a list of all equipment needed, showing the kinds of airplanes, types of engines and instruments, and an estimate of the raw materials required for the make-up of such planes, including armament and radio, with notations on the probable time it would require to construct them. This complete program was prepared and sent to Washington by April 20th, ten days after my arrival in Paris.

The French were making two-thirds of the airplanes used by the Allies. They were the most practical and efficient planes obtainable, and had we adopted these types and immediately begun production of the necessary planes in French factories, the value of our assistance to the Allies would have been immeasurably increased. While we were organizing our own factories in the United States, we could have immediately augmented French production by sending mechanics and raw materials to their factories. I recommended that this be done and that the Spad, Bréguet and Salmson types of planes be adopted as our standard. Subsequent events proved these recommendations to be sound.

No attention was paid by Washington to these suggestions from me, the person on the ground, familiar with the conditions in Europe. It was the beginning of a series of blunders made by those directing aviation in Washington, which culminated later in that department being virtually removed from the authority of the War Department and put into the hands of businessmen.

The feeling was prevalent in the United States, helped on by British propaganda, that the English, possessing as they did the powerful bond of a common language and common descent, understood us better than the French did. Therefore, our instinct was to favor British equipment and British methods of doing things. This led to a foolish and disastrous move on the part of those in charge of aviation, that is, taking an English airplane for production, which had been made for an English engine, and attempting to put into it an entirely new American engine which had never even been tried out, much less designed in connection with this particular plane. I refer to the De Havilland airplane and the Liberty engine. As it was, this one decision held up the delivery of American equipment to the air forces for an entire year, and constituted one of the most serious blunders that has ever occurred in our military service.

Anticipating that something like this would happen, and knowing that every day counted, I consulted with Daniel Vincent, French Secretary of Aviation, and told him what I thought the United States contemplated doing. In view of this, unless he manufactured a surplus of aircraft, we would be without planes to fight with. On his own initiative and really without authority, Vincent immediately ordered overproduction of

French planes, without which our air forces would have been totally without equipment until just before the Armistice, when the first unsuitable American planes began to arrive.

During this time, France was a prey to all sorts of rumors and agitations, and we were requested to keep wearing our uniforms and talk a great deal about the thousands of men who would come from America in a short time.

Having sent in all the data necessary to start our aviation in Europe, I applied for and received permission to join the French army on the front. I was determined to learn at first hand all I could.

The following ten chapters are based on my diary of ten tremendously eventful days in my life, April 20 to 30, 1917. They constitute the record of the first American officer to serve with the Allies under German fire, and to participate in the tremendous but fruitless offensive launched by the Fourth French Army in the spring of 1917. In this great attack, the French lost about three hundred thousand men in three weeks.

3

The French Army Launches
Its Great Attack

Friday, April 20, 1917

The train was ready to start for Châlons when I reached the
Gare de L'Est in Paris, at 8 A.M. Nearly everyone on the train
was returning to regiments after a ten-day leave in Paris, which
they were allowed about every six months. I was in a compart-
ment with four other officers.

We wound our way forward up the valley of the Marne
River through Meaux, the headquarters of the Prussian army
in 1870, the scene of Von Kluck's operations in 1914 during
one stage of the battle of the Marne, but now a quiet, relatively
unimportant town.

As we proceeded, the signs of the presence of a great army,
which had been growing more distinct, took definite form.
Railway trains laden with wounded men and broken material
passed to the rear, the personnel to the hospitals, the materials
to the factories to be repaired. Going in our direction were new
men and materials to take the place of the maimed and broken.

In the interior of France, everything had given me the impression of being much worn. Things looked old and in need of
repair; but as we approached the great army, this appearance
changed and the nearer we got to the front, the newer things

looked. Here was the whole life of the country, this splendid army which the Republic had kept in being for nearly three years.

When our train stopped in Châlons station, the sound of artillery at once became very evident, as the battle was even then proceeding with great violence. The station was manned entirely by military personnel and among them were two officers from the Aeronautical Headquarters to meet me, Captain Olivier Raulin and Captain de la Colombe.

After introductions, we went to lunch, which was laid out in a little mess building that the air outfit had for themselves. While at table, we saw a battery of long four-inch naval guns, pulled by heavy tractors, going to the front. The guns and carriages were painted in blotchy designs to look like the ground they stood on. The French navy had little to do, and many sailors had been placed in the heavy artillery.

At the end of the luncheon, Major Bose, the senior officer, drank to the United States with champagne made on the neighboring hills. I responded by drinking to France, and those present, and said a few words about the bonds that for another time had brought the two great republics of the world together.

After lunch, we took a motor and started for the front. As we rolled along, the artillery fire became louder and louder until soon it was a continuous roar. Organizations of all kinds, especially artillery, kept going forward. The Germans had made a powerful counterattack and heavily reinforced their lines, and the French were bringing up troops from several directions.

The "sausages" soon came into view, and we could see how steady they were. Each had two baskets and two observers, and they could rise to a height of six thousand feet if necessary. Each balloon was protected by a pair of machine guns on the ground, and the observers carried automatic shoulder rifles with them in the baskets. In case of attack, the balloons could be lowered rapidly, therefore it was quite difficult for airplanes to attack them with success. On clear days, it was possible for observers to see over twelve miles.

We stopped first at the airdrome of the French Fourth Army Corps. The hangars were the usual sectional wooden-frame, canvas-covered affairs, very practical and handy for this work; twenty-eight men could erect one in a day.

The squadrons consisted of fifteen airplanes; each pilot had a machine which was never given to another. Each pilot also had his particular mechanician to whom he intrusted the whole care of the machine. The planes that I saw—and I looked over about fifty in the afternoon—were in splendid condition. Each squadron had a personnel of from sixty to eighty men, depending on the size of the airplanes and what they were doing. They had from four to eight motor trucks, two or three touring cars and two motorcycles. The army park (the repair unit) carried all the heavy repair parts, extra fuel supply, and contained the machine shop.

We saw the airplanes coming and going, bringing back reports and photos. The latter were immediately developed in an auto-photo outfit. There was also a little board house fixed up as a dark room. Cameras with a focal length of from twenty to forty inches and 8 x 10 plates were used. Machines came down to about six thousand feet, or lower, to take photos and ran the risk of getting hit. The photos were very good and were carefully pieced together to give the most detailed information of the ground.

While we were at this airdrome, Captain Victor Ménard, in command of all the pursuit squadrons in the French army, came over to pay me a call. He announced his presence by making a steep glide in his new Spad from ten thousand feet to about five hundred, then did two vertical banks, looped, then throttled and glided slowly to the ground. These Spads were said to have a landing speed of sixty miles an hour, and they certainly did not look to be going any faster. They gave one the impression of being easy to control, very strong and very dependable with their Hispano motor. The Nieuports looked like a thing of the past beside them. I believed that if our pursuit triplanes were equipped with the same motors, they would be even better, although they might not be as stable or as well balanced.

I had quite a long talk with Ménard. He had been a prisoner in Germany and escaped. He had to scale walls, swim rivers and pass through many dangers before he reached Holland, where he secreted himself, finally getting back to Belgium and France.

He considered at least a year necessary for making a good pursuit pilot, and thought no men should be in any of the air services who were not alert physical specimens with good training in athletics and sports.

He left in his Spad, climbed almost straight up to 7,000 feet, then made a spinning dive with his fuselage as the axis. This was absolutely vertical and the rhythm perfect; he then straightened out into a straight nose dive, came out of it, made a couple of steep climbs and descents, then sped away. The Spad was regarded by all pilots with something approaching reverence.

Pilots were encouraged to do all the acrobatic flying possible, to keep their hand in. From what little flying I had done, I believed this to be correct. I saw many of the pilots returning, and all made some maneuver to break their speed as they approached the ground. Their flying appeared to me to be excellent. In America, where our pilots had been trained under non-flying officers who knew nothing about aviation, acrobatics and maneuvers in the air had been frowned upon as being dangerous. The result was that pilots became afraid to fly as they should, and when they got into a dangerous place and had to maneuver, they were incapable of doing so, and disaster ensued.

We left the airdrome and began working our way forward toward the front, through firing artillery, consisting of 340-mm. mortars, tremendous cannons on railway carriages, 200-mm. new and old mortars, 150 and 105 guns and howitzers, while the 75's were spitting everywhere. The guns were firing against the German batteries to cover the advance of the French heavy artillery to new positions, and the Germans were replying with pretty well-placed shots, most of their fire being directed at the very front line.

The tops of the hills and the whole terrain around us looked as though it had been withered by the blast from a mammoth furnace and harrowed by giants. It was like some of the country I once saw devastated by an eruption of Taal Volcano in the Philippines. All trenches and entanglements had been leveled. Not a tree was left standing. It seemed incredible that a flourishing countryside could be transformed so entirely into a desolate waste, resembling a combination desert and lava flow. When they added gas to the implements of war, they could have destroyed the productivity of the soil for years after.

Concealed near us were some thirty of the new French tanks, ready to go forward. Every effort was being made to shield the men from hostile machine-gun fire when they attempted an advance. Never had a more deadly instrument of war been invented than this automatic weapon of destruction, the machine gun. All sorts of body shields of steel and other metals were devised. Some of the shields were pushed along on little wheels and some were held out to the front on short staffs while the men crawled along behind them. This was another indication of the great change that had taken place in ground warfare: no longer could men, unprotected by shield or gas mask, advance against a prepared position. Bit by bit the army was losing its mobility and, therefore, becoming incapable of quickly obtaining a decision over the enemy.

Overhead we saw French pursuit planes heading for the front. They worked in groups of five, which flew in a formation that is difficult to describe. All the machines were at different heights, each about one hundred yards from the other and all kept their eyes on the leader. It was a combat group formation hard to keep, but capable of meeting an attack from any direction. Several of these groups of five could be seen over the lines, also an occasional German machine. The German pursuit

planes fought in groups of three. Every German machine, of
every type, had at least one Vickers gun with five hundred
rounds in the belt. The spring of 1917 had seen the real beginning of grand tactics in air warfare, that is, large numbers of
airplanes acting together under a common leader. This was the
first war in which aircraft had been used, and their scheme of
working and fighting had to be developed as the necessity arose,
and as the planes became more powerful and maneuverable.

At 5:30 P.M. the artillery fire usually grew more intense.
Activity was evident everywhere, as all prepared for the evening.
The shooting up of everything within range occurred just before dark, because both sides knew that the other would con-
solidate and perfect their positions under cover of night, when
their working parties could not be seen. The engineers would
make communications to the front, their telegraph groups busy
stringing wire forward. French equipment, including their
pontoons—the boats used for making military bridges—appeared superior to ours. Where we were woefully deficient in
equipment was very apparent after only a few hours at the front:
it was in aircraft, artillery, machine guns, anti-aircraft guns,
bombs and grenades; in fact, about everything pertaining to
modern war.

We then proceeded to the airdrome of the pursuit squadrons.
There were four here attached to the Army Headquarters. The
commanding officer of the entire French air organization in the
field, Major Paul-Fernaud du Peuty, had flown up in his Spad
from Compiègne to see me, and with him was the famous
Major Felix Brocard who had brought down so many German
machines. (Major du Peuty was an extremely interesting character. He was the only real fighting head the French aviation
had during the war. The others were ground officers, selected
for various reasons with no particular reference to aviation. Du
Peuty finally became so dissatisfied with the conduct of and
interference with aviation matters by these non-flying heads,
that he requested to be relieved from his position in aviation
and returned to his former command, a regiment of chasseurs.

He was killed a few days later, leading his battalion against the enemy. France lost in him not only her greatest air officer, but a man of the highest genius along these lines, whom she could ill afford to spare. I felt that until air forces were removed from the control of ground personnel, this condition would continue to exist. There should be just as distinct a line of demarcation between the air force and the army, as between the army and the navy.) After a good talk together on matters connected with aviation and our participation to the best advantage, du Peuty and Brocard took the air to return to Compiègne, sixty miles away. Major Brocard did not make a very good getaway but the French fliers had complete confidence in their motors, which seemed well warranted.

All the pilots swore by the Hispano-Suiza motor, its only drawback being that they had to watch that the water did not freeze at high altitudes. Each pilot had a different arrangement for reducing the area on his radiator. Most of them had some aluminum strips running in grooves on the periphery of the radiator which could be extended at will so as to cover the front.

The Hispano-Suiza was invented in Barcelona, Spain, and submitted to the French Air Service. It was such a sensitive and complicated motor that the French mechanics had difficulty in making up the first examples; so they took it to Switzerland, to the Swiss watchmakers, who, in the exactness and delicate precision of their work, are unexcelled in Europe. They made the first satisfactory production model; thus, as it originated in Spain and was perfected in Switzerland, the name Hispano-Suiza was a very appropriate as well as a euphonious one.

I formed an impression that the French Air Service was very efficient. This was due to their excellent planes, their splendid mechanics and their well-trained aviators. They were very short of personnel and their losses from air battles and other causes were very heavy. Not every officer was capable of becoming an airplane pilot, very few in fact. Beside such physical and mental characteristics as alertness, splendid eyesight, initiative, endurance, they must have a natural aptitude for the air. This class of men was almost exhausted in France. It was impractical and foolish to attempt to use mediocre personnel for this work, because they would only be killed off, one after another, and added to this would be the loss of the good planes they flew.

The French believed that young Americans coming from universities, proficient in sports of all kinds, would be especially adapted to work in the air. They wanted us to bring our pilots over just as fast as we could train them, as they felt that the war could be ended only by a decision in the air.

We returned rapidly in our auto, reaching the mess shack at Châlons at 7:40 P.M. our time. After a good dinner, Captain Raulin accompanied me to the hotel where they had put me up.

I spread my effects around the room at once and prepared to do all the work possible in the time I was to be on the front, because now that we were in the war, every day counted tremendously. I felt that our people would have more confidence in the actual observations and deductions of one of their own officers and citizens.

The people in the hotel at Châlons at first did not know exactly what to make of me, as I was a different breed of cat from any of the others they had seen. Deep into the night they could hear my typewriter clicking as I wrote up my notes. They speculated a good deal on that, arriving at the conclusion that it must be some strange radio telegraph. One of the women finally spoke to me about the peculiar noise, and I showed her the typewriter and read her some parts of what I had written, which cleared that mystery up. Many of the people really expected to see us with feathers in our hair, like the pictures of American Indians in their books.

4

General Situation at the Front

Saturday, April 21, 1917

When I first arrived, my French was not particularly good. As a little boy, I had spoken French better than English, as my parents had taught us all to speak two or three foreign languages. I lived in Milwaukee, Wisconsin, and at the age of four or five could hardly converse in English. The other little boys made long noses at me and called me "Froggie." This so irritated me that I would not say a word of French for years, but I had always been able to read it, and it came back to me rapidly.

The morning dawned dark and a little rainy, with few indications for a good day, so we decided to see the parks and other organizations of that kind. A park, as the French called it, was a repair unit that accompanied the fighting forces as closely as possible. It repaired things which did not have to be sent back to the factories in the interior, performing much the same service that a garage does for automobiles.

We went to the army photographic headquarters for the aviation, run by a Lieutenant Pepin, who was directly responsible for much of its development. Although I had watched this end of the work and knew as much as I could without actually having seen the latest phases, I was surprised at its excellence, its accuracy of course, the ingenuity displayed on the part of the man in charge of it, and above all its absolute necessity.

In former wars, reconnaissance of the enemy's position was made by mounted men who rode into and around the enemy lines, or by observers stationed on the tops of hills, who drew sketches of the enemy's disposition, or, in some cases, from balloons. Photography was never used. Now every detail of the enemy's establishment was photographed from airplanes and no attack was made until the most complete aerial-photographic reconnaissance had been made. Nothing escaped the camera's eye, and the greatest precautions were taken by both sides to conceal their permanent works which had to remain in position for more than a day or two.

It may be said that no assault was made, nor was one possible, until a complete pictorial record was made of what had happened. From the photos taken of the position, the whole system of artillery preparation was worked out, and as the preparation was continued, the work done was checked up from day to day. I saw one series where it took twenty-one days to destroy the opposing works. It was a terribly wasteful method of advancing. Even when the destruction of everything which could be reached or that was within ten feet of the surface was complete, machine-gunners could come up from twenty-five feet below the ground and cause heavy losses among the attacking troops. Photography is the surest and almost the sole method of determining what has happened.

From the photographic section, we proceeded to the park of the pursuit squadrons. This was installed in the drill area and riding hall of a former artillery post. It was quite similar to a post in our service. Here heavy repairs of pursuit machines were being made. Some Spads had been badly shot up, one in particular, the pilot of which had almost miraculously escaped being hit. The bullet must have gone between his arm and body and cut his safety belt. These belts are like ours, only with a buckle; I think our safety clasps are better. The radiator of the Hispano was all shot up, as were the water jackets and sides of the body. General repairs were being made to this motor and a new one installed. I noticed about a dozen spare Hispano motors in their cases on the floor. All the power tools were being run by electricity from the motor truck machine shops. The usual number of trucks and touring cars were on hand, likewise a good many spare parts. Truly a modern army must carry its factories with it.

There was also a five-ton truck equipped with a generator and eight eighteen-inch searchlights, with stands, to be used for airplanes landing at night. They put two or more lights on the stands about four feet above the ground and far enough apart to give room for landing between. When the landing signal was given by the pilot, the lamps were directed along the ground in the direction of the wind and the pilot landed between them. Signals were given with a form of Very pistol. The cartridges were about ten bore and had charges for one, two or three balls of various colors.

The field tents used at this park were like little hangars, with their wooden frames, glass windows and a door. They were sealed inside by cotton cloth and were as tight as a house. The aviation service was the only branch that was allowed them. They were very careful of the personnel of the Air Service, even the mechanics, as they were very hard to get.

From the park, we went to the army pursuit squadrons. There were four of them, commanded by Captain de la Colombe, who impressed me as a most efficient and energetic officer. His duty was to protect the army photographic machines and to carry out certain attacks. It is a principle that the best defense is a vigorous offense. (In six months the Captain's losses among his pilots amounted to 125 percent.) He was also charged with very distant reconnaissances, and of course this involved photographing. His equipment consisted of Spads, Nieuports, a couple of two-seater Sopwiths, and some Morane Parasols because they could get nothing else. These are two-seaters and armed with a Vickers machine gun in front and a Lewis behind. They had lost a pilot with his observer in a Morane two days before, because the place where the wires are concentrated above the top plane was shot away by a German pursuit machine, and the wings collapsed.

Orders began to come in for certain tactical missions, so I left to look over the army meteorological station. Each army had one, with from five to seven substations that had sounding balloons in addition to the ordinary anemometers for measuring the velocity of the wind, hydrometers for measuring humidity and ground temperature thermometers. The latter were used to tell how much frost was in the ground, from which an estimate could be formed about when troop movements could take place, when considered in connection with the weather predictions.

Meteorological information was furnished each hour to all air and artillery units. Daily reports were made to Army Headquarters and General Headquarters, and a daily prediction chart was made out. There was a radio antenna up for getting the time from Paris. The time, by the way, had been set ahead an hour and the hours were counted from one to twenty-four, beginning with 12:00 (or here 24 o'clock) at night. I think for military work it is a good thing, as no doubt exists as to whether A.M. or P.M. is meant.

During the time we had been at the station, the weather had cleared, and the pursuit squadrons were beginning to take the air in groups of five machines, so we bade good-bye to the Lieutenant and the dozen men who ran the station, and went up to the pursuit airdrome. As we walked up, the French anti-aircraft batteries that had moved forward earlier in the day suddenly opened fire on German airplanes that had appeared overhead. Their fire was quite different from the German. The latter fired successive salvos which burst in groups. The French opened rafale fire with each gun and there were a couple of hundred rounds in the air at once, covering a tremendous area vertically and horizontally. The enemy machines went on however.

One of the German pilots had his machine painted black all over and ornamented with white crosses (the iron cross). He was very expert and used this way of challenging his opponents to individual combat, in which he excelled. One of the best French pilots, Lieutenant Armand Pinsard, was having his machine painted red, as a challenge to the German whom he was going to try to kill, as he had destroyed so many pilots of Pinsard's outfit.

We heard at supper that three German planes had been brought down that day. One was undamaged, but the pilot had been badly wounded and his arm broken. We made arrangements to see the machine the next morning.

As I came to my lodgings, it was very evident that all precautions were being taken to prevent anything being seen by enemy airplanes, which do a great deal of their reconnoitering and aerial bombing at night. No lights were allowed to be shown from windows or doors, and the patrol in the streets kept a strict watch. Signals have been made to the Germans at times in this way. A little flash lamp that I brought with me came in very handy in getting around.

5

I Take Part in a French Infantry Attack

Sunday, April 22, 1917

As I mentioned before, we had heard that a German machine had come down with the pilot badly wounded. We found out where it was and this morning Captain Raulin and I started out for it, picking up Captain de la Colombe on the way. After about three-quarters of an hour, we found the machine near Suippes. It had landed near a tree, in fact the pilot had run it into the tree. He had been badly wounded through the left arm and had lost a great deal of blood after landing. Leaving the machine, he had dragged himself to the vicinity of the tree, as the puddle of blood on the ground showed, apparently with the forlorn hope of hiding himself. He was observed however, and captured by the nearest infantry group, which sent him to the rear and put a guard over the machine to keep souvenir hunters from spoiling it.

The machine had two little metal name plates on the side of the fuselage, forward of the plane:

ALBATROS–WERKE   MILITAR–FLUGZENG
g.n.b.h.   D2096/16
BERLIN–JOHANNASTHAL
Type Dill No. 1440

This indicated to us that it was a German pursuit machine of the latest type, with the famous six-cylinder 170-horsepower vertical Mercedes motor. It was in splendid condition and although the water jackets had been pierced by machine-gun fire, we had no trouble in starting the motor, which ran like a watch, all parts functioning perfectly.

The armament consisted of two German Maxims, each having a belt with five hundred rounds. Only a few had been used. The belt had webbing loops for the cartridges and metal between them. The firing cam arrangement, which allowed the guns to shoot through the propellers, was the same as used by most machines which operated it from the main shaft end. The sight was an ordinary open one between the guns and along the top of the motor.

The cockpit had a comfortable and large seat, and the two safety belts, made of webbing, crossed from rear to front so that pressure came on each hip and thigh. It looked like a pretty good arrangement and the French pilots approved of it. The only instruments were a tachometer, or engine-revolution counter, an aneroid, or altitude indicator, and a compass. There was nothing special about any of them, but they were well made. The fuselage was entirely of wood and very smooth. The fixed planes, both horizontal and vertical at the tail, were very large and the rudder and elevator small, which among other things made the stick control easy indeed.

The control installation was similar to the French. The stick itself had two handles, each with a little lever, which actuated a wire which pulled the triggers of the guns. The landing gear showed nothing unusual, but the shock absorbers, instead of using rubber cord, had a circular spring cord in its place. (The Germans were very short of rubber.) The radiator was in the top plane, the exhaust came out in a bell-shaped pipe to one side on the right, while the whole upper part of the motor was exposed. That undoubtedly had a good deal to do with cooling it, but after taking so much care with the rest of the structure to get streamlined effects, this seemed strange. The propeller was constructed of alternate strips of walnut and maple and was said to be very good; it was made in Berlin. The wings were blotched green and yellow, to render it inconspicuous, and on the side in large letters was painted the word *Vera*. This, the French pilots told me, was the name of the German pilot's sweetheart. I wondered what she would think when she received word he was missing over the line, and did not know that he had made a safe landing.

French pilots said that these machines had a ceiling of twenty thousand feet. They did not have quite as much speed as the Spad but more than the Nieuport; they climbed better than the Spad; they also dived better than any machine, probably, and were extremely sensitive to control. They were considered very formidable, notwithstanding that their motor was so heavy (about four pounds to the horsepower). I suggested that *Vera* be sent to America for inspection and to show our people a trophy of the war.

As we prepared to leave, two Spads landed nearby to act as escorts to the German plane, which was to be flown back to the park. If it had been flown without escort, naturally it would have been attacked at once by French planes on the lookout for enemy ships. They started off, the Spads flying close on either side of the Albatros, ready to warn off any French planes they might encounter. I heard afterward they had made the journey back to the park successfully, but had narrowly escaped being attacked by a flight of Spads, who, approaching them against the sun, did not glimpse the German plane until they were almost on top of it. They apparently did not notice the escort ships as they turned to give battle, and were barely averted in time by signals from the accompanying planes.

Our next objective was the military hospital in Châlons, where the funeral of the two fliers killed two days before was to be held.

The little Gothic church was about fifty feet long by twenty-five broad, with a high vaulted ceiling. I looked around it and thought I had never seen so may images of the various saints.

The caskets, in the center of the little chapel, were of plain wood with a brass cross and name plate affixed, and were draped with the tricolor, surmounted by the uniforms and caps of the deceased. Both had the Military Medal and one the Legion of Honor.

Behind them was another casket, containing the body of a private soldier who had died of wounds the night before. We ranged ourselves around the caskets while Captain Max Boucher, commanding the aviation units of the Fourth Army, stood with the mother of Captain Febre, one of the dead pilots, on the right.

There were high, burning candles on each side of the caskets and a choir boy holding a cross at their head. Two infantry soldiers, with their rifles at reverse and in their field uniforms with helmets, stood guard at each side. The high altar was decorated with candles and a Sister attended to the flowers, which on account of their scarcity here, had been procured with the greatest difficulty the preceding day. The whole service was in Latin and few could understand what was said. At last both priests advanced to the caskets, made the sign of the cross, dropped some holy water on them and led the way out.

We came after them in a column of fours, our heads bared. After a five-minute walk, we reached the cemetery, a military one, crammed full of graves. To the left stood a plain dignified obelisk, with a patriotic inscription on it. We found our way to the open graves and the bodies were removed from the hearses. This was the first time I had seen the mother of the dead pilot shed a tear. She stood erect, a fine picture of a French matron, only one or two tears running down her cheek. Her husband had been killed in action about eight months before; now her only son was gone and she was alone.

The priests said a few words in Latin and Captain Boucher stepped forward. Just then a Spad came out of the sky toward us at full speed. It was about ten thousand feet up and, when right above us, made a straight nose dive of a couple of thousand feet, ending in a spin on the axis of the fuselage, followed by three beautiful loops. He then shot his motor in, flew level for a little way and made several vertical banks. When he returned, he flew upside down at a height of fifteen hundred feet, rolled out and left.

This was the way they rendered homage to the departed from the air. Aside from the sentiment it was a wonderful exhibition of flying. The pilot of this plane, Lieutenant Pinsard, was said to have brought down, within those last five days, four airplanes and one "sausage" of the enemy's.

Captain Boucher then told of the military exploits, fine qualities and noble characters of the departed and exhorted everyone to follow their lead in this great crisis. We then proceeded to the front of the coffins and in single file took the holy water baton, threw a little on each, walked by the mother, halting and bowing individually, and then started for the gate. Near the gate, one officer asked all the others to look at a bracelet he had taken off the body of a French aviator who had been shot down between the lines and had been burned up. No one could identify it. This is the way many a pilot's life is ended.

After lunch at the mess, we started for the lines. I carried my helmet, gas mask and field glasses. I asked Captain Raulin to take me wherever an attack was going on, so I could see what was necessary in this kind of warfare. He said earnestly that they did not want an American officer killed at this stage of the game, because of the bad effect it might have on sentiment in America toward the war. I pointed out that we were at war and their allies, and that no Americans had ever actually been with their men at such a time, so it was necessary to go in order to find out about things at first hand. To which he replied that I was the judge.

By 3:30 P.M. we reached the beginning of the communicating trench and started forward to General de Gallais' division headquarters. We found the headquarters in a deep dugout. It was quite an elaborate affair, containing offices for the various staff officers, a mess room and bunks for the officers and their attendants to sleep in. While these underground chambers are safe from the fire of explosive shell, they can be reached by gas. They are damp and unhealthy, and a long stay in them is certainly destructive to the morale of officers and men alike.

General de Gallais, a handsome man about fifty-five years old, seemed very much worn and a little nervous from the great tension to which he had been subjected. His staff, consisting of ten officers, were all hard at work on various duties, and all looked worn out from the strain. We were in the zone of heavy artillery fire and the noise was great, although no missiles were falling close to us at that time.

The General cautioned me about the very heavy fire through which we would have to pass, and then he discussed the tactics which had to be employed at the front:

"*Mon Commandant,* the battle today is decided entirely by the artillery. Three things are necessary in its employment. First, counter-batteries to obtain the ascendancy over the enemy's heavy artillery, because unless these are put out, almost nothing of a lasting nature can be accomplished; second, the enemy's works must be demolished; and third, there must be a very efficient barrage fire of field artillery to help the infantry to advance and occupy the ground. Without this, nothing can be done."

He continued: "Day before yesterday, I received orders to take a redoubt in a little wood. The airplanes were unable to take good pictures of it. We know it is there but when it comes to a question of telling within ten yards where the actual parapets are, we cannot, and to destroy the whole woods is almost impossible.

"I ordered heavy trench mortars to be placed in the front line which throw one hundred and fifty pounds of explosive. We began an artillery preparation, fired the mortars and then advanced the infantry. I had a battery of thirty-six 75's prepared for the barrage fire. When the assault was started by my brave 227th Regiment of the Line, and these are very experienced men, five hundred out of thirteen hundred were destroyed, my trench mortars demolished and sixteen of my 75's blown up by the enemy.

"When we started our last attack, the Germans put in an

entirely new division brought from the rear the night before we started the operation and also increased their artillery. Today I received orders again to assault the same work while the troops on my right carried the hill. I replied that unless fresh troops could be given me with a plentiful supply of artillery, my men, both because of deficient numbers and on account of fatigue, could not do it, but were even put to it to hold their works."

I told him that the 12th Corps was on the way to reinforce this army and he replied that that was none too much as the Corps are very small now.

Again we started forward, guided by a Captain of engineers. After proceeding for some seven hundred yards in the sap (communicating trench), we came to the abri of the brigade headquarters, which was a dugout with six meters of dirt and two layers of railroad iron (rails) over it, supported on the inside by large pillars of wood.

One had to stay in these abris night and day. They are barely high enough to stand in, as the entrance is made as low as possible and as small as possible to guard against the entrance of shell. The air is bad and when a great deal of rain falls, it is almost impossible to keep them dry.

Within this abri was the first wireless buzzer telegraph instrument I had seen, a very large one, about three times the size of ours. This army had only had them, they said, for eight days. They were all cussing them out because they had no good telegraph operators and said it took too long to train them. But as the wires were all being cut by artillery fire while we were speaking, it became impossible to use anything else. From the sending I heard then, they could not work more than ten words a minute, but of course they would improve with practice.

I told them about the instruments, how long it took to make operators, but what they could do with good operators. They made a note of this and sent it out to all stations.

The regiment was disposed on each side of the brigade commander in a fire trench within which the entrance to his abri was cut. The traverses were made of sandbags about four feet thick. The parapet was high. A few men, about one every forty yards, stood guard, and when an especially close shell came, they dodged into little recesses gouged in the scarp. The rifles, pretty well muddied up, were in stacks against the scarp. They grabbed any rifle when they came out, in case of sudden attack.

The fire of the heavy artillery was steadily increasing and was directed largely at a point where several trenches came together, through which we had to pass. To get forward now was an operation requiring a good deal of exertion, because one had to run across the places where the trenches had been knocked in, or almost certainly would be knocked down. I had seen a good deal of artillery fire before—the most rapid fire that our field artillery, or the Japanese, could put up—but never anything that equalled this.

These large shells, 210's and 305's, were falling around us as rapidly as any fire of small field artillery that I had ever seen or could imagine. This artillery fire was truly a terrible thing. To get away from it, veritable caves had to be dug, twenty-five to thirty feet underground; it was the only means of living. The recesses were stocked with food and water for many days, when a battle is on. We worked our way forward, stopping occasionally when we reached an abri on the side of the connecting trench, placed there for this very purpose.

We passed three first-aid stations, which displayed little Red Cross flags, in the main trench and located to one side in a deep abri. Each had heavy trails of blood running to them. We had already passed several trenches held by the Germans five days before, now we came to their former main trench. The change from the French trench was very noticeable. The whole scarp was revetted with excellent concrete, intact everywhere. The abris were deeper than the French and very well made. The parapets had ammunition recesses all along them. The French occupied them and used the old gorge as their new parapet, just using it the other way around.

The Colonel of the 227th Regiment of the line was a man of about fifty, not very tall but well knit and very energetic, and strong, although at that time he looked as though he had been pulled through a knothole. He came up out of his abri to meet us and said that he had no idea that any foreign officer would come of his own free will through such a fire to see them, and when Captain Raulin told him that this was the case, he sent a man along the parapet from the abri to tell his men that an American officer was there.

The word spread rapidly and smiling faces appeared wherever we went, looking out of their gopher holes. I say smiling faces, but one could hardly discern the look on the men's faces, so heavily were they covered with the grime of the trenches. These men had been in a continuous battle for six days. When they lay down, they slept in their tracks. No rifles were cleaned; mud was the great enemy of these individual machine guns and officers had to keep their eyes on them continually, or they would jam.

Suddenly the field-gun fire of the enemy was shifted from us. The reason was very soon apparent. The attack ordered for 5:30 P.M. against Mt. Cornouillet was being launched. The hill, for the last few hours, had been under a tremendous artillery fire by the French, while the Germans were shooting up all approaches, including our own, with the heavy field artillery and using field guns with shrapnel mostly against the fire trenches to circumvent attack from them.

The left flank of the French attack was about three hundred yards from my position. The Colonel and I got up where we could see over the parapet and saw the men jump out. They were covered in a cloud of dust. Within an instant a great number of white calcium fire signals were sent up, one ball at a time. These rose about fifty feet in the air. There was a short wait, possibly a minute, and then all the French 75's behind us began the barrage fire, about one hundred and fifty of these guns firing against an enemy front of about four hundred yards. Nothing but the bursting of the shell could now be heard. The German heavy guns fired with about the same rapidity as formerly, but their field-gun fire had stopped.

We went forward to the battalion where we saw the Major, who was all caked up with the Champagne clay. In fact, none of the officers could be distinguished from the men without looking twice. All carried automatic pistols or revolvers which they used not only in the advance but sometimes for another purpose: often the Germans would come out of their deep abris days after they had been taken by the French, watch for small parties, kill them and attempt either to get back to their own lines or make a diversion in favor of their comrades who were counterattacking.

The fire of the big guns suddenly shifted directly to our position and we jumped into the Major's abri. The ground shook to where we were, thirty feet below the surface; several tons of metal landed within a radius of fifty yards while we were there. Within about ten minutes it slackened a little and we ran forward to the first line trench, the Major with us. He impressed me as a splendid example of all a battalion commander should be, strong, agile, cool and educated.

After some two hundred yards of trench, we reached the first fire trench. The men had been in it two days and were attempting to deepen it. Very little could be done during the day, on account of the enemy fire, and the men were lying in excavations under the parapet. The great width of the trench was due to its construction under fire, with the enemy guns continually knocking down the work. A few dead bodies of Frenchmen were scattered around and a good many dead Germans lay in front of the trench, the result of the counterattack just delivered.

The companies here had only eighty men left, no grenades, but plenty of rifle and machine-gun ammunition. The machine guns were thrust forward about ten yards in front of the trench in shell holes and were ready to fire. From their position they could bring a flanking fire to bear. Every forty yards, signal rockets lay propped against the parapets.

The men were very tired and slept in their little niches, under all this fire. Their rifles were all clotted with earth. I tried a couple to see if they would work, which they did, but with difficulty.

One operator was a man much older than the rest of the soldiers, who had distinguished himself in handling machine guns in every action they had been in. They told me it was his machine gun alone which practically stopped the German counterattack a little while before. These guns, if ably handled by cool men, were this war's most grimly efficient agents of destruction, and it was entirely impossible to advance in front of them over open ground.

While we looked along the trench, frequently getting into a niche, the French barrage fire was moving forward slowly. The attacking line was armed solely with the individual machine guns, grenades and pistols. All of a sudden, a German barrage began and German machine guns opened strongly all along this sector. Grenades were bursting over the ground where the French were attacking.

We had a direct view of the side of the hill where the attack was taking place, but few individual men could be seen. The place was covered with smoke, dust and bursting projectiles. It was a fantastic and very uncomfortable inferno. The French sent up lights which asked for more artillery and a few more heavy pieces were turned on the positions; possibly their barrage grew a little more intense, although not much.

Having seen everything possible, we started back and had gone about halfway to the Major's, when all of a sudden the air above us was full of small shells. The major shouted to hurry, as the Germans were throwing a barrage over that place, thinking that reinforcements were coming to hit them in the flank from our position. When we were within seventy-five yards of the Major's abri, at a point where a good many trenches met, the fire of the heavy guns grew more intense and we sought the nearest cover. This proved to be a listening post for detecting German mining operations. It was the usual abri, but had a tunnel reaching inward and down to a length of about twenty yards, with a gradual slope downward about ten yards or more from the surface. At the end of the passage, there was a sharp turn to the right and at the end of that was a well about seven yards deep. We were then over fifty feet below the surface. At the bottom of the well was the listening station, consisting of a microphone, an amplifier, a sort of seismograph or instrument such as the ones that detect earthquakes, and a double head telephone receiver, similar to that used on radio instruments.

Both the Germans and French drove long tunnels under the opposing trenches and ran galleries out on each side of the head of the tunnel, directly under the enemy's position. They filled these with explosives and at the moment set for an attack, exploded them, demolishing the positions sometimes for one hundred yards. This was often decisive in attacking a certain locality.

Operators in the listening posts said they could hear German mining operations far away with their instruments, depending on the intensity of the work, the hardness of the soil and the expertness of the workmen. It was hard to detect good men who knew the game, as they took care not to strike the ground hard with their tools but applied the pressure gradually.

Truly, this war was being waged under the ground and over the ground. The men on the surface did the least actual work. Life could not exist in the presence of the dreadful weapons of modern war, and men were forced to burrow in the ground like gophers. Above in the air our pilots could penetrate deep into the enemy's country. In other words, the immemorial battleground was being displaced, rendered obsolete—war was being thrust beneath it or lifted above it.

The same applied to the sea; a submarine paid no attention to a battleship but dived straight under it in search of its prey, the merchantman.

The ground shook while I was inspecting the tunnel, more than thirty feet down. It felt like an earthquake. We were again in the midst of the heavy gun fire.

As I went toward the entrance, I found everyone well within

the tunnel. The earth shook more than ever and they told me
that several heavy shells of 210 caliber had hit the top of the
abri. After about fifteen minutes, this fire let up and we got out.
By letting up, I do not mean that it ceased—the same routine
rate of fire kept up as formerly. We looked back at the top of
the abri and sure enough there were two big shell holes, clear
down to the railroad iron, about five feet in depth and twelve
feet in diameter. I picked up a couple of hot shell fragments and
shrapnel bullets from the barrage fire and went on.

We finally reached the Major's abri. I noticed that a man had
been carrying a German steel trench helmet back from the
first line trench, and now the Major said that there was little
to give and what there was did not amount to much, but he
thought this was as good a souvenir as anything, so he wished
to present it to me in token of our meeting under those circumstances. In accepting it, I congratulated France and himself
on having such brave and accomplished soldiers to man her
trenches.

The Major observed that there was a limit to all things,
meaning the endurance of the French army. He knew full well,
he said, that we could not send a large army over at once, but
even if we did, how long, in my opinion, would it take for
our men to become accustomed to this sort of thing? I thought
a little while before answering. We were way down in the abri,
above us were bursting the heavy shells of about as perfectly
served an artillery as could exist, manned by a brave, determined and well-instructed foe, the Germans. The Major said,
"Answer me truly." I thought of our men, officers and equipment and what they were trained to do, then answered that I
believed our regular infantry could be depended on to hold
their own alone after six months, or if serving alongside of
French troops, in about one half the time. As to our artillery,
about three months, and the same for our technical troops, if
acting with or near French organizations.

To act alone there, on the offensive, successfully, with artillery of our own manufacture and all our own equipment, in-

cluding efficient machine guns, I believed would take a year for preparation and training. To do it in less time would have been a slaughter house performance.

At about 7:00 P.M., we arrived back at the division head-quarters. The General and his staff were at dinner. Captain Raulin told where we had been and what we had seen. The General said that they had been subjected to a heavy fire, as the Germans had greatly reinforced their lines. He again em-phasized the necessity of artillery and mentioned that he had served in both artillery and infantry, had always studied his profession hard and that he was sure of what he was talking about. More airplanes were needed, he said. Lately the Ger-mans seemed to have things a good deal their own way, and it would make a great difference if the men could see their own airplanes over them.

The comment of the General, that the men liked to see their airplanes over them, was a usual one with ground officers. They did not seem to recognize the fact that planes had to go far into the enemy territory to engage hostile planes on their own side, and prevent them from crossing and attacking our observa-tions planes. Consequently, the observation planes were left alone over the troops and it looked as if they had few planes near them. It was impossible to convince ground officers of these facts. They thought each time they looked up out of their dugouts, they ought to see a lot of planes hovering over them. They knew little or nothing about air tactics. They did not know, for instance, that the planes had only two and one-half hours' fuel; that they had to act in large bodies if they were not to be pounced on by the enemy and destroyed piecemeal.

After bidding good-bye to the General, who had kindly asked us to stay to dinner, I started to leave by the most direct route to the village, as there was no fire at that time. Our automobile was within fifty yards of the village. The driver grabbed my dispatch case and jumped into a ditch as the frag-ments of shells and masonry had reached the auto. We had to run through the village at high speed, several walls toppling over as we hurtled by. An old man and woman were the only inhabitants left there and they ran out of it and got in a dugout whenever a shell hit.

It is remarkable how these French people cling to their homes and little pieces of ground. Even when a village has been completely destroyed and the houses levelled to the ground, if the armies go a sufficient distance away from it, the inhabitants return and try to build up their old homes. It is pathetic, as these poor people have nothing else to depend on for their existence.

This was the hour for "ravitaillement" in food, forage and ammunition, and the wagon trains were all along the roads to the front. These go to where the communicating trenches begin, about three or four thousand yards behind the first line fire trench. The roads are all concealed by camouflage, such as I described before. Notwithstanding this concealment, the Germans had made good practice with their cannon, as the bodies of horses just killed and thrown to one side of the road plainly showed.

In that one day alone, I saw and asked about enough to write a book. What struck me most forcibly was the utter helplessness of the infantry when attacking over open ground, against modern machine guns and cannon. Neither side had yet developed a system which would protect the individual foot soldier, so with him it was simply a case of being sacrificed for an infinitesimal gain, as an advance of a mile or two into those elaborately entrenched positions did not mean anything.

The artillery, on the other hand, was well protected and suffered comparatively little loss. While in action, they lost about one-twelfth as much as the infantry.

The men in the infantry regiments knew all these things full well and talked a great deal about the utter futility of this kind of war. They saw no alternative, however, and felt they must keep it up or be defeated. Everyone from the humblest private up seemed to feel that the air service was going to be the one thing that would bring the war to a speedy close when they got great numbers of new and more efficient planes.

Anyone who thinks that war is not more "heller" than ever, should have been in the first lines during these battles and tasted a little of what it was. Our people hadn't the remotest conception of it. It sounds as if I may be overstating things, but I think that is impossible with the words we now have in our language.

I later received a citation for my part in this operation. It was the first Croix de guerre given to an American officer for participating in the war.

6

The French Air Force

Monday, April 23, 1917

My next visit was to the bombardment squadrons. They were stationed at Villeneuve, which in time of peace was one of France's largest aviation schools. The prewar hangars were still there and several more had been added. The former were made of wood, and the latter were the wooden-frame and canvas covered construction, called Bessenau after their inventor.

In addition to the bombardment squadrons, all machines of the 12th Corps had just arrived. They were reinforcing this army with air equipment as fast as possible, and there were over three hundred machines with their pilots on the line.

Upon my arrival at Villeneuve, we were met by Captain Mayol in command of the garrison. He had been one of the first aviators in France and used to fly a good deal; now he never goes up.

We first inspected the night bombardment squadron. These were all machines with large wing surfaces, many of them twin motored, and some Farman pushers. For night work they needed a very slow landing speed, and as they were not exposed to the attack of pursuit machines high speed was of no particular advantage. They were equipped with four electric light projectors six inches in diameter, mounted under the front part of the fuselage. These were used principally to give landing signals but illuminated the earth from about four hundred and fifty feet altitude. Their instruments were luminous and consisted of an altimeter, a tachometer, a compass and, when they could get it, an air speed indicator. They had one machine gun but it was hardly necessary, unless they got caught out in the daytime. They usually had only one person aboard, the pilot; another man meant fewer bombs. They had an average of three and one-half hours' fuel and went about seventy-five miles per hour, or a little better. They went on their night missions independently and alone, choosing moonlight nights whenever possible.

They had no special bomb sight or direction instrument; each pilot had his own system. Some had a plumb bob in a tube in the fuselage, many had nothing; some had a piece of glass in the floor with cross hairs, to sight through. They said they could do just as well without any instrument, and that they could not see through an instrument at night anyway. Sometimes they went down to within three hundred feet, but no lower, because they had to allow for sufficient distance for their bombs to turn over and arm themselves. This usually required from one to two hundred feet.

These bombs were by far the best I had ever seen. The explosive was made when two liquids, separated by a tin diaphragm, were mixed by puncturing this diaphragm in the middle of the bomb.

When the pilot wished to drop one, a lever was pulled; this pressed a plunger down into the bomb and ruptured the diaphragm so that the liquids mixed and formed the high explosive; at the same time the door was opened and the bomb left the fuselage, head up. The tail fins then pointed it nose down, the little propeller turned and armed the base fuse, and the bomb exploded on contact. It was simple, sure and very safe, the most practical thing I have seen. (On the other hand, some said it was more dangerous, especially as the bombs could be punctured by machine-gun fire and the liquids mixed without the pilot's knowing it.)

The bombers claimed that their projectiles, weight for weight, were four times more efficient than artillery shell, for the reason that their bombs could carry so much more explosive within their comparatively light walls.

There was a great *esprit de corps* in the French service, and each branch had all sorts of confidence in its own outfit. The bombardment people were sure that if they were given enough planes and explosive, there would be nothing left of Germany in a short while.

Still, landing at night was no fun, and resulted in a good many accidents. The squadron was out the night before and had lost three machines in Germany and two were hurt on landing, even though the pilots of these machines were not novices but carefully trained and selected old pilots.

I went, next, to the day-bombarding outfit. They had Sopwiths, one- or two-seaters. The single-seaters carried twelve small bombs, and the two-seaters eight. All the bomb outfits and instruments were the same as on the night machines.

The theoretical men who did not have to fly the machines into Germany held that the single-seaters were the best, because more bombs could be carried and the pilot could drop them as well as anyone else. The pilots who had to go into Germany said they were always exposed to the attack of pursuit machines during the day; they were of course unable to maneuver as fast, or climb as high, as a pursuit, therefore they had to depend on heavy armament. They wanted a gunner in the back seat and a good one.

The pilots said that they had raised the mischief with the enemy, and reported with pride that they had dropped a thousand kilos, a couple of days before, on some town whose name I cannot remember, forcing its evacuation and destroying its ammunition factories. They were very enthusiastic about what they would be able to do in the future, but thought that the night system had more in it than the day, as they could approach their targets more closely and carry more weight.

We drove back a little after noon, through the beautiful Champagne country toward Châlons. Old men, women and children were working in the vineyards, which require a great deal of care and of course are the great wealth producers of this part of France.

In the afternoon we went to Vardeny, where the school for balloon observers was stationed. It was almost too well located. From the school balloons the field of battle could be plainly seen, and it was within the extreme range of the German heavy artillery. Also it was frequently attacked by enemy pursuit machines.

Major Jacques Saconey, commanding the entire French balloon organization of eighty-seven companies was there to greet me. He told me that to turn out trained observers, men who can be depended upon, required careful selection and at least a six-months course. Either officers or enlisted men who are thought suitable are selected and sent with balloon companies on the line for three months. Here they learned various duties of the company and were taken up in the balloon to get used to the motion (many get seasick) and to get an idea of perspective from the air. If they came through these preliminaries successfully, they were sent to the school.

The course began with a series of lectures and practical exercises in map reading, map making and the selection of points on the ground from maps, and the ideas of perspective formed from a map or horizontal projection. They had to be able to look at a flat map and then draw a picture of how the country would look—its hills, woods, houses and trench lines.

Next, a point on the map was marked where a balloon ascends. The altitude of the observer in the basket was known. The student had to figure out how much his line of sight dropped for each kilometer he ascended; they then estimated how high the hills were in the line of sight and whether they hid certain

areas behind them from the view of the balloon observer. Sometimes aerial photos were thrown on a screen. The student had in
front of him a map, representing the area shown in the photo; a
point would appear on the screen, and he had to tell where it
was on the map. Next, shots would be shown on the screen
picture by a moving slide, and the student would have to
locate these on his map. In another more realistic exercise,
they were put through the exact operation necessary in indi-
cating to a battery of artillery where the shots go.

Only enough was taught the student about the balloon to
enable him to know what to do if something went wrong with
it while he was up.

These balloons were left out of doors all the time and had
little wind breaks built around them. Whenever possible, they
were put in a creek bottom or the side of a valley, and tree
limbs and brush were erected around three sides of the position
to break the wind. They looked like gigantic eggs in a nest.

When a balloon company set itself up at a new place, the
inflation site of the balloon was first selected. The gas group got
its outfit and gas tubes ready, the balloon group cleared the
ground if necessary, got the balloon and its net out of the wagon,
with the sandbags for ballast and the anchor ropes. The winch
truck was backed up near the balloon. The telephone wagon
went to the place selected and made its connection, while the
anti-aircraft machine guns were set up and a guard established
around the place. When the balloon was entirely inflated, the
wagon towed it to its place, the observers got in the baskets and
off it went. I went up in the balloon and had a problem with
simulated artillery fire carried out at eight thousand meters.

The battle line was between twelve and fifteen thousand
yards away and could be plainly seen, as the day was perfect.
The battle was still going on for the summit of Cornouillet hill.

The observers wore belts that ran from their thighs to their
shoulders and around the waist, with a loop at the back of the
neck to which a parachute was attached. If anything happened,
they jumped overboard. I have never heard of one of these

parachutes failing to work. I cut one loose from the basket, which had a sandbag attached instead of a person. It opened up within ninety feet.

The other day a balloon was attacked successfully by a German pursuit machine, which set it afire with incendiary bullets and shot the pilot through the leg. The pilot took his camera, jumped overboard, and photographed the burning balloon while descending in his parachute.

The officers said that very few of these balloons were ever destroyed by airplanes. In the first place, they could be pulled down very rapidly; they always had anti-aircraft machine guns around them; the observers were armed and fired from their baskets; and last, there was usually infantry near them. From what I had seen, however, I thought planes would shoot a good many down in the future.

7

Viewing the Great Battle from the Air

Tuesday, April 24, 1917

On the way to Mt. Sans Nomme to observe aerial reconnaissance, I saw forty-eight of the New French tanks hidden in a little wood. We stopped to examine them.

They were armed with one full-size 75-mm. cannon, having one hundred and six rounds of ammunition. It could fire direct for 2,000 yards, and was operated by a man in a conning tower which was just on the left of the gun. The gun port was on the right of the chassis pointing forward and could be traversed in azimuth sideways about fifteen degrees on each side of the center, or thirty degrees and ten in elevation.

They carried four Hotchkiss machine guns with seven thousand rounds of ammunition, one on each side, one to the front and one behind.

The driver sat in front on the left side. There was a guiding wheel in front of him, clutches and throttle on the right side and on the left a lever to manipulate the port through which he looked. Between his little conning tower and the gun director's was an eleven-inch searchlight run by the generator.

These tanks had a little wireless outfit for communication, the wire being thrown out to the rear. They carried enough fuel

for twenty-five to thirty kilometers (fifteen to eighteen miles),
and had a crew of eight men. They weighed twenty tons, and
could cross ditches nine feet wide. They resisted rifle, machine
gun and shrapnel fire, also shell fragments if these were not too
large. Several tanks in that group had been hit by shell fragments, the outer armor being pierced, but the inner was intact.
One was hit on the top the other day by a 105 shell, torn open
and the whole crew killed.

There was a good deal of controversy about tanks in general.
The officers I talked to believed that the British tanks were not
much good, being entirely too large, and having their driving
mechanism exposed. They liked little ones and wanted a number of them.

In a few days, these tanks were to be employed in another
grand attack. Enthusiastic tank officers think that in their arm
of the service they have a branch that will revolutionize land
warfare. It is no longer possible, they say, for infantry to advance on the ground, alone, against machine-gun fire, and to
employ them in this way is mere butchery. The future, they
think, will see tanks attacking positions very much the way a
fleet of battleships attacks a coast. After the tanks take a place,
they will establish a post, which will be supplied by transport
tanks bringing up food, fuel and ammunition. These tank
officers are strong believers in aircraft also and think great
results could be obtained, with comparatively little loss of life,
from its use in conjunction with tanks, the aircraft striking at
the enemy's rear areas, while the tanks make the direct attack
on the front.

Near the tanks we heard heavy explosions and looking over
there, we saw that two large 340-mm. French railway batteries
had gone into action. These tracks had been built abreast about
forty yards apart. Projectiles weighing some eight hundred
pounds were fed to them from a railway car just behind. Their
fire was directed at an enemy railway junction about nine miles
away; a "sausage" was making adjustments for them. The
recoil seemed to be very easily taken up by the carriage, which

moved to the rear about fifteen feet. I could not get on the carriage itself without interfering with the firing, so did not inspect them closely.

Around noon, we went to see the "camouflage" or disguising studio. Where this word came from, I have not yet been able to discover. Any method or ruse that puts a different appearance on things so as to deceive the enemy, is camouflage.

For instance, there was a dead body of a horse somewhere that offered an excellent position for an observatory. An exact duplicate of this body was made, all hollowed out, with observing ports in it, through which a man, concealed inside, could look. This was substituted some dark night for the original. A tree located between the lines was copied exactly and the tree substituted might be a steel tower that had an observation station in it, but from the air it looked exactly like the original tree. Periscopes were put in trees. Steel observing posts were covered with stuff that looked exactly like the Champagne clay. Real artists did this work and a good many lives were saved through their ingenious devices.

Finally we reached the army group whose machine I was to go up in. It was stationed at La Cheppe and particularly charged with the spotting of fire for the heaviest long-range cannon. The machines they flew were three-seaters powered by two 140-horsepower engines. The observer was stationed up front with one Lewis gun, a compass, map, speaking tube and radio; the pilot sat in the center, and the gunner, with two Lewis guns, sat behind.

We left the ground at about 5:30 P.M. The pilot, Lieutenant François Lafont, took the machine off the ground in fine style. He jumped her up pretty well, then straightened out to get speed and climbed up in long spirals, with the two Hispanos buzzing regularly. The fuselage was so constructed that most of the wind was blown up over one's head. The pilot and gunner wore no glasses. I took some as I was used to wearing them, but soon pulled them off. There was very little vibration and I found I could see very easily with field glasses. These were eight-power instruments with large rubber eye pieces that fit closely and let no wind in.

At six thousand feet, we started for the lines, passing the row of "sausages." I was impressed by how plainly I could see the flash of the guns. We were still climbing up when the German anti-aircraft guns opened on us at long range. The shells burst about three or four hundred yards away, and the pilot immediately turned at right angles and went parallel to the lines. Just then our own anti-aircraft ordnance filled the sky with little puffs of smoke, and about one thousand yards off we saw two German pursuit machines. They were above and ahead of us, but left when they saw a patrol of five Spads arriving. A little later we saw a single German pursuit machine that was not being bothered by anyone. He did not attack nor were we bothered with anti-aircraft guns again.

The hits of the shell on the ground could be spotted perfectly; observers told me they could estimate within ten yards of where they struck—at a distance of from eight to ten thousand yards.

Mt. Cornouillet was still under heavy fire. The French batteries were shelling the concentration points behind the enemy line, while the Germans were doing the same thing. I saw no motor trains on the German side and no troops.

There were certainly no signs that the Germans were short of anything except rubber. They had plenty of ammunition, aircraft, and balloons, and used them in a military way, with care and at the places where they would do the most good.

While we were over the lines, several units of French pursuit machines came by us, for my benefit I believe. I was impressed with the compact formation that the flights of five were keeping. The machines were not more than one hundred yards from each other, sometimes not over fifty, and passed very close to me, both under and over.

We could look down the Marne river and see Reims plainly at a distance of ten miles, in spite of its being in the direction of the setting sun. All about were villages of which there was nothing left except crumbling walls. The enemy destroyed them to prevent their being used for shelter or points of supply and concealment. Villages were shot up at distances of ten miles or more behind the lines, particularly places where roads or railways joined.

At 7:00 P.M. we started back. The wind was blowing at twelve meters a second at six thousand feet, according to the sounding balloons, or about twenty-eight miles an hour. I asked the pilot how the big machine handled when he threw her around a little, and he said that looping had been done with one, but he could not do it then because the gunner was not tied in. He made several vertical banks, nose dives and extremely tight spirals, however, and the machine handled beautifully, with little vibration. He said it was almost impossible to get into a tailspin with it, and anyway if it did, he could stop it quickly by applying opposite control.

We came down at very slow speed. He used his motor until within three hundred feet of the ground, gave her a kick just before we landed; and we did not roll more than one hundred feet. It was a beautiful landing. A Sopwith landed alongside of us with a bang, "pancaked" as it is called, bounced about ten feet and then came to rest. I expect the pilot with me was the best in the organization.

We had dinner with the squadron officers in their mess, a small frame building by a clear little stream. On the walls were hung pieces of a couple of German machines that had been destroyed by the large observation machines.

The conversation was all about the tactical use of airplanes. The Commanding Officer considered that the observation part was well worked out, that is, the map, radio and seeing end of it. He wanted more performance from his machine, more armor, and above all, armament. He wanted a gun of ten to twenty barrels, each one of which could fire as fast as a Lewis or Vickers. He only fought defensively and needed all the fire he could get.

A few days before, one of his machines had been engaged by

five enemy pursuits; they attacked both from above and under-neath. Those underneath would stick their machines straight up in a stall and let go their guns, while those from above at-tacked in the usual manner. It was impossible for the pilot to keep all of them under the fire of his guns. Soon the observer was killed, the gunner shot through both arms and the pilot's left arm broken; the wires to both ailerons were shot away, and the gas tanks of both motors punctured. He glided for the ground and when making a landing, turned the machine upside down. The pilot yelled to the gunner to come and let him out, as he could not release his belt with one hand; but the gunner was wedged in the cockpit and, on account of both his arms being broken, could not get out. Some infantry were near them, and came over and released them.

This was a normal happening in the war, something that could be expected to happen every day. Everyone knew when he started on a flight that there was sure to be a fight if he was looking for one, or if his mission was such that he had to carry out some special thing regardless.

One flight over the lines gave me a much clearer impression of how the armies were laid out than any amount of traveling around on the ground. A very significant thing to me was that we could cross the lines of these contending armies in a few minutes in our airplane, whereas the armies had been locked in the struggle, immovable, powerless to advance, for three years. To even stick one's head over the top of a trench invited death. This whole area over which the Germans and French battled was not more than sixty miles across. It was as though they kept knocking their heads against a stone wall, until their brains were dashed out. They got nowhere, as far as ending the war was concerned.

It looked as though the war would keep up indefinitely until either the airplanes brought an end to the war or the contending nations dropped from sheer exhaustion.

8

Terrific Fighting Continues

Wednesday, April 25, 1917

In the morning I went out to Mt. Sans Nomme, a continuation of the same ridge of which Mt. Cornouillet forms one end. Mt. Sans Nomme itself had been taken by the French and the Germans were on the other side of the eminence. It rises gradually for about two hundred feet and is, or was, covered with a growth of young pine trees. There is not much left of the pine trees now.

I walked through former German wire entanglements and was struck more than ever by their efficacy. The wire was strung on iron posts which screwed into the ground. When hit by artillery fire, they bent up and made a great mess of the wire. There were merely narrow avenues smashed in the wire through which the infantry could advance.

The characteristics of the Germans' trenches were straight revetments, narrow profiles, deep abris and a great deal of concrete and iron work. They offered wonderful cover. The French and Germans had been fighting so long that each had more or less the same system, when they could get it. The French, of course, could not get the amount of concrete and iron the Germans could, so they used wood instead. This did not hold the revetments as well; consequently the profiles were broader, and, as the artillery fire could enter them more easily, there were heavier losses proportionately among the personnel.

Still all former siege methods are valueless against such works, without a tremendous artillery preparation. This does not mean a few batteries, but hundreds of guns of huge caliber firing against a front of only a few hundred yards.

In fact, the artillery lesson of all wars has been the same. In peace, the talk has always been of lightness, mobility and the inability to supply ammunition; in war, it has been weight of projectile and still more weight. That was what was asked for then. Even the common soldier in the trenches knew it and asked: "When will America begin to send her heavy artillery over, and are they building lots of it?"

The debris of battle lay all around and shells were bursting on top of the hill about one hundred yards distant. The bodies of the dead had been removed, but the ground was strewn with torn German helmets, pieces of clothing, French helmets full of holes from machine-gun fire, broken rifles and bayonets, mess tins and all sorts of camp paraphernalia. The bodies of the Germans had been thrown into their old abris, in which some of them had met their deaths.

Between the lines lay many inert forms, those especially brave ones who had paid the forfeit for their unsuccessful daring.

At one place in the German trenches, I heard someone talking down in an abri. I looked for some time, as I could not make out what language was being spoken. At last I saw a red fez and the uniform of the Moroccan infantry. Some of them were looking around to see what they could find: a little plundering on the side. As a matter of fact, they could have hidden there as long as they liked. I have no doubt but that deserters did get into the deep dugouts and stayed to avoid going into battle.

As we returned, we passed the soup kitchens and supply trains. They were proceeding up the road, first in horse-drawn vehicles, then further back in splendid motor trains. These had all been organized into groups of twenty. Each group had its own symbol painted on the truck; one had a dog, another an elephant carrying what looked like an onion in his trunk; another a naked lady bringing up a 12-inch shell.

Long trains of trucks, each carrying three small hogsheads of wine or beer ran up behind the lines every day, were emptied of their contents and returned for more. The French soldiers are as used to their wine as ours are to their coffee.

After lunch at the *popote*, we started for Reims, about twenty-eight miles away, passing through Épernay en route, where many of the former inhabitants of Reims were congregated. From there we took a side road to Reims by mistake. It was very interesting, however; we followed a chain of hills over which the Champagne grapes are grown, and watched the people toiling hard to get them in shape for the coming summer. This work went on whether they happen to be under fire or not.

After several kilometers, we came to the top of Reims hill, or mountain, from which we had a remarkable view of the Marne valley and of the city, with its old quaint houses, the cathedral and other churches. This mountain is a tremendously important place from a military standpoint. It forms a position that can be easily defended, with plenty of room for large forces to be quartered on it. From it, roads radiate to the north toward Germany and to the south toward Paris and the interior of France. The Germans had always had their eye on the mountain of Reims and all French officers thought then that sooner or later the enemy would attempt to capture it, and using it as a base, would strike into the interior. Reims is a very old place; its quaint houses, cathedral and other churches stood out clearly.

We were surprised to find the town under heavy bombardment. Shells from the large German artillery were bursting all over the lower edge of the city. As we entered, it seemed like a town of the dead; no one was about except an occasional soldier. Every wall bore the evidence of shot and shell, and the farther we penetrated into the town, the more ruined were the houses. At last we reached the cathedral. I had expected of course to see it damaged to some extent, but was shocked to find it in such a wrecked condition.

The marks of the German 305 howitzers were stamped into the court in front and around the statue of Jeanne d'Arc. She had not been hurt much, as she is defiladed by the towers. The only bit of damage sustained was where one of the bridle reins had been cut by a shell fragment.

All sorts of projectiles, from 77's to larger guns, had hit the area. Captain Raulin told me that he had been there eight days before and that in the short time since then there had been more damage done than during the two years preceding. The shells were bursting around the town at a pretty lively rate even then, but none closer than a block off.

I was taking a photo of the cathedral from the front when Captain Raulin came over toward me with a French soldier, who said he thought I had better not stay there too long, because the heavy shells had fallen there in the morning and the cannonade might begin again at any moment.

When he saw that I was an American officer, he told us that he was a Dominican friar. They all have to serve in the army now. We learned from him that the Cardinal was there in a house close by and could give us an audience at once, under the circumstances. Accordingly we went to his house, and Cardinal Lucon came to us at once. His house had been damaged a little by shell fragments that morning, not very badly however. He conducted us into his study, which was heated a little. There was no coal then anywhere, and no heat except for cooking.

The Cardinal seemed to appreciate our coming to see him at such a time and was very gracious. He told us about the heavy bombardment of the cathedral itself, which had started anew a few days before. He had remained through it all, and when the shelling became very heavy, he went into his cellar. So far, he had escaped serious harm. I thought if he lived through it, he would be one of the historic characters of the war; his devotion and disregard of danger were wonderful. His whole conversation was about the cathedral and its chances for ever being reconstructed, or even standing up. He showed us pieces of shell of fantastic shapes that had hit all parts of the building and cloister.

After a half-hour's talk, punctuated every minute or so by a Whizzzzzzzz-Boom! of the heavy shells striking only a little way off, he proposed that we go into the cathedral and see the havoc wrought. From what he said and the way the shelling was going on, I did not think it was an especially healthy place, but I was anxious to see it and I went.

The caretaker, himself a priest, was summoned by the Cardinal and he conducted us in through a little wooden door. No one was allowed to enter without permission from the Cardinal, which was granted to but few persons. The sight that greeted us was distressing, even to an outsider. The roof of this fine old twelfth-century cathedral had been riddled by shells from heavy artillery, some of the holes being large enough to throw an ordinary house through. The floor had been smashed to bits and was littered with the remains of the wonderful windows, centuries old; the altar and its properties were in ruins. A bronze statue of St. Peter, at one side, was still in good order, with his right toe still showing signs of having been kissed. Fragments of shell were lying all about.

The Cardinal showed me where Clovis, King of the Franks, had been baptized after accepting Christianity; where Jeanne d'Arc had entered and stood when she came to Reims. Every part of the edifice has some historical association connected with it. After looking about, I took a few photos of the interior.

I believed that if three or four more 12-inch shells hit the towers, a great part of this famous and much-loved structure would cave in.

The caretaker told us that a few days before he had had some boys working in the cathedral, trying to sweep up some of the debris; in the midst of their work several 77 shells crashed in, killing or wounding all the boys. He gave me some pieces of glass from the famous rose window which he picked up from the floor. These were regarded as precious relics and little fragments were mounted in brooches and worn as ornaments by their fortunate possessors.

As we came out, a patrol of five Spads came over us, flying low. We bade *adieu* to the soldier priest and ran across the court and got into our automobile on the side street.

We left with rather a sad feeling, and took a road that parallels the front of the armies for a long way.

We passed through a village entirely occupied by Russians. It did not look as well as the places occupied by the French. None of the Russians that we spoke to knew a word of French and looked just as wooden and stupid as they always do. I doubt if the sending of this handful of Russians had a very beneficial influence on the French morale, because they saw them, knew they were picked troops from the Russian Army, and compared them in their minds with the Germans. Consequently they thought that Russia could do very little against Germany, an estimate that was entirely correct. High intelligence in the individual is necessary nowadays.

A Visit with Pétain

Thursday, April 26, 1917

Early in the day I visited a listening post for aircraft. These posts were put in advantageous positions and were supposed to detect the presence of aircraft long before any other means on the ground. All sorts of peculiar schemes had been tried to detect the approach of aircraft. One which particularly amused me was this: pheasants are very susceptible to sounds of any kind, so for a while they tried putting pheasants in a cage, with the idea that if they heard an airplane or Zeppelin a long way off, they would fidget around and thereby indicate its presence. I think a good many other things besides airplanes made them fidget, so this form of detector was not entirely successful.

The listening post was equipped with a listener which consisted of several megaphones grouped in the same frame with a diaphragm and ear pieces attached like a stethoscope. Very minute sounds could be heard with it. A whisper could be heard for several hundred feet; the noise of the town in the distance was very plain. This instrument was designed, first, to detect the presence of airplanes, then to tell their direction and their height, from a succession of readings they took. The faculty of determining direction in a human being is said to depend on the distance between the ears, which is about eight centimeters in the average person; so this listening device, which was a megaphone at each end of a bar about two meters long, was supposed to give, theoretically, about twenty-five or thirty times the power to determine direction possessed by human ears. These were fixed up with telephones in a similar manner. They had two devices for determining the direction of an airplane, one for the horizontal direction and the other with a bar stuck up vertically to determine the height of the plane.

I listened carefully in these devices but was not much impressed with them. All sorts of sounds could be heard, but to determine what each was, was a different thing. The men in charge agreed with this.

With these listeners, were the ordinary telescopes and optical instruments used by the artillery for observation of fire. These were used to train on the point where the airplane was located. A 60-inch searchlight with its automobile generator was always kept ready to begin operations, and there were anti-aircraft guns alongside.

The whole outfit was situated on a commanding position, on a hill back of the town. The French were always trying out some scheme for defending a position from the ground against aircraft. At that point, they had not hit on a successful one; everyone I talked to about it said that although a few hits may be made, the only real defense against aircraft is other aircraft.

In the afternoon, I went over to Army Group Headquarters and talked with Major Paul Armengaud, the aeronautical officer there, a man of exceptional ability and foresight, who was a General Staff officer before the war. What they all wanted to know was how soon we could help them. I told him of the problem confronting us at sea, and the industrial conditions; how we had recently obtained a substantial appropriation for aviation and schools for the training of pilots. He told me of conditions on the French front and expressed the fear that the German production of equipment and personnel might surpass the French, unless substantial aid were given by the United States.

As I was leaving Major Armengaud's, I met Mr. James H. Hyde of Paris, who had come up to Châlons to dine with General Pétain. Mr. Hyde was probably the best known American resident in Paris, having a wide acquaintance among French officers, by whom his knowledge of conditions and judgment was greatly respected. Mr. Hyde's advice and assistance were invaluable at the beginning of our work in France. Whenever a difficult question arose and it was necessary to assemble French officers, no matter what party they belonged to or what their views were, Mr. Hyde was always able to arrange a satisfactory discussion and often to bring about a solution of the questions being considered.

We chatted a few moments, and the Chief of Staff invited me to come to dinner that evening with General Pétain, which I accepted.

At 7:00 P.M. we went to the large house, occupied by General Pétain, for dinner. The French laws allowed houses in the zone of fighting to be taken and occupied by the army; officers and men could be billeted in private houses even though the owners were living in them. When a military organization came into a town, it was preceded by officers of the administration who marked on each door how many officers and men could be accommodated, and on the stables how many horses could be taken in.

General Pétain, it will be remembered, is the one who defended Verdun against the great German assault of the year before, when a new epic was written into the heroic legends of the human race and the whole world thrilled to the superb and ferocious courage of that slogan "They shall not pass." He was one of the three Army Group Commanders and I believed ranked next to General Nivelle. He was a Colonel when the war started and was promoted more rapidly than any other officer.

As we arrived General Pétain was just returning from a visit to the lines. The United States flag was flying in our honor from the front door, which was within a little court removed from the street. He received us under the flag in a very pleasant manner. I was at once struck with his forcefulness and positive ways. When talking about anything, he went straight to the point. In a few minutes, we were ushered in to dinner. His whole staff of twelve officers was there and had ranged themselves around the table according to rank. They impressed me mostly as office men, except the Chief of Staff and two liaison officers who had come over from neighboring armies.

Mr. Hyde sat on the General's right and I sat on his left. The General seemed very much preoccupied and was thinking about the military operations. General Pétain made his great reputation as a defensive soldier and while he had commanded small offensive operations before, this was his first command of a great attack against a prepared position. He well knew its strength, the terrible losses that had to be incurred and the small advantage that would result. As a soldier, he felt he had to push the attack in the way he had been ordered, but he considered it was being made more for political reasons than as a strictly military move. I do not believe he ever had the idea that it would succeed, or even be of advantage to the French. On the contrary, he was terribly afraid that the losses in men, munitions and morale would encourage the Germans to counterattack and enable them to smash the French front. This I believe he was guarding against. Naturally this detracted somewhat from the spirit of offense, but I believe was the correct thing to do at the time.

He asked the different officers of his staff for the particular information each was charged with obtaining. They made short, concise reports, the general tenor being that things were at a standstill while the artillery was being prepared for a new attack. Meanwhile, local battles were taking place for the possession of tactical points, a necessary step in preparing the ground for the general attack all along the line.

I had the impression that the General was largely his own chief of staff, that is to say, he prepared and laid out all operations himself. Some generals entrusted their chiefs of staff with the duty of drawing up all the operations, all the orders, and seeing that the various staff officers coordinated their work; while others merely required them to coordinate the work in the staff. General Pétain himself prescribed exactly what should be done and the staff carried it out.

At the beginning of the dinner, the General was a bit withdrawn, and reflective, but after a while he entered into conversation in a general way. I knew he wanted to find out what the United States could and would do and how soon. He had prepared a study on the manner in which we could coöperate, a copy of which he gave to me.

I explained the way a man in the middle of our country felt about sending his son or going himself thousands of miles away to the European continent to fight and probably die there. The French were fighting for their homes and cities on their own soil, for which their fathers fought before them. General Pétain replied that it would be difficult for France to send a conscript army to our Pacific coast, if we were in a great war with a Pacific power. As I understand it, the conscription laws of both France and Germany provide that only soldiers volunteering for such service can be sent on expeditions outside the country, except in a defensive war. Of course, war between France and Germany is always regarded as a defensive war by either side, no matter which is the aggressor; but it would be hard to stretch popular imagination into believing that the war in Europe was a defensive one for America, no matter how truly it might be in fact.

I told him about our armed forces, our sources for officers, and what the instruction had been in the past. He replied that it was much superior to what England had at the beginning. They were always brave enough, he said, but it took a long time to train suitable officers.

He thought we could help the French most quickly with aircraft and artillery. Of course what they needed most urgently was men, in the interior and on the lines. He kept emphasizing that if we could even send industrial personnel here, it would release Frenchmen to go to the front.

We talked all through dinner, at the end of which he picked up the little menu card, signed it, and asked me to accept it from him. We went out into the *sala* and soon departed. We all had a good deal to do.

10

The French Artillery in Action

Friday, April 27, 1917

This morning we started out for Suippes, where the regiment of heavy artillery commanded by a Colonel Escouroux had its headquarters. We went to a group of 155-mm. guns, which were firing at about eight thousand yards' range. The fire was for adjustment. A Farman airplane was giving the directions to the radio receiving station which worked with it. This station was temporarily established in a trench just built, until the bomb-proof under construction for it was ready. A man from the telegraph regiment had the equipment and did the receiving. The receiver was a pyrites detector with tuning coils and head telephones. The note from the airplane radio set was clear and easily distinguishable.

In a depression about five hundred yards from the batteries, three men with pieces of cloth, called panels, stood ready to spread them on the ground for signaling to the airplane. The station was put at this distance so that if enemy airplanes saw the panels, they would not necessarily spot the battery at the same time. The whole operation was protected in the air by pursuit airplanes flying toward the enemy, while the spotting plane was about six thousand feet up, directly overhead.

The ground signal station was connected to the artillery group by telephone, with an officer at our end. The airplane signaled "Fire by salvo," which meant that all guns should fire simultaneously, in one volley. In a few seconds, the report from the battery came over the phone that the shots had left, coincident with the bark of the guns. The telephone officer shouted: "The shots have left," and the men arranged the pieces of cloth on the ground instantly in the shape of the Roman figure four. (Each group had its own identifying cloth on the ground, so the airplane would make no mistake as to which battery the shots they observed belonged to. The battery panel or mark stays on the ground all the time, while the signals referring to the fire are placed near it.)

In another few seconds, the airplane signaled: "Over one hundred and fifty meters, twenty-five to right." This meant that the shots were hitting one hundred and fifty meters beyond the target and twenty-five meters to the right of an imaginary straight line drawn from the battery to the target.

Another fire by salvo, the report, and then another done the same way. Then from the airplane "One piece is out, fire by piece." This indicated that three guns out of the four were firing uniformly, but the other one was not being laid properly or its sights were out of adjustment. Telephone officer, to the battery: "Fire by piece." Back from the battery: "Number One has fired, sir; Number Two has fired . . ." and in each case the men with the cloth made the appropriate signal.

When the fourth piece had fired, the airplane said: "Third piece out, fire it for adjustment." Two shots were then fired by Number Three when the airplane instructed "Fire for destruction," and off went the battery as fast as the pieces could be loaded and fired, with the airplane watching and moving in long spirals. The airplane signaled "Firing effective," and we went over to the battery. The companion battery had been put out of action by the German artillery fire the day before, and the Captain, five noncommissioned officers and several privates were killed and a number wounded. The place was in great disorder, but all the guns and material could soon be fixed up when new personnel arrived. The German fire against it had been very accurate and had come in a perfect deluge. An enemy airplane had located the French battery, had communicated with its own artillery, and within less than a minute the position had been smothered with fire, from guns up to 305-mm. caliber, which made craters thirty feet broad by twelve feet deep.

I mentioned to the Captain that the real commander of these guns was the observer in the airplane above, who told them exactly what to do. To which he replied, "Yes, all we do down here is to perform the work of laborers."

Next we visited the position of the infantry supports. These acted as guards for the artillery, to protect them from destruction in case an unexpected assault was made by a German raiding party. The road over which we went was under fire, and several shell holes were in the middle of it; a wrecked ambulance was piled up to one side—it had been hit a short while before and the driver killed.

The batteries were all camouflaged, the guns themselves being painted in blotched colors, while over them all was grass matting in camouflage colorings. They were all very ingeniously hidden, but it is much harder to conceal from the observation of aircraft than from the ground.

Each little railway to the guns was carefully camouflaged near the position, a false railway being built out to a fake gun emplacement a few hundred yards away, to fool the hostile aircraft. The ammunition and other supplies for the battery were concealed in the same way. The clever, inventive French mind is the parent of all kinds of devices to deceive hostile airplane observers; who else would have thought of camouflage shell holes? These were painted pieces of canvas that were laid on the ground. Often a German battery firing at long range would send an airplane over to photograph the holes where the shells had burst. If the French suspected they were coming and for any reason they wished to divert the fire, they immediately covered these real holes with pieces of cloth which looked exactly like the ground around them and then put their painted shell holes out a long distance away; so the photograph showed these and not where the shells actually fell.

We returned by way of Suippes, and as we approached the town a splendid regiment of infantry passed us on their way to the trenches. These men were the real thing, veterans of nearly three years of war, well trained, well equipped and with a morale that made them able to stand almost annihilating losses. Many troops were being brought up for a new attack, which was soon to take place. As we approached Châlons, the famous auto train of five hundred trucks, with twenty infantrymen to each truck, came into view. They had traveled a long way. The dust was very thick and the men in the trucks looked like gray statues. All the townspeople and soldiers in the city turned out along the streets to cheer them and watch them go by. They said a division of infantry, about ten thousand men, was in these trucks, but I doubt if French divisions had more than seventy-five hundred men then. It took several hours for the whole train to get through. They stayed well on one side of the road, so the traffic could pass, and made about twelve miles per hour.

The men in the trucks, the famous Moroccan division from Africa, furnished a good example of the races who were fighting the war on the side of the Allies. These were the shock troops *par excellence* of the French Army. They were always given the post of honor in an assault and suffered losses accordingly, but nothing seemed to deprive them of their élan, their tremendous fighting spirit. They were composed of all sorts of men, white, tan and a few blacks, who inhabit the French possessions in North Africa. Many have in them the blood of the Arab conquerors of northern Africa, of the aboriginal Berbers from the hills, of the Carthaginians and Romans, Vandals and Goths—all potent fighting strains originally. Only occasionally traces of kinky hair and thick lips, indications of a negroid strain, were seen.

The drivers of the trucks were Annamites, imported from

French Indo-China. They are silent, industrious little fellows, who look a good deal like the Japanese or Filipinos. They were not used directly against the enemy but for all sorts of work behind the lines.

It was not difficult, I think, for the Germans to detect this movement of the truck train, either from balloons or aircraft, so great was the dust cloud formed. It could be told from the character of the dust thrown up what kind of troops were going forward: whether infantry, cavalry, wagon trains, artillery or automobile transportation.

Arriving at the aviation mess, we had a good dinner, prepared by French cooks. What a difference it makes in one's morale, not to mention anything else, to have good things to eat, excellently served, as was the case there. In our American campaigns in the Philippines and Cuba, and even along the Mexican Border, bacon and hardtack were often the sole items on our menu, as our forces moved so quickly from place to place. In France, although the losses were terrific in actual battle, living conditions behind the front were not bad. It was rather like the treatment which is accorded a condemned criminal, who is allowed every kind of delicacy he desires to eat.

In the discussion that took place after dinner, it was the consensus of opinion among the flying officers that movements such as that of the truck train would have to be made at night, in order to utilize the element of surprise. They had seen German airplanes hovering around, watching everything. Even if these movements were made at night, they thought the airplanes might see them, as they could drop calcium lights that illuminated great areas of the ground. With the element of surprise taken away from their operations, the progress of ground armies was greatly hampered. This fact, combined with the great defensive power of modern firearms and the consequent necessity for tremendous artillery preparation before an infantry assault, made it almost impossible for ground troops to make any appreciable advances in a short time. War on the ground is an obsolete system and improvement must come through the air.

11

Military Instruction of Troops
Near the Line

Saturday, April 28, 1917

The school for grenadiers, as it is called (really an infantry attack school), is located at Mailly. I was anxious to see what
was done there and after lunch we left Châlons and drove over.

At the school, Major Favry was commanding an attack by a
battalion of infantry against a simulated position of the enemy.
Two infantry companies were put in the attacking column, with
one in support; a machine-gun company was placed on each
flank so as to sweep the front; two machine guns were held with
the support.

For attack, the company was formed in two echelons, or lines,
of two ranks each. The first echelon had men deployed on a
three-yard interval, the individual machine-gun men and rifle-
grenade men being in the first rank, the ammunition carriers
and hand grenadiers in the second rank, deployed on the same
interval about ten yards to the rear. Behind these, a couple of
squads called cleaners of trenches followed. They were armed
with pistols, knives, blackjacks, brass knuckles, etc. and carried
sulphur bombs to throw into the abris of the enemy to force
them out. They also had *flamenwerfers* (flame-throwers), in
fact, carried any weapon they fancied for hand-to-hand combat.
(The actual fighting between these "trench-cleaners" and the

remaining occupants of the enemy position was about as rough individual combat as anything that went on. Both attacker and attacked allowed no quarter; it was death to one or the other.)

The second echelon followed the first at a distance of from fifty to seventy-five yards, and was composed of riflemen. They acted as a holding and reinforcing force. The supporting company was formed according to the same method.

In an attack, the companies jumped out of their trenches at a given signal and went forward; the machine-gun men fired from the hip when a certain point was reached about ten yards from the trenches, so as to avoid hitting anyone coming out in front of them.

The first line of enemy trenches was supposed to be destroyed by artillery fire and they jumped over this at a run. The cleaning-out squad got busy with the enemy underground, if necessary; if not, they followed the attacking echelon.

When the attacking line, on its way to the enemy second line, was stopped by the fire from the enemy trenches and machine guns, the men lay down, and the large Hotchkiss machine guns, which were carried forward in parts by the men, were instantly brought into action. Together with the individual machine guns and the rifle-grenade throwers they opened up with a terrific fusillade. The rifle-grenades are remarkable weapons and the grenadiers were very accurate with them (up to one hundred and fifty yards) putting up the same awful fire that I saw in the attack on Mt. Cornouillet the other day.

In this exercise, the enemy was supposed to have been rendered incapable of holding this trench and the first echelon went ahead and occupied it, while the second jumped into the first trench, crossed and started to improve it and open up communications by digging with their entrenching tools. This was as far as this battalion was supposed to go. A definite task was given to each and when the objective was attained, they went no further. Great care had to be taken in assigning the amount of ground to be covered and held, because if too great an advance was undertaken, direction was lost by the troops, they were scattered and became an easy prey to the enemy.

The exercises used service ammunition all through. A few men got hurt by the grenades once in a while, but that was war.

Three years of war had shown this system to be the best for this kind of work. Whether or not it would be the best in a war of maneuver is hard to say. I think it can still be improved upon. For the attack of a Mexican town, for instance, it would be cruel as well as useless, because at the end there would not be left a vestige of either the town or the Mexicans.

On the way back to Châlons, I stopped at a charcoal-burner's (he was a soldier and had soldiers under him; some German prisoners were also being worked there). They burned the charcoal in the ordinary way, making a conical pile with a chimney in the middle, covering it with moss, then mud. They then dropped a fire down the chimney and punched some holes near the base to make a draft. After ten days it is finished. Charcoal is very good fuel near the line as it burns with practically no smoke.

These charcoal-burners constituted something like a separate guild. They lived deep in the woods, apart from the people and led a hermit-like existence. They were looked on with awe by the peasantry, who sometimes attributed to them supernatural powers, gained from association with elves and spirits of the woods. Almost every charcoal burner had a collection of quaint and delightful stories that would do credit to any fairy book.

Sunday, April 29, 1917

Captain Dourif of the French Air Service came down to see me the next day. He had been in the United States for a long time, and was a very superior, energetic and well-posted officer.

He called a spade a spade. He told me what the conditions in France really were, which, however, I had already discovered for myself, from observation and from conversation with officers in the mess, who after the second day treated me as one of themselves.

French aviation was on the defensive, or at the very best holding its own. Its tactics and strategy were defensive, as I found out. The pilots in the squadron had been at this work too long, and had lost their nerve, in most cases. A new source had to be tapped for pilots—the United States. The losses were so tremendous that if only a few of our men were sent at a time, they would get the nerve taken out of them also. The thing to do was to get enough organizations together to clean up the air and then hit hard, with everybody fresh and willing to take a chance.

The whole thing was a straight military problem: it was necessary to have command of the air; the enemy had such a force, we had to have an equal force. The lessons of the last three years made this no longer a matter of guesswork, but a sure thing.

To gain the mastery of the air, the air service had to be made more than five times as strong as it was at that time, in men and material, and maintained at that strength. The numbers seemed appalling even in such a great war. We should have had between eight and ten thousand planes on the line all the time. The German curve of aircraft production appeared to be going up faster than the others.

German strategy seemed to be to let the French butt their heads into a stone wall, to encourage them to do so; then when their resources were exhausted, the Germans would strike.

I also had quite a talk with Captain Ménard, who explained to me how he ran his pursuit groups.

One group was stationed at an altitude of six thousand feet, covering the artillery spotting-planes. Its role was defensive. The second group was at twelve thousand feet, its role also being defensive. The former group was twice as strong as the latter. Above the latter, he allowed certain pairs, such as Lieutenant Pinsard and other expert pilots, to take the offensive. The tactics of the squadron patrols of five machines each, as practiced then, was purely defensive in the majority of cases; they faced the enemy and opened fire on him, rarely attacking. If they got a German machine alone, they might attack, or if the enemy machines got behind them, they might be forced to attack in order to get away.

In either case, to signal the attack, the patrol leader made a small bank of his plane from one side to the other successively. The others did the same thing in acknowledgment. The leading machine dived for the enemy, who might try to avoid it by making a vertical bank and quick turn, or a straight nose dive, rotating his machine as he went. The number-two machine was then supposed to attack, then the third and so on.

When pursuit machines engaged in single combat, the fight was usually a series of acrobatic maneuvers between two good men. Where a great number of machines had effect was in taking up the fight successively.

This type of defensive role, while necessary at the time for French aviation, could never be successful in the end. Aircraft had to act on the offensive. It could not dig a hole in the air and go on the defensive as the infantry does on the ground. The Germans knew this full well and rather than keep patrols in the air the way the French did, they kept their men on the ground until such time as they could send a strong patrol capable of breaking through the scattered detachments of French aviation.

While I was at the airdrome, four machines were smashed up. One pilot, while getting off in a new Spad, did not hold his rudder exactly straight on the ground. His machine took a sudden turn and ran into one of the temporary barracks. It went clear inside and smashed up wings, propeller and a good part of the machine. Neither the pilot nor a man who was inside the building was hurt.

A Sopwith, getting up, had engine trouble, and as the pilot was climbing steeply, it stalled and smashed up the front part of the fuselage; neither pilot nor observer was hurt.

Two Spads made poor landings, one turned over and the other had its wing smashed. Neither pilot was hurt. Two pilots came down with their machine guns firing, one full speed; both were nervous and tired, as they had been in the air about five hours that day. The whole army was attacking and using its aircraft overtime.

The new Spad planes that had just been sent to the front were very strong in construction and stood hard usage, but were a little tricky to handle on the ground.

The percentage of loss in machines during an attack was extremely high. The rate of supply, in accordance to the losses to be expected, had to be figured out at least one year ahead. I think the loss in pilots per month amounted to one hundred percent or more, during intense fighting.

Pursuit squadrons are essentially an offensive element, and to enact their role successfully, they must take and maintain the offensive. They should seek the enemy and wherever found, attack and destroy him. A man cannot stand this pursuit game very long at a time without becoming over-careful, and when this stage is reached, it marks the end of a good offensive pursuit pilot. One must have young men, with a good sporting instinct, willing to take big chances; their average age, around twenty-two years. If one can assemble a large enough number of men, with good machines which they have confidence in, they will do wonderfully well. When fatigue and the terrible casualties they must endure begin to affect their nerves, they must be taken out and allowed to recuperate.

Captain Dourif and I returned to town, and by the time we had finished dinner at the little mess, it was night and a beautiful moon had risen. We remarked that it would be a good night for bombing (the French bombers would soon start on their errands themselves). I went back to the hotel to write up the occurrences of the day.

The shades in my room were tightly drawn to prevent any light from shining out and being seen by hostile bombers. I was using my small Corona typewriter by the light of two candles.

As I wrote, I heard the hum of a strange airplane motor and almost immediately—Zing! Zing! Zing! and all the windows and doors shook. The extremely heavy explosions seemed quite near. I looked at my watch; it was just a quarter to eleven. Searchlights were immediately turned on the sky. The hum of many motors became very plain and the anti-aircraft guns opened. Another series of strong explosions, then machine-gun and anti-aircraft fire.

I went out to see what was taking place. The whole town was in darkness, and everyone had taken to the caves or vaulted wine cellars under the houses.

The enemy planes returned at twelve and again a series of heavy explosions shook the place, while the sky was lighting up with bursting shells. Large shell fragments fell in the streets. One small piece hit me on the leg as I stood in a doorway. This I picked up and kept.

The anti-aircraft guns were firing at the sound of the airplanes as much as anything else. A little before one, a great buzzing of motors was heard; I could distinguish the sound of rotary motors and decided they must have twin German Gnome machines. Bombs dropped again, a lot of machine-gun fire was heard overhead, and the antis filled the sky with shells.

I found afterward that the rotaries I heard were the French bombers returning from a raid on the German side. They got all mixed up with the Germans just above Châlons. One enemy machine and a French machine were shown by the same searchlight beam and began firing at each other. This was the first occurrence of this kind that we knew of and we thought it might open up a new field of night airplane combat.

I was impressed with the well-nigh impossible problem of searching the sky at night. To see anything in the sky at night required that all secondary lights be screened from the observer. He should be put down a pit or well with no lights around him. If the searchlights are used, they should be directed by one person, who should assign to them the area to be swept, and have them ready to concentrate on one point whenever told. I believe that calcium bombs with parachute attachments could be arranged for the 75-mm. guns, which, with their rapidity of fire, could shoot them up to any height desired and fill the whole sky with them. This would light up the area as bright as day. It would show the ground below also, but that is very easy to see from airplanes when a bright moon is shining.

As a defense against aircraft, the Germans were said to have used captive balloons in pairs, which carried a wire between them. From this wire were suspended many aluminum barbed wires, which of course were a very formidable obstacle to any aircraft flying through them, as they could break the propeller and smash the wings.

Another scheme, said to be German in origin, designed to protect certain factories which manufactured explosives, consisted of hanging nets over the tops of the buildings, which would explode the bomb before it reached the building.

Airplane hangars were highly vulnerable and one small bomb recently destroyed a hangar and twenty-one French machines inside it; while another one blew up one of the largest ammunition depots the British had accumulated for the Somme offensive.

Many buildings were hit and destroyed in Châlons that night. A shell hit near the aircraft park and did a great deal of damage. Parts of the railway station were demolished.

Some men, attached to a radio station, were sitting playing cards at a table. An airplane bomb came through the roof, tore through the center of the table between them, embedding itself in the ground under the house. Its fuse failed to work and it did not explode.

At a place of amusement, there were assembled fifteen or twenty men who had been safely through hundreds of battles; practically all of them were killed.

Not only was the material effect of bombardment to be reckoned with, and it was constantly increasing, but the moral effect on the people was even greater. Women and children were paralyzed with fear. It was a menace from an entirely new quarter. Fighting on the ground and on the water had gone on since the beginning of time, but fighting in the air had just started; and several generations will have to be born and pass away before people can adopt and maintain the same attitude toward this form of warfare as they exhibit toward the old familiar ones.

12

The French Attack Moronvilliers

Monday, April 30, 1917

This was the day scheduled for the grand attack against the Moronvilliers position, the line of heights of which Mt. Cornouillet was the dominating feature. The Bois de la Grille, in front of which I witnessed the unsuccessful attack the other day, was made one of the principal objectives of the operation; it had a very strong German closed work in it.

These strong works that the Germans built at various critical points on their lines were most interesting. Some of them had three and four decks of floors in them, going down into the ground for sixty or seventy feet. They were lighted up by electricity, had artificial ventilation and were completely equipped to resist a siege, with food, ammunition and all necessities for a couple of weeks' stay. Some of them held more than a thousand men and had machine guns, grenades, bombs and flame-throwers—even heavy artillery. It seemed impossible to dislodge a force from one of those positions by artillery or infantry attack. The only feasible means of conquering it was through the use of gas, laying down such a heavy concentration that the furthest corner and crevice would be penetrated.

We proceeded to the Mt. Sinai Observatory, situated about seven thousand yards from the line.

As we made our way to the observatory, the sound of the great guns became an incessant roar. The only individual discharges we could identify were those from the French guns of very heavy caliber which were firing in the immediate vicinity.

It is impossible to describe this roar of artillery or convey an adequate impression of the monstrous quality of sound that assaulted one's ears. It was grand and appalling and, at the height of an artillery preparation, could be heard for miles and miles. It had a stupendous effect on human nerves. It was as though this inferno of sound was something that had a separate malignant existence of its own, which, not content merely with taking life, had to also exact a toll from every individual nervous system exposed to it. The elements themselves seemed to be affected, as almost always at the end of such an artillery preparation, great storms with heavy rains occurred.

Nearby, men were working on trenches about four feet deep, into which they were placing lead-covered telephone wires. Our way took us through the woods by a little path which was concealed from overhead and lateral view. The trees were just beginning to bud and a few wild flowers were coming through, while many migratory birds were actually singing in the trees, in the midst of the heavy detonations.

We entered the observatory, which was made of concrete, steel and earth; the concrete was reinforced and about two meters thick, and all this covered with about three meters of earth. The observation port, or aperture, was about ten feet long by ten inches broad. Looking out of it were several telescopes and scissors-shaped optical instruments. The view from this observatory was truly remarkable and may be likened to that from a captive balloon. It was on the brow of the mountain of Reims, some three hundred and fifty feet above the plain below, over which it looked. Roads, railroads, villages, hills, creeks, woods, meadows, farms and trenches were spread out before us. Our artillery seemed to literally fill the valley and surrounding hills, as from every nook and corner a flash shot out, followed by another and another.

This fire had been kept up for two days. The Germans replied to it deliberately and steadily but with no such whirlwind of fire as the French were directing against the Bois de la Grille. The front trenches were subjected to constant, heavy field artillery fire, but little of the light 77's. A German balloon was in the air for a while and then was pulled down because of the haze; later it went up again. There was no lack of airplanes of any kind on the German side.

At 1:00 P.M. the heavy fire suddenly stopped, and within a minute the first wave of infantry could be seen leaving the front trench; the tanks began to move from their concealment. For an instant as I looked through the glasses, the attack looked as though executed by troops at drill, so perfect was the alignment. Tanks smashed through the barbed wire entanglements and the infantry began to split up into small bodies, as it was delayed by the wire.

In another minute the infantry disappeared in the dust and smoke of the attack, and the lighter smoke from grenades thrown by the soldiers became noticeable. Soon rocket signals for the barrage to move forward were sent up by the infantry. It was almost as easy to see them at this distance (eight thousand yards) as when I had been close to them the other day.

Red rocket signals, sent up by the French infantry, indicated that a counterattack was coming, and the French artillery fire was turned on again with all the guns possible. Little spouts of earth now merged into a great upheaval of the ground. Trees, denuded of their leaves and branches, were rooted up bodily and flung into the air. Men and tanks alike disappeared from view.

An airplane went forward at about one thousand feet over the infantry to see what was happening. It carried long cloth streamers under the wings, showing it wished to communicate with the infantry below. Four times I saw the airplanes of "commandment" go forward and come back, each time making

it without being destroyed. Most of the fire went over them, although they must have been directly in line with a good deal of
the artillery fire. Aircraft were the only means of conveying
information from front to rear at a time like this, because all
telephone and wire lines were destroyed, and it was impossible to
install radio or other stations.

The fight now seemed to be confined to the Bois de la Grille,
the Germans either throwing the French back, or the French
being able to hold only the front line of the Germans, which
they appeared to have captured during the first attack. Try as
they might, they were unable to gain the crest of the hill; the
German fire swept them down every time an attack was tried.

The tanks attacked with the infantry in this operation. It was
very difficult to tell what they actually did after they started,
as all that could be seen most of the time was a terrific melee of
bursting shells, dust and grenade smoke.

The attack impressed me as a very well-managed affair, tacti-
cally, for a frontal fight such as it was. From a strategical standpoint, however, there was no doubt that it was another piecemeal affair, and merely resulted in a great waste of life, without
accomplishing any lasting result.

We left the scene after two hours, and the fight was keeping
up as violently as ever, without any appreciable gain by the
French. The crux of the matter is that the French had only
sufficient artillery to attack the line at certain points, all the rest
being let alone while the one place was attacked. The Germans could wait until the attack was well developed and then
meet it, even to the extent of taking men away from other places
on the line.

Although the loss of life was difficult to estimate and no figures could be obtained at the time, I think, from the casualties
that were inflicted during the previous attack, there must have
been at least fifty percent casualties in the assaulting columns.
There were at least four thousand men deployed from each of
the seven divisions attacking, and therefore, about fourteen
thousand were killed or wounded that afternoon while I

watched, with the number constantly increasing as the evening wore away. In spite of the tremendous showing the artillery made, the fire had not been sufficient. During the preparation, most of the Germans had retired to their deep dugouts, where they were comparatively safe from the artillery fire. When the French infantry was upon them, they emerged with their machine guns and engaged in combat from behind their parapets.

If the French were going to take the offensive, they needed at least ten times the amount of heavy artillery they then possessed, a corresponding increase in aircraft, and a strategical plan that would stop the piecemeal attacks. The German front had to be attacked all along the line and the deep formation placed against the vital points.

We returned by the route over which we had come. All the roads leading to the front were filled with columns of wagons containing artillery ammunition, while the small arms ammunition and cartridges for machine guns went forward in little carts.

A stream of wounded was already beginning to make its way back to the rear, some of them walking, some terribly mangled ones in the ambulances. We passed several field hospitals, where the surgeons were busy with cases which had to be attended to at once.

After supper, the moon rose bright and clear, and the people of Châlons were convinced that there would be another bomb attack by the Germans. Sure enough, at a quarter to ten the leading German machine was heard, after which the bombs began to fall.

This time the anti-aircraft defense was not caught unawares. They had nine searchlights instead of three, and instead of trying to shoot where they thought the German machines were, they threw a barrage fire around the town; that is, the batteries were so arranged as to keep up a constant fire covering certain areas, both longitudinally and in an upward direction.

The airplanes returned three times but their numbers were much smaller than the night before. Anti-aircraft guns failed to bring down a single German plane, although thousands of rounds were fired, both from cannon and machine guns.

In the evening after the raid, I worked most of the night getting my papers and equipment ready to leave. I had seen everything possible with the Fourth Army.

Tuesday, May 1, 1917

After making final arrangements for departure and bidding my new friends *au revoir,* I started with Captain Raulin by train for Paris—a journey of three hours.

A Japanese Colonel of engineers was on the train with me. I thought I had seen him once at Port Arthur, a good many years before. After keeping quiet for a long time, he remarked to me in French "that France had no spring climate, winter immediately passing into summer." I asked him if he were thinking about the cherry blossoms of Japan, and he said he was. Japan at that time of the year, he said, was the most pleasant part of the whole world, and he felt very bad whenever he had to be away in the springtime.

Later, our conversation veered to many subjects, and he showed me the prize thing he had obtained during his stay at the front. It was a piece of concrete from a German trench, which he said he had had analyzed and was sending to Japan, for them to use as a model in the future.

These little fellows were observing every detail in each branch of the service. They were becoming particularly interested in aviation, and I am told had some pilots in the French service, one of whom was very good and had obtained several victories over the Germans.

13

War Politics

May 1917

The month of May, 1917, proved to be one of diversified and intense activity in preparation for the coming of the American forces. We heard few words from the United States directly. Occasionally a telegram came to Mr. Sharp, our Ambassador, but even he seemed to be overshadowed by Colonel House, who came over to find out about things for somebody; nobody knew exactly whom—whether it was for Colonel House himself or the President of the United States or for some group that we knew nothing about. Our Ambassador, of course, felt the matter quite keenly but naturally could do nothing about it.

It has always seemed to me that if a diplomatic representative in a foreign capital is not capable of exercising his functions, he should be removed and another person put in, rather than have the ground cut from under his feet by secret emissaries, and his influence and prestige with the foreign country and his own people reduced to almost nothing.

We had received a great deal of information from the French as to what was going on in the United States, and some from the British. All were impressed with the prodigious effort that was being put forth. The only question was whether our assistance would reach Europe soon enough to stop a German victory. The submarine operations were keeping up against Great Britain and she was on the verge of starvation. Many of her people had no potatoes, their great food staple, nor had many of them had meat for long periods. They could not hold out for many months at the rate the submarines were sinking their ships.

Everyone was saying that the attack of the French armies was a political attack and not a military one. It was well known that the soldiers heartily opposed a main attack by the French army alone against the German army. The majority of them were against attacking even in combination with the British at the time because these attacks were just what the Germans wanted. They would lead to tremendous losses with no advantage to be gained and might give the Germans a good chance to defeat them if they were weakened too much.

Conditions in France were so entirely different from those in the United States that few of us understood the manner in which their government worked.

The whole policy about what should be done in case of war with Germany was determined by the Chamber of Deputies really before the war ever started. It must be borne in mind that every country in Europe prepared with their greatest energies for this contest long before 1914.

In France, it was well known that the Germans would be able to concentrate their armies and assume the offensive much more quickly than the French, because the German centers of population were closer to the frontiers than were those of France. The bulk of the French people live in the southeastern part of the Republic, and they could not possibly be mobilized and concentrated on the northern frontier of France before the Germans would be upon them.

Everyone knew that the Germans would come through Belgium because all the European nations when at war had always gone through Belgium. Napoleon did it; Caesar did it; and it was certain it would be done in any coming war. The French military men, knowing this, wanted to concentrate their army along the line of the Seine River, get it together as a fighting machine and then move north and engage the German army. In this way, although territory would have to be given up to the enemy, the French army would be entirely intact, fighting on its own soil, close to its magazines and depots, while the Germans would be correspondingly removed from their own country and supply points. The French politicians, however, did not want one *pouce,* or inch, of French territory given over to the hated barbarian (as they still regard the Germans) and the deputies tried to have the army agree to concentrate on the northern frontier. This the French General Staff refused to do, as it would have been practical suicide, but they compromised by concentrating the French army along the line of the Marne River, which is halfway between the Seine and the frontier.

The Germans calculated that the French would do this very thing, also that they would offer battle there, because if there was one thing the French armies had always done, it was to offer battle whenever they had a chance. So the Germans laid their plans to swing their army completely around the French army. The pivot or shoulder was in the east near Toul and Épinal, the hand in Belgium and the elbow around Charleroi. The French army was to be strangled by this grip.

The movement started on the first day of August, 1914; the Germans went through Belgium as rapidly as if there had been nobody there. Their cavalry overran it, supported by some infantry and motor trucks. The forts that the French had helped to construct were speedily reduced to powder by the mammoth German howitzers.

During the first ten days of August, 1914, the French army faced almost certain destruction. The one man that saved France at that time was old Papa Joffre, an engineer officer by profession and a defensive soldier by nature. It was one time that the country needed a leader of that kind. Instead of offering battle on the line of the Marne, he ordered the French army to make a rear march and take up a position along the Seine. Such a

thing had never been heard of in French history. It was a movement fraught with the greatest difficulty, for if the army were
caught in the retrograde movement and a hole made in it, certain destruction would result. Everything hinged on getting the
various army corps back to the Seine in an orderly and organized
way. This move astonished the Germans, who at once realized
that the French Army was escaping them. Their only hope was
to hit it while it was moving.

The German troops performed prodigious marches, the
greatest the world has ever known. The swiftest marching in
history before that was during Napoleon's concentration against
Ulm, when his army, marching from camps near Boulogne-
sur-Mer, opposite England, averaged fourteen miles a day, to get
up to Ulm and destroy the Austrian army under General Mack.
The right flank of the German army averaged thirty miles a
day, in their attempt to catch the French army. Finding that it
was entirely a question of speed and that a great number of their
troops in France did them no good from the middle of August
on, the Germans detached five army corps and sent them to the
Russian frontier, which was being seriously menaced.

The Joffre movement kept up and a line was being re-formed
and organized near the Seine when the first divisions of the
German army made their appearance. Everything was thought
to be closed up when suddenly it was found that a hole existed
toward the right of the line. The Germans had found it and
began pouring troops into it. Just at this juncture the great 20th
Corps came up, filled the gap just in the nick of time, and old
Joffre ordered the whole army to attack. That is what saved
France and all the people know it. The politicians did not give
old Joffre credit, nor did many of the professional army officers,
because Joffre was originally an engineer, but the old fellow's
name will go down in history in the list of the great captains.

The French have fought their own wars in times past, and
no more glorious pages have ever been written in the book of
military annals than those placed there by the French armies;
but the birthrate in France had fallen off so that they only had

about one-third as many males available for military service each year as the Germans. They had to make up this difference by getting men from some other place, and their chief source of man power was their colonies in Africa. In addition to these, Mongolian troops had been brought into France from Indo-China. Their British allies had brought in East Indians from India, and Chinese laborers from China.

Now France was faced with an influx of Americans, both black and white, although many French think we Americans are red Indians, just as when Columbus discovered the new world.

Think what this great flood of foreigners on their soil meant to a people with the great pride and traditions of the French. It is true they seemed to fraternize and associate with them, but this is a tolerance born of desperation. Always within themselves, they feel they are the superiors of any people on earth and it wounded their sensibilities to feel that their country had come to such a turn. The French are exceedingly sensitive but make remarkable comrades. They are constant, true and dependable, although in carrying a point they sometimes employ methods of circumlocution that we do not understand. I wondered how our Americans would do with them.

Both the English and French were attempting in every way to obtain the greatest influence with the United States, because after the war when the commissioners would sit around the table determining what should be done, whichever side had America behind it would unquestionably carry its point; that is, providing the Allies won. If they did not, it would be all off with them anyway. Consequently there was the greatest amount of pulling and hauling, propaganda and inside work going on both in the United States and with our emissaries in Europe, to get the inside track with us. The English had a great advantage in that they speak our own language. Many of our men were unable to speak French and they had the old Anglo-Saxon suspicion of any Latin, which was aided and abetted by our English cousins calling the French "frogs" and deriding them in the way they always have.

Logan and Churchill had been working hard with the French General Staff and the British representatives as to what part of the line the American army should be put into. Both the French and British, particularly the latter, were attempting to influence our government to send them men to put right into their own regiments as individuals, so as to bolster up their rapidly falling numbers. They argued that if men were not put in at once, the Germans would win; that it would be impossible for the United States to create a fighting army within a year to cope with the German troops, and if we waited a year it would be too late.

I felt that we were over here fighting our own fight just as much as fighting the fight of the French and English, because if they were whipped, we would be the next; furthermore, we were over here as Americans and not as French or English. We had to insist upon having our own army, as I was sure the American people would never stand to have their sons killed on foreign soil under foreign leaders. As a matter of fact, if the reverse situation existed and our Pacific coast were being invaded by the Japanese, and our existence threatened, it would be impossible for the British and French to conscript men to serve in our army, and next to impossible to send any military forces at all on account of the feeling of their population. Consequently, we had to make an American army because when this particular squabble ended, another one might start soon after. We need to keep our powder dry, keep it in our own possession, and get weapons that we can use with it.

We had impressed this upon our Allies, so the question was, where would this independent American army fight? The next question was, where should our troops be debarked from the transports?

These matters, among others, occupied me for the first ten days of May at our little offices at 138 Boulevard Haussmann, in the building of the American Radiator Company. One floor had been turned over to us gratis by the president of the Paris branch. Up to this time we had received practically no assistance from America. It seemed probable that we might not for some time, so we had gone ahead organizing our own show in France. Each day was full of work from morning until night. When we left our office and went to the Hotel France et Choiseul on the rue St. Honoré, where Logan and I lived together, we spent hours talking over the matters that lay before us. Logan was a man of unusual ability in dealing with the French and British, and he combined a knowledge of business methods, transportation and military matters to a remarkable degree. He had a broad acquaintance in the French army, and during his tour in Europe had been careful to create a good entente everywhere.

Many volunteers were appearing to help us, some of whom had seen the conscription coming and thought they might get easy jobs away from the enemy by volunteering for some desk position before the American forces arrived. Few of these had been taken, because on looking them up through the Paris police and intelligence service, we found many of them to be the flotsam and jetsam of all sorts of defunct war contract companies, or mere adventurers.

There had been some notable exceptions, however. As I sat in my office one day, my assistant came in to tell me that there was an elderly gentleman outside who wished to volunteer his services, whom he thought I should talk to, being greatly impressed by the man's earnestness. He was a man of about sixty, in robust health and of pleasing address, who said he was Laurence W. Miller of New York, that he had been a Captain in the New York infantry in 1887, and that he had been engaged in foreign trade for some time and was familiar with conditions in France. He wanted to fight the Germans, he told me very seriously and gravely; he could support himself and did not need any pay. He knew, he said, that aviation was going to be the great decisive element in the contest, and he wanted to be with us and help us in every way he could. Being quite impressed with Mr. Miller, I asked him to come back the next day, after we had had him looked up by the police, as was the custom with every applicant. The report came in from police headquarters that he was an excellent individual in every way, so upon his arrival I had him get a desk and appointed him business manager of the office, in charge of keeping track of all the personnel, installing a uniform system of indexing and filing, and keeping up the daily journal of all we did. Laurence Miller stayed with me from that time until the end of the war in the same capacity. He was later made First Lieutenant and then Captain, being discharged in the United States after the conclusion of the contest. No more efficient or honest person ever served under the American flag.

Another interesting volunteer was Boyreven, a sergeant in the French army who was terribly wounded at the beginning of the war. He was recovering, but was not yet able to do full military service. Captain Jacques Maurice Boyreven, his brother, was one of the leading French aviation officers. Sergeant Boyreven spoke English quite well, had a very good education and was an artist of considerable note. He was an excellent draftsman, and I assigned him the duty of drawing up graphical studies of all the aeronautical organizations in Europe and the graphics of what our organizations should be when our air troops began to arrive. These drawings were used by us in Europe and are still being used in the United States. Boyreven also remained with me in the capacity of a personal aide during the whole war. His service was always remarkable in every way; he was a master of detail, of tact and understanding. Nothing in the relations between my staff and the French ever escaped him, and I think it was due largely to him that my staff never had a misunderstanding with the Allies all during the war.

Another Frenchman who had come with us was Adjutant Victor Fumat of the French Flying Corps. I had applied to my friend, Daniel Vincent, French Minister of Aviation, for some airplanes, a good instructor and a good mechanic. I had been able to flounder around with the animated kites that we called airplanes in the United States, but when I laid my hand to the greyhounds of the air they had in Europe, which went twice as fast as ours, it was an entirely different matter. Vincent acted at once and assigned Fumat to me as pilot instructor and a sort of general chaperon in the air, ordering him up from Pau, where he was an instructor of pursuit aviators.

He was the best instructor I have ever seen in any country. He was a man well past forty, one of a family of eighteen children, a Basque, with typical Basque thoroughness, loyalty and personal interest. He took charge of me and we began flying from the French airdrome, Le Bourget, in Nieuport airplanes. Each day we went out and flew a little while. To reach Le Bourget, we had to pass through the slaughter-house district, where the population was almost on the verge of revolution; then through a series of graveyards, with tombstones sticking up, sort of beckoning to us; then through a lot of worthless anti-aircraft guns, lined up around the city of Paris. It seemed strange that flying fields were habitually put next to graveyards, considering the effect of this on the pilots. Those selecting airdromes probably did it with a prudent eye to the saving of time as the departed pilots did not have to be carried far when they crashed.

Fumat brought with him his mechanic, Louis Blanc, an extremely efficient workman. Blanc tended to my airplanes throughout the war and I never had a forced landing from engine trouble during the hundreds of hours of flying I did in France. This was a remarkable record.

Each day we became more efficient, and the Americans in Paris helped in every way possible. Mr. Hyde brought me into contact with the chiefs of the French army, General Foch, General Weygand, his Chief of Staff, and others. At his house I met many of the leading politicians, Royalists, members of the Clerical party and Socialists, and people from Great Britain and Italy.

Dr. Edmund Gros, an American living in Paris, one of the founders of the Lafayette Flying Squadron, used the funds of that organization and his own money toward helping out our office force and getting Americans in the French Flying Corps concentrated at French flying schools; so that when our new squadrons come, we can make use of trained leaders who have had experience over the lines.

I met Mr. James Gordon Bennett, who was one of the pioneer aviation enthusiasts of the world. He was in his declining years, but was just as interested in aviation as ever. He wanted to know every detail of our work and frequently asked to accompany me on my visits to Villacoublay, the great French aeronautical experiment station where all their new planes were tried out. Mr. Bennett had an intense personal dislike for William of Germany. He thought there was nothing too bad to say about the Kaiser and he could certainly say bad things when he wanted to. As nearly as I could make out from what he told me, Mr. Bennett and the Kaiser became involved in a discussion about some yacht races at Kiel many years ago, and in some way the argument was continued until they got down into the engine room of the Kaiser's yacht, where they had a personal encounter until separated by some of their friends. Mr. Bennett's whole idea was to whip Germany so as to get rid of "Bill."

Another person for whom I formed a great and lasting admiration was Daniel Vincent, Minister of French Aviation, patriot and man of action. Some manufacturers of aircraft and engines had been attempting to monopolize the government's orders so as to control the aircraft industry. One of these men was Louis Renault, a great industrial figure in France. His works made the best large aeronautical engines in Europe. I had an accounting made of what these engines cost to produce and considered that what we were asked to pay for them was excessive. The manufacturers on their side took the attitude, "Why not make America pay? They have been charging us exorbitant prices for the war materials we have bought from them; why shouldn't they pay us back some of our own coin, now that they have to have our equipment?" I told Vincent that these ideas might be justified to some extent, but that the American government was entering the war to whip Germany, and her loss of men on French soil would be terrific; that if the American people got the idea that the French were profiteering in this way, it would be a decided check to their enthusiasm and would probably affect American participation, which would be extremely serious for France. We had no idea of beating them down, I pointed out, and when a man turned out an excellent airplane engine, such as Renault's, he should get a fair profit on his investment; but in time of war anything beyond that would not be tolerated.

Vincent was of my opinion, but the strength of the Renault combination in the Chamber of Deputies was almost greater than that of the government itself, and was a very difficult thing for one Minister alone to handle. However, he saw far ahead what the results would be and prepared accordingly. There was a law on the French statute books that any factory which did not conform to the government's orders could be requisitioned and run by the government. This had never been put into force by the Aeronautical Department and to attempt such a thing with Louis Renault was something very few people in France would have done. I am told, however, that Vincent drew up the articles of requisition, sent for Renault and told him straight out that he would either conform to what we wanted or his factories would be immediately requisitioned. Renault was astonished but bent his sails to the wind and we never had any further trouble with his concern. In fact, everything that Renault turned out, whether it was aeronautical engines, automobiles or tanks, had in it the best possible materials and workmanship.

14

I Visit the British Army

May 1917 (Continued)

Toward the first of the month I had put in a request to go with the British army, which took several days to come through because it had to be sent from the British Mission in Paris to the British army headquarters, then back again to Paris. Immediately on receipt of my permission and orders, however, I departed from Paris to visit General Hugh Trenchard, commanding the Royal Air Force of the British army, whose headquarters were near Abbeville.

As we entered the zone of the British armies, the appearance of the troops changed materially. The men were well turned out, wore good shoes, and their weapons, leather and equipment were spick and span. The officers looked particularly smart. All the automobiles and trucks looked as though they had just rolled out of a garage and the traffic was beautifully handled. The motor cars were all well closed up, kept to the right and proceeded at exactly the rate prescribed. The horses presented an excellent appearance, being well fed, well groomed and shod, with their harness, bits and equipment wonderfully cared for.

All this was in marked contrast to what I have seen in the

French army, particularly the horses, which receive very little attention in the French service. This struck me as strange because the French knew more about the scientific training of horses than any other people, yet they took poorer care of their animals than our American army, which is saying a good deal.

The men in the British ranks I found to be only about half the size of the French infantrymen. We think of the French people as being small, but in the British Isles not only is the average inhabitant small, but the ones who come from the mining district where the people have been so poorly nourished for years, are almost midgets.

General Trenchard's headquarters were in a nice country house, off by itself, about twenty miles from the front. The General, having been notified of my coming, was awaiting me when I arrived. He was a man of about six feet in height, erect of carriage, decided in manner and very direct in speech. His judgment inspired my immediate confidence and his whole personality my deep respect, and we became fast friends at once. He was really the father of the British fighting aviation. At the beginning of the war he was a man of about forty-five, a pilot and thoroughly convinced of the enormous value of this great arm of the service. Under his impulsion, the British air service grew from a few second-class planes to a great force, with more than two thousand airplanes on the line.

General Trenchard asked me what I wanted to know, and I told him I desired to learn about his organization, his equipment, his system of supply and that also I wanted to participate with his aircraft in any operations that were taking place at that time against the Germans. He replied that this was quite a big order, and asked me how much time I had to give to it. I told him I thought the first part of it could be gone over that afternoon and evening and the next part might be started the following day. He asked me if I thought he had no other duty except to show me around and tell me everything they knew, to which I replied that he had such an excellent organization that it should not need his leadership for the space of a day or two, no matter how serious the condition might be. This made him laugh a good deal and he observed that he guessed I would get what I wanted.

In his office, large maps of the entire British front were spread over the walls, showing the lines held by the ground troops and the positions his air forces occupied. He explained the system to me in great detail and outlined the policy which had been pursued by the air forces from the beginning of their military operations. What few airplanes there were were employed merely for observation, like elevated movable platforms which could see and report the movement of the enemy to the ground troops. When the airplanes began to attack each other and drop bombs, the troops on the ground yelled for protection and brought the air forces to task for not keeping all enemy airplanes out of the air near them. He read me the following paper, containing his opinions and policy at that time:

"It is sometimes argued that our aeroplanes should be able to prevent hostile aeroplanes from crossing the line, and this idea leads to a demand for defensive measures and a defensive policy. Now is the time to consider whether such a policy would be possible, desirable and successful.

"It is the deliberate opinion of all those most competent to judge that this is not the case, and that an aeroplane is an offensive and not a defensive weapon. Owing to the unlimited space in the air, the difficulty one machine has in seeing another, the accidents of wind and cloud, it is impossible for aeroplanes, however skilful and vigilant their pilots, however powerful their engines, however mobile their machines, and however numerous their formations, to prevent hostile aircraft from crossing the line if they have the initiative and determination to do so.

"The aeroplane is not a defense against the aeroplane but it is the opinion of those most competent to judge, that the aeroplane as a weapon of attack cannot be too highly estimated.

"A signal instance of this fact is offered to us by the operations which took place in the air at Verdun.

"When the operations at Verdun began, the French had few machines on the spot. A rapid concentration was made, and a

vigorous offensive policy was adopted. The result was that superiority in the air was obtained immediately and the machines
detailed for artillery coöperation and photography were enabled
to carry out their work unmolested, but as new army ground
units were put into the line which had less experience of working
with aeroplanes, a demand arose in some quarters for machines
of protection, and these demands were for a time complied with.
The result was that the enemy took the offensive, and the French
machines were unable to prevent the hostile raids which the
enemy, no longer being attacked, was now able to make. The
mistake was at once realized and promptly rectified. A policy of
general offensive was once more resumed, and the enemy at once
ceased to make hostile raids, all his time being taken up in fighting the machines which were attacking him. Superiority in the
air was thus once more regained.

"On the British front, during the operations which began with
the battle of the Somme, we know that, although the enemy has
concentrated the greater part of his available forces in the air on
this front, the work actually accomplished by their aeroplanes
stands, compared with the work done by us, in the proportion of
about 4 to 100. From the accounts of prisoners, we gather that
the enemy's aeroplanes have received orders not to cross the
lines over the French or British front unless the day is cloudy
and a surprise attack can be made, presumably in order to avoid
unnecessary casualties. On the other hand, British Aviation has
been guided by a policy of relentless and incessant offensive. Our
machines have continually attacked the enemy on his side of the
line, bombed his aerodromes, besides carrying out attacks on
places of importance far behind the lines. It would seem probable
that this had the effect so far on the enemy of compelling him
to keep back or to detail portions of his forces in the air for defensive purposes.

"When Lille station was attacked from the air for the first
time no hostile aeroplanes were encountered. The second time
this place was attacked our machines encountered a squadron of
Fokkers which were there for defensive purposes. This is only one
instance among many.

"The question which arises is this: Supposing the enemy, under
the influence of some drastic reformer or some energetic leader,
were now to change his policy and follow the example of the

English and the French, and were to cease using his aeroplanes as a weapon of defense and to start a vigorous offensive and attack as many places as far behind our lines as he could, what would be the sound policy to follow in such a case? Should we abandon our offensive, bring back our squadrons behind the line to defend places like Boulogne, St. Omer, Amiens and Abbeville, and protect our artillery and photographic machines with defensive escorts, or should we continue our offensive more vigorously than before? Up to now the work done by the Germans compared with that done by our aeroplanes stands, as we have seen, in the proportion of 4 to 100, but let us suppose that the enemy initiated a partial offensive in the air, and that his work increased, compared with ours, to a proportion of 30 or 50 to 100, it is then quite certain that a demand for protective measures would arise for protective squadrons and machines for defensive patrols.

"One of the causes of such demands is the moral effect produced by a hostile aeroplane, which is out of all proportion to the damage which it can inflict.

"The mere presence of a hostile machine in the air inspires those on the ground with exaggerated forebodings with regard to what the machine is capable of doing. For instance, at one time on one part of the front whenever a hostile machine, or what was thought to be a hostile machine, was reported, whistles were blown and men hid in the trenches. In such cases the machines were at far too great a height to observe the presence of men on the ground at all, and even if the presence of men was observed it would not lead to a catastrophe. Again, a machine which was reported in one place would certainly, since it was flying rapidly, be shortly afterwards observed in another part of the lines and reported again, but the result of these reports was often that for every time the machine was sighted a separate machine was reported, leading at the end of the day to a magnified and exaggerated total.

"The sound policy, then, which should guide all warfare in the air would seem to be this: to exploit this moral effect of the aeroplane on the enemy, but not to let him exploit it on ourselves. Now this can only be done by attacking and by continuing to attack.

"It has been our experience in the past that at a time when

the Germans were doing only half the work done by our machines that their mere presence over our lines produced an insistent and continuous demand for protective and defensive measures.

"If the Germans were once more to increase the degree of
their activity even up to what constitutes half the degree of our
activity, it is certain that such demands would be made again.

"On the other hand, it is equally certain that were such measures to be adopted, they would prove ineffectual. As long as battle is being fought any machine at the front has five times the
value that the same machine would have far behind the lines.

"If the enemy were aware of the presence of a defensive force
in one particular spot he would leave that spot alone and attack
another, and we should not have enough machines to protect all
the places which could possibly be attacked behind our lines, and
at the same time continue the indispensable work on the front.

"But supposing we had enough machines both for offensive
and for defensive purposes. Supposing we had an unlimited number of machines for defensive purposes, it would still be impossible to prevent hostile machines from crossing the line if they
were determined to do so, simply because the sky is too large to
defend. At sea a number of destroyers will have difficulty in preventing a hostile destroyer and still more a hostile submarine
from breaking the blockade. But in the air the difficulty of defense is still greater, because the area of possible escape is practically unlimited, and because the aeroplane is fighting in three
dimensions.

"The sound policy would seem to be that if the enemy changes
his tactics and pursues a more vigorous offensive, to increase our
offensive, to go further afield, and to force the enemy to do what
he would gladly have us do now. If, on the other hand, we were
to adopt a purely defensive policy, or a partially offensive policy,
we should be doing what the French have learnt by experience
to be a failure, and what the rank and file of the enemy, by their
own accounts, point to as being one of the main causes of their
recent reverses.

"Moreover, in adopting such a policy, it appears probable
that the Germans are guided by necessity rather than by choice,
owing to the many fronts on which they now have to fight, and

owing also to the quality and the quantity of machines they have to face on the Western front alone. Nevertheless, one cannot repeat too often that in war nothing is certain, and that the Germans may, either owing to the pressure of public opinion, or the construction of new types of machines, or the rise of a new leader, change their policy at any moment for a more aggressive one."

The Germans were beginning to adopt a more aggressive policy with their bombardment aviation, attacking principally at night when they needed no pursuit protection. In some cases the Gothas, German twin-engine airplanes, inflicted thousands of casualties in one night by bombing British troops that were huddled up in their bivouacs in preparation for an attack the following morning.

Some remarkable individual attacks by German airplanes had taken place. One was against a railroad train proceeding from northern France to Rouen, filled with hundreds of wounded and disabled soldiers. A two-seater German plane flew down close to the train and during the approach the pilot fired his front guns. As they passed the train, the observer fired his machine gun from the turret. The men on the train had very few weapons, nothing of course that could affect the airplane; consequently, some two hundred men were killed and wounded by this one enemy plane.

General Trenchard held the opinion that aviation should be carried just as far into the enemy country as possible. He considered it a perfectly practical thing for airplanes to attack the rear of the German army through the air and destroy all its means of supply, subsistence and replacement.

With the capacity for ten-hour flights making an increase in the radius of operation, Berlin could be reached, which would mean the whole interior of Germany. These things could be accomplished. All that was needed was development of the planes and methods of handling them. But certain difficulties stood in the way. For one thing, it was difficult to persuade Great Britain to build the planes the troops needed, due to the conservatism of the people. For another, the army opposed the plan of sending airplanes into the interior of Germany, because they thought it would leave them unprotected. The ground troops did not yet realize that they were perfectly incapable by themselves of dealing a blow at the heart of the enemy country, or its vital centers.

Another element that militated against a development of air power was the navy, with their Royal Naval Air Service. This service was not acting at sea with the navy, but had organized squadrons fighting on land, detailed with the Royal Flying Corps, and really a part of General Trenchard's organization at the time. They had their own way of operating, their own system of supply and their own corps of officers. It complicated matters exceedingly to have two organizations doing exactly the same work at the same place. The navy wished to control all air operations against the enemy and opposed any that were not under their control. It was General Trenchard's opinion that eventually air power would be much greater than sea power. The old conservative elements in the British navy saw this and opposed any change.

As a result of this division of authority over British aviation between the army and navy, German raiders over England had things pretty much their own way. The navy claimed jurisdiction over all the air that lies over the water, with the army restricted to that over the land. Thus, if a German plane flew to England, the navy was supposed to attack it over the English Channel, but as soon as it reached land, it became the army's job to shoot it down. As this worked out, the Germans crossed the Channel too quickly for the naval planes to reach them, and bombed the cities before the army air service could get to them. If the army planes did give chase, they had to quit at the water's edge and there were no naval planes waiting to take up the pursuit, as there was no unity of command. So the Germans flew over England as they pleased, with practically no losses.

The only way to handle air power, in Trenchard's opinion, was to unify it all under one command. The air covers everything and is one substance in which movement takes place irrespective of what is under the flying machine, whether land or water. I thoroughly concurred in General Trenchard's ideas, because this same spirit of controversy between our army and navy was holding us up in organizing our air forces for the war and if it was continued, would set us back many months and seriously affect the outcome of the war. In America an independent air department should have been established at once and aviation developed to attack the enemy far inside his territory, not just to play around the lines where the infantry was ensconced in rabbit warrens and fox holes far below the surface, where they could not easily be hurt or hurt anyone else.

General Trenchard, in handling air forces with troops, placed with each army the minimum number of airplanes necessary for the use of ground troops in action—for their own domestic use, as he expressed it.

The bulk of the aviation General Trenchard had assembled consisted of all the bombardment aviation and as much pursuit as he could get together, so that he could hurl a mass of aviation at any one locality needing attack. His idea was to send them across in one big formation which attacked the object with bombs and machine guns, fought whatever air battles were necessary and then got back as best it could. This is the proper way to use air power and I am sure the future will see operations conducted in this way by thousands of airplanes.

The following day I went to the Fifth British Army, holding the section of the front opposite Cambrai and south of Arras, and under the command of General Gough, to whom I reported. He was a small, energetic, well-knit man, and of course was intensely interested in what the United States would be able to do. He had a pretty good knowledge of things American and a firm conviction that not only should we be able to do a great deal in increasing the supplies for Great Britain, which were running dangerously low on account of the submarine menace, but that our men could be used to great advantage at once, not only behind the front in the supply system, in the repair depots and as motor-car drivers, but could be fed in with older units, where they would take the stiffening, as he put it, from the experienced soldiers and veterans.

This was just what I had heard all along the line, which meant that if we concurred in their plans, we would have no American army, and not only lose our identity as a fighting force but have no organized and experienced units at the end of the war. I did not discuss the matter at any length but merely listened to what the staff had to say about it.

Most of them considered the German position as almost impregnable to attack by the old methods of artillery preparation, advancing the infantry and assaulting the works. Their tanks, however, offered a means of pushing through the enemy's machine-gun nests, pill boxes as they were called, which was possible in no other way. Some thought that the tanks could carry on almost independent operations; that is, be pushed forward in fleets, seize the strong points and hold them, having their supplies brought up by other tanks. In this way, the positions could be held until the infantry could come up and entrench.

Their conception of handling tanks was almost like the navy's method of handling the battleship fleet on the seas. I liked this characteristic of the English—their leaders were not bound down by tradition as those of the older French and German armies certainly were. Their minds were much more elastic and receptive to new developments and new methods. Of course, if the new methods did not work, the danger was greater than if they had not been attempted. If somebody got some new method or equipment that did work, however, the older systems instantly gave way. The great captains were those who thought out new methods and then put them into execution. Anybody can always use the old methods. That is the trouble with old regular army officers; they can never get out of the rut, but always go into a war with the methods of a former war and consequently they are sure to be whipped whenever they come up against an elastic-minded, constructive leader on the other side.

I drove around the front to some extent and observed the terrain. It will be remembered that the Germans had retired in front of the whole British army, from fifteen to twenty miles, and destroyed everything that intervened. All the houses were blown up so they could not be used as shelter for troops; all the roads were destroyed. All the population had been taken out of the area. The thing that looked most pitiful to me was the fruit trees, sawed or chopped down. In many cases the sap had run up them or a little piece of bark still remained attached to the stumps, and they were in full bloom, lying on the ground, of course never to bloom again.

An attack of a part of the Fifth Army was to take place the next day and I asked to be permitted to see it or take part in it, either in the air or on the ground. The task assigned the attacking troops was to capture a salient of the German position, formed by Bertincourt, which controlled the roads about eight miles south of Arras, and just north of Bapaume, another important point which controlled the road to Amiens. It was quite an important position and had to be taken by the British if they were to hold the Arras area. An Australian division, who had an excellent reputation as assault troops, had been assigned to this duty.

Both the Canadian and Australian troops I had seen looked much stronger physically than the units from Great Britain. They were bigger men, seemed more intelligent and better educated, and were extremely proud of their organizations. Although their camp and march discipline was not as good as that of the British troops, and their equipment not so well cared for, I believe their battle discipline was better. There is a decided difference between battle discipline and camp discipline. Troops may present a wonderful appearance in camp but go all to pieces when heavy losses are incurred. The measure of battle efficiency is the ability to stand the terrific losses and still carry on. If I were going into a ground fight, I believe I would take the Australians with me in preference to the others, particularly if much maneuvering, open warfare and marching were necessary.

General C. A. H. Longcroft, the Commanding Officer of the

Air Brigade, looked after me during this attack. He was an excellent pilot and thoroughly conversant with all details of the air work. When the ground attack started, he put me in the back seat of his own plane, which was an old BR-2 observation ship, very slow in the air but very sure on landing. It was a good sort of bus to go from one place to another in, but no ship in which to be caught over on the enemy's side. It would not last a minute against the German Albatros pursuit machines. We had a good look along the lines from one or two miles behind them, and could plainly see the bursting of the shells and the troops fighting.

The British and French systems of identifying the explosion of shells on the ground for the artillery were entirely different. The British system did not fix the command of the artillery in the air to the same extent that the French did, but was really spotting the hits, in much the same way that the navy conducted its fire from battleships. On the other hand, where great precision was required on a certain target, I believe the French system of coördinates was better.

General Longcroft and I obtained an excellent view of the trenches where the battle was going on between the Australians and the Germans. We could see that the Australians had taken the position they were after; whether they could hold it or not was another question, as they were being deluged by artillery fire.

The British balloons were all up, from four to five kilometers behind the front, or a little less than three miles. As we were well in advance of these, we could see no other airplanes near us, except some British two-seaters, which were spotting for the artillery. Naturally we were quite exposed to any German attack. The British were not protecting their observation machines with pursuit aviation close to them, but were pushing the pursuit aviation away over on the enemy's side, so as to force the air fighting to a distance away from the troops. The British two-seaters had to protect themselves.

While we were looking over the battle lines, a patrol of German Albatros pursuit planes suddenly made its appearance coming directly for us. General Longcroft's vigilant eye caught them, and he turned toward the line of balloons, looking for a place to land. I think he expected that the German planes were coming to attack the balloons and if they saw our unprotected and helpless aerial jitney, they would just shoot us down in passing. We came to earth safely in a field and saw that the Germans had become involved in a contest with the British observation planes, instead of coming to the balloons. The German artillery, however, saw our airplane on the ground and began firing at it. We ran to a road nearby that had steep banks, in which there were a number of dugouts. Crawling into one of these, we remained there while the bombardment proceeded. After a while it stopped and we emerged from our retreat, and found that the airplane had not been hit at all, although there were several shell holes close by.

Ambulances were passing to and fro, carrying back the wounded, the little packages of flesh and bone which still contained a certain amount of life. As I noted the excellent care they received, I compared it with what had been given our troops during the Spanish War and Philippine Insurrection, which was quite primitive. I thought of the terrible suffering of our Civil War wounded, who had no anaesthetics or powerful drugs to alleviate their pain. They were carried in springless wagons, pounding over the Virginia mountains and almost impassable roads, to what they called hospitals, places little better than cow barns. Few people today realize what a terrific contest the Civil War really was. The losses incurred in it were greater in proportion to the troops engaged, than those being incurred in this war, and for that matter, it was just as important a war. If we had been split into two nations, we might have had little subsequent influence on the progress of world events, but I feel sure that from now on we are going to be a great determining influence.

General Longcroft and I decided we had seen enough at the front for one day and proceeded to our airplane, cranked it up and went home.

15

To Paris Again

May 1917 (Continued)

Never had I spent a more instructive four days than those with the British, nor have I ever met a man with whom it was a greater pleasure to talk and associate than General Trenchard. He promised me every assistance in future and invited me to come back whenever I wanted to talk matters over with him, or see more of the British air operations against the enemy.

I returned to Paris and found that reports were coming in to the French government about the prodigious effort America was putting forth. There had been doubts in the minds of a good many as to whether conscription would be adopted by us, but this was assured. Four million men were to be called to the colors. One difficulty with which we were faced, however, was in transporting them to France. Many advocated the building of wooden ships, on account of the great forests available in our country. When I suggested to some of my French friends that the old forests near Fontainebleau be cut down and transformed into wooden ships, they were horror-struck at the mere idea of these sacred trees being touched.

Speculation was rife as to who would command the American forces. Many of the French think that if Theodore Roosevelt could just make his appearance on French soil in a general's uniform, the effect on their people would be tremendous. Some expected General Wood to come, but political conditions in the United States precluded the possibility of these leaders being given any of the dominant positions. If they were successful, as would be quite likely, it would lead to the President's chair; and both Wood and Roosevelt were Republicans.

My second visit this month to the Allied front was in company with Dr. Ames of Johns Hopkins University. He arrived in Paris as the head of a mission to look into the aeronautical situation. Dr. Ames was a man of excellent judgment, with a considerable knowledge of air matters and great breadth of view. His was the first mission to come over, and they investigated the subject more thoroughly, I believe, than any that came afterward. I do not think but a very few of Dr. Ames' recommendations were followed, although all were excellent.

We looked over the different branches of aviation and their attendant supply organizations connected with the French army in the vicinity of Châlons. Again I had the opportunity to fly along the front of the Fourth Army, in the Champagne, which continued to attack. Their losses had been frightful and their gains almost negligible. It was now certain that General Nivelle, in command of the French Armies, would be relieved and another put in his place.

During this visit to the Fourth Army, I was formally presented with the French Croix de guerre. I had to obtain permission from our government to keep it, since it was against the law for us to accept any foreign decoration or patent of nobility. I thought a special law should be passed to allow our officers and men to accept marks of commendation and decorations from foreign governments for meritorious service.

Upon returning to Paris, I was brought in contact with many of the leading French political figures. The French politicians are brilliant men, without exception; they are great inside

workers and leave no stone unturned to find out everything they
want to, some being quite unscrupulous about it. The French,
as a people, are great students of personality, of the intimate
personal characteristics of the individual. They are much more
personal in that respect than we Americans, who sort of strike
an average between everybody and go ahead on that assump-
tion. Mr. Henry Franklin-Buillion, the leader of the Socialists in
the Chamber of Deputies, was about to make a journey to the
United States to investigate conditions. He wanted to know about
all the individuals who were controlling matters, from the President down; how they could be approached, what they were
interested in and how he could gain the maximum amount of
information, and do the most good for his country. We had several meals together, at which I gave him some idea of conditions at home and he acquainted me with the aims of the Socialist
Party in France.

Another person I met was Senator Baron d'Estournelles
de Constant, the head of the Senate Committee on Aviation, who
was intensely interested in air power and its development. His
son was attempting to become a pilot, but he had a bad crash
and I doubt if he ever became proficient. Senator Constant gave
me a great deal of information on conditions pertaining to the
manufacture of French aircraft and engines. Of course, there
was manipulating by all of the various manufacturers to get
orders just as in other places. It was a good thing to know about
this because it is necessary for us to use a great deal, if not all,
French equipment with our aviation.

The Committee of which Senator Constant was head asked
me to come down to the Senate and talk to them on the subject
of aviation. This was rather a large order for me but I was glad
to accept and on the sixteenth of May I talked to the Senators in
the Senate Chamber about aviation and our participation in the
war. I established relations with the various members of the
Senate which unquestionably would do us a great deal of good in
the future. Although having practically no legislative power, the
French Senate studies all the political questions that arise, and

can give more mature and sober judgment on them than can the
Deputies. There was a strong Royalist sentiment in the French
Senate. Although France is a republic in every way, the old titles
of nobility are still used, and people pay as much deference to
the counts, barons, marquises and dukes, as though they were
real nobles in a kingdom or empire. A republic, in many ways,
seems artificial with the French people. If they had a constantly
increasing birthrate and were a world power, an expanding people, they might be better off under a monarchical form of government, but now outside of Europe their effect is not very
great. With their diminishing population, their world influence
politically is growing less.

Later in the month I visited Avord, the great center of aeronautical instruction in France, in company with Mr. Sharp, our
Ambassador; Colonel Girot, in charge of French training; and
Dr. Gros. On the way to Avord, we went through Fontainebleau, where Napoleon bade farewell to his old guard in his first
abdication and then went into exile on the Island of Elba. His old
chateau is just the same as it was then; the Napoleonic "N" with
the laurel wreath around it still decorates each portal, and the
same flagstones pave the courts that resounded to the tread of
his invincible grenadiers. We had a pleasant luncheon in a restaurant opposite the chateau, which formerly was one of the
buildings belonging to it. The walls were covered with prints
and etchings of all sorts of French subjects, while the furniture
and other articles all had historical significance and were price-
less in value. It was kept by an old lady, who, when she found I
was an American aviation officer, told me she would knit me
some heavy socks for the following winter. She kept her promise.

We arrived at the aviation school in the afternoon and were
greeted by the Commander, Captain Max Boucher. I was struck
by the immensity of the place. There were several flying fields,
hangars stretching for miles, and five or six hundred airplane
in use all the time. Men were being instructed from every
branch of the service in the ground army, and also many that
had never served in the army at all. A good many Americans

were there who had enlisted in the French Foreign Legion, probably two hundred of them. These were the men I was so anxious to get for our own aviation as they would have several months start on any we could get from the United States, besides their experience in actual air fighting.

The system of instruction here was quite different from ours in the United States. They started the student, alone, in what is called a Penguin, an airplane in which the wings are too small to allow it to fly, and which is equipped with a low-power engine. The controls were the same as in a full-sized airplane. These things were difficult to maneuver on the ground and when the student first started out with them, he would go every which way. Gradually he got so he could go straight from one place to another at a speed of from twenty-five to forty-five miles an hour.

After the students became proficient with the Penguins, they were put in what are called Rouleurs. These machines had bigger wings in comparison with the Penguin and could get off the ground a little. The object was to have students make little hops off the ground and keep a straight course. After they got through the Rouleur stage, they were put in Découleurs. This machine was similar to the one before it but the student could hop it off the ground a little more. First, they went up four or five feet, flew a little way, throttled the motor and landed, then took off again. Gradually the student took the airplane a little higher, each time while flying straight from one end of the field to the other. After this stage, the student, who had really taught himself so far, was put into one of the larger machines, some into two-seaters with an instructor. These were supposed to graduate into bombers and observation airplanes. Those destined for the single-seaters, or pursuit, were put into Bleriot monoplanes and after this into the fast Nieuport *chasse* or pursuit planes.

I believe that this system produced excellent pilots, although it took a great deal of time, going from one kind of machine to another. Five or six different types were used before the pilot was graduated. I went through this same sort of instruction myself and know it taught me more about flying than any other system could possibly have done; but I believed we should get one kind of training plane and graduate our pilots from that right into the service planes being used against the enemy. Although the French system is very thorough, like everything else they do, the cost is tremendous.

The Americans who were undergoing instruction here seemed to be pretty well pleased with things. The food was not what they were used to at home, and the quarters, in some cases, had a good many insects in them, but the men were treated very kindly and considerately by their French instructors. All had nothing but praise for the flying ability of the men over them.

We arose next morning at daylight, about 3:30, to watch the instruction, which began at four. Everywhere we looked the sky was full of airplanes. They were landing, taking off, getting more gas, rolling around on the ground, some of them crashing, at which ambulances would rush out to drag the unfortunate pilot from the wreck. We visited classes where the students were taught about motors and airplanes, how to read maps and what to do when they joined their squadrons.

After the classes, we motored back through the old city of Brughes with its tall church tower rising above the tiled roofs, about which hundreds of cawing rooks were flying back and forth. On the way to Paris, the roads were almost deserted of traffic. There were few men left in the interior of France. The fields were being tended by women and children, while old men did what they could on the police force, in the mills and at home.

The month of May was drawing to a close and still no troops had come from the United States. We hoped that at least a brigade, possibly a division, might come. It seemed an interminable while to wait but at the time every minute seemed an eternity. The battles were still raging and the French hospitals were full. The French kept asking, with more insistence, "When are the

Americans coming?" Some added, "What good can they do when they *get* here? Everything has been taken away from us already and the coming of a few more men will only continue the agony."

We heard that some men in the army had to be shot for mutiny, also that two regiments mutinied and refused to go into the front line, but this I was unable to substantiate. Naturally there are some such happenings in every war and rumor always magnifies them, especially with people so conversationally inclined as the French.

My own little air office was in excellent shape. We had all the information we needed, our plans of organization worked out, and everything written up as to how we could work. In regard to the several hundred Americans in the French aviation schools, I had made arrangments with the Minister of French Aviation to equip them with French airplanes and within a month or two we could put five or six American squadrons on the line and be fighting the Germans with our own men, regardless of the delay in sending troops from the United States.

16

We Hear that Pershing Will Command

June 1917

France had contracted to produce, for the use of the British, Italians and Belgians, a great many more airplanes than she used herself. When we came into the struggle, another country had to be supplied. The output which the French were capable of was prodigious. France showed that she could produce more per man day of work than any nation in the world.

With so many nations involved in the purchase and use of French aeronautical material, it was necessary to create an Inter-Allied Board, to apportion the equipment and fix the method by which it should be handled. M. Flandin, a brilliant member of the French Chamber of Deputies, was made head of the Board. He had to reconcile a great many elements—military, political and economic—with manufacturers of France and other countries. He and I had a great many disputes, which were pretty sharp at times, because I insisted that we get the best airplanes that could be manufactured at the earliest possible opportunity. I did not want to brook any delay and we were getting into one misunderstanding after another, when some of our friends began inviting us to luncheons and dinners, so we could discuss these affairs more at our ease. Among those who did a great deal to iron out these misunderstandings was the Marquise de Brantes, who was a Schneider of the iron-and-gun-making family of that name, and the "Bertha Krupp of France." She brought us together at frequent luncheons at her Paris residence, 5 Place des États Unis, where we discussed our differences unofficially and did a great deal toward smoothing them out.

Early in the month we heard that General Pershing was to command the Americans forces and that a division of regular troops would soon be landed at St. Nazaire, which had been selected as the port of debarkation for our army. The French had hoped to see Roosevelt and Wood. They had never heard of Pershing and wanted to know who he was and what he had done. They place much more emphasis on personalities than on systems and organizations, and after all are quite right in their viewpoint, because an organization is only a means to an end, not an end in itself; the best sort of an organization will get nowhere in the hands of poor men, whereas a poor organization handled by excellent men will always do something.

The French began saying that now we would have two *peres* running the war, "Pere Joffre" and "Pere Shing." This phrase has caught the imagination of the French, who are great people for bon mots or catchy expressions.

On June 6th, I sent to the United States a complete list of the raw materials necessary for making the following aircraft engines: Clerget, Renault, Lorraine, Hispano-Suiza. This included such things as soft and hard steels and chrome-nickel, in bars, tubes and forgings; aluminum, bronze, cast iron, brass and copper, and woods. France was getting very short of spruce wood and was immediately in need of more.

Complete lists of the amount of gasoline and oil required for these engines was also submitted. Together with the Salmson, these motors were the best then made for aircraft work, and their production should have been augmented immediately to meet the requirements of American aviation. Instead of this, we heard that an entirely new engine was to be made in America which would require months of trial before it was perfected, and which then would not fit any airplane in existence. It was to be made by engineers entirely unfamiliar with the aviation conditions of the war.

Our office was outgrowing the space donated free of charge by the American Radiator Company, and with the coming of the American Expeditionary Forces, we needed much larger quarters to accommodate the offices of our air service. Besides, the American Radiator Company really needed this space for their own use. So I looked about Paris for a suitable building and at last found one at 45 Avenue Montaigne, a fine new six-story structure, which was condemned for war use by the Minister of Aviation. Captain Benedict was detailed to furnish it for our purposes.

After completing these arrangements, I requested and obtained permission to visit the British front again and see how their air operations were being conducted, from Flanders, against the submarine base at Zeebrugge and along the channel ports. Arriving at Dunkerque I proceeded to the air force headquarters, commanded by General C. L. Lambe. I had known Lambe years before at Hong Kong, China, where he was a Commander in the British navy, in charge of torpedo boats. At that time we had international polo games between the American teams in the Philippines and the British Asiatic Team at Hong Kong. Lambe and I played opposite each other and became great friends. Lambe was an expert on submarines and when the air service developed, he saw its possibilities and took it up.

The air force headquarters, a large house on the beach near Dunkerque, had been hit several times by German artillery. This long-range artillery fired practically every night at 9:00 P.M. It was said that the British observation station could see the flash of the cannon, and on a signal by telegraph that the projectile was starting, everyone would run into the cellar and all the lights would be turned out before it hit.

One thing that struck me as both amusing and interesting was the fact that French troops held the city of Dunkerque. It is away up in the corner of France, practically on the Belgian

border and of course nearer to England than any other part of
the line. One would think if the English were going to hold any
place, they should hold Dunkerque, but it seems there is a tradition which has come down from the middle ages that whoever
controls Dunkerque, controls France. The French, in the back of
their minds, are still afraid that the British may again control
France, so they allow no British force to occupy this place.

Near Dunkerque, we crossed the Belgian frontier. The Belgian gendarmes made a great fuss over inspecting all our passes,
both for ourselves and the automobiles. They wanted us to
know that it was their country although they had only a ten-
mile slice of it.

That afternoon I saw the first heavy bombardment squadrons
of the Royal Flying Corps. They were Handley-Pages, with two
Rolls Royce engines, capable of carrying over two thousand
pounds of bombs, with enough fuel to last eight hours. Since
they could make sixty-five miles an hour, they had a radius of
about two hundred miles. They were so slow, and consequently
so easily shot down by the German pursuit aviation, that they
were mostly used at night.

They were making nightly raids on Brughes, in Belgium,
which was the center of German activity for that part of the
line. Railroad yards, barracks, ammunition dumps and depots
of supplies had been demolished and set on fire in that vicinity.
After each raid, a De Havilland would be sent out in the daytime
to photograph the damage done, and the following night the
attack would be made in accordance with the information obtained from these photographs.

I was told they had recently received a bomb that weighed
sixteen hundred and fifty pounds and this had been carried
across the lines on a Handley-Page, with a view to dropping it on
Brughes; but the pilot had been picked up by the searchlights
there. To get out of them, he had to maneuver his plane rapidly,
but could not do so with this large bomb aboard, so he dropped
it. There was a terrific explosion and immediately all the searchlights went out and he was let alone. It was claimed that when

one of the huge bombs was dropped within half a mile or a mile of a searchlight, the concussion smashed the glass in the light and otherwise rendered it useless.

A short while before, they told me, a super Handley-Page with four engines had been made and flown over from England; but the pilot, instead of flying it to France, went directly into Germany and landed it at a German airdrome, thereby giving the Germans complete information on the latest type of bomber that the British were developing. It was intimated that this pilot had been tampered with by the Germans and in reality was a spy.

Spies were said to be carried over by airplanes and dropped behind the lines in parachutes. It is remarkable how volunteers can be obtained to do almost anything in war, even though it means almost certain death. In this spy business, women were used as much as men; in fact, the women were usually better. They were very nimble-witted and could meet almost any emergency that arose, hence were able to get through many places with ease where men would have been detected.

General Lambe was sending a large flying boat, with two engines and two five-hundred-pound bombs, from Dunkerque to attack the submarine base at Zeebrugge, about forty miles distant. It had to go in the daytime in order to get a good view of the place; the wharf at which the submarines lay was only about one hundred feet wide. It was really a mole, constructed of concrete blocks and closing the mouth of this shallow harbor.

It was a great sight to see this seaplane start. It ran along for a considerable distance on the water, then took the air, accompanied by two or three squadrons (forty or fifty British pursuit planes). They usually used Sopwith-Camels because these were the best the British had for "dog-fighting." They were light, could turn very rapidly, were quick on the ailerons. It was necessary to send them with the flying boat, otherwise it would have been shot down by German pursuit machines. Practically every raid meant a fight.

The flying boat, accompanied by its land planes, went well

out to sea, then came in from the west or the north to Zee-brugge. If the expedition went over the land or even within hearing distance of the land, its presence would have been re-ported at once by German listening posts and it would have been stopped. There was a good deal of trepidation felt at first about sending the British land planes out over the sea, but there was less loss in these operations due to forced landings than there had been over the land.

At first, the flying boat used an escort of seaplanes, and when they approached the enemy coast, the Germans immediately attacked them with their single-seater pursuit planes and caused great loss among them; the big, heavy, lumbering, un-maneuverable seaplanes could in no way protect themselves against their fast adversaries.

It therefore appeared that seaplanes or flying boats could only be applied in war where land planes were unable to go. In other words, wherever seaplanes had to fight land planes, they could not hope to conquer. This is interesting because it means that air forces acting from the water can do nothing against land air-dromes unless they are equipped with similar planes. They must either use seaplanes or fly off the decks of ships with land planes. In the latter case, only one or two at a time can get in the air; whereas from land airdromes, hundreds can take the air simultaneously because they may use any number of flying fields. Therefore it is evident that no naval air force, no matter how transported, can hope to do anything against an air force based on shore. This is extremely important, because if naval vessels cannot control the air over them, they cannot operate against shore establishments. Airplanes are necessary for spot-ting the fire of their great guns and in order to prevent the land batteries from operating they must drive the opposing airplanes out of the air.

Airplanes now carry torpedoes of the same size and weight as those used on naval vessels, and are able to aim them with great accuracy. No decided attempt was made to do this, except in the Baltic Sea, where it was reported the Germans sank several vessels with torpedoes launched from airplanes.

British officers were convinced that with the coming of long-distance bombers, the Essen district in Germany, with its magazines and ammunition works, could be reached and destroyed. Dunkerque certainly was a decisive area for the operation of aircraft because with a flying radius of two hundred miles, the whole position of the Germans in northern France could be covered, and if sufficient aircraft were gotten here, every supply point, every camp and concentration point of the enemy could be effectively bombed.

On the following morning I went up through the infantry positions in front of Dixmude. Here I ran into mustard gas for the first time. The Germans had been using it in large quantities in this locality. It lay about in shell holes and its effect on a person was very much like a burn from a hot iron or scalding from hot water. It affected all parts of the body but particularly the eyes, and wherever there is excessive perspiration, such as under the arms. It is said that wounds from gas were more numerous than those from all kinds of artillery and infantry projectiles. A shell, when fired, bursts in a certain area which is affected by its explosion and a certain number of fragments that can be counted definitely, we may say fifteen hundred or two thousand. But if a gas shell hits, it projects millions of bullets, as it were; its area is infinitely greater than that of an explosive shell and with mustard gas, it is effective for ten days to two weeks afterward.

The British had had a terrible experience with gas in 1915, the first time it was used by the Germans. It came as a total surprise and they had no masks or equipment to counteract it. Great waves of the deadly stuff rolled over their troops, killing or incapacitating them by the thousands. In fact a great gaping hole was torn in the British line, large enough for the Germans to pour whole army corps through had they known the measure of success that attended their gas attack. It worked better than they had expected and they were not prepared to follow up their tremendous advantage. Even at that, had they had more gas, they could have retained their advantage, but the chemical warfare service in Germany had not been able to persuade the German General Staff to allow them sufficient manufacturing capacity to turn out great quantities of this new and most dangerous weapon. It had never before been tried in war and the old conservative army officers were skeptical. They said to the chemical officers, in effect, "If we give you factories to manufacture as much gas as you want, we shall have to cut down the manufacture of our gun powder. We do not know what the gas will do and furthermore we do not believe in the kind of warfare which steals up on a person when he is not looking and asphyxiates or paralyzes him. That is no way to make war."

This is much the same sort of cry that went up from the armored knights in the sixteenth century, when a peasant with a musket could shoot through his steel cuirass and roll him off his charger a dead man. That also was taking a mean advantage. The use of firearms was then considered inhuman warfare, but it obtained a much quicker decision than did the old hacking tactics of the armored knights, with their maces, their axes, their swords and pikes.

The British made a great noise about gas when the Germans first used it, but the British themselves then used it and there was a great question among military men whether it was not a more humane form of warfare than any other.

The countryside of Flanders was absolutely flat and covered with shell holes. It looked from the air the way the moon does through a telescope. It was wet and damp. The troops were subjected to a great deal of discomfort and disease as a result of these conditions. They got diseases of the feet, in which the feet really rot off; they had rheumatism, colds, catarrh, and sinus troubles.

Towns near the lines were merely heaps of stones. Ypres was entirely destroyed. If the Germans could have pushed into Lille, then down the coast and seized the Channel ports, they would have had a tremendous advantage, but I doubted if they could, as the difficulty of bringing forward supplies was so great.

Assisting the British in this area were some French pursuit squadrons under Major Brocard, of the *Cigogne* or Stork group, which took its name from the fact that each airplane had a stork painted on its side. The various squadrons had different kinds of storks. Georges Guynemer, the leading French ace, whom I met first in Paris, was with one of these squadrons. He was a little, thin fellow, about five feet seven or eight, with remarkably bright and alert eyes, and was a wonderful pilot. His family came from Compiègne. It is said he was not at first accepted for military service on account of weak lungs. He was very nervous from overwork and I thought he should leave the front and rest up. It would have been a great thing if he could have come with the Americans and given us the benefit of his experience in forming and training our pursuit aviation.

Guynemer was a remarkable shot and took photographs of his victims at the time they were hit. He was said to be able to put the bullets of his machine guns in a space as big as a hat, at one hundred meters range. He was always accompanied by two excellent mechanics, who kept his Spad airplane in the best of condition. They also sized and carefully fit every round of ammunition that was used in his machine gun. In this way he seldom had any machine-gun jams. He had a new airplane equipped with a .37-mm. cannon. The propeller shaft of his geared Hispano-Suiza motor was hollow and the cannon shot through this and through the middle of the hub of his propeller. This cannon was effective not only against airplanes, which of course it could blow up with its shells, but one shot from it would set fire to and destroy a Zeppelin.

I returned to Paris well pleased with this profitable second trip to the British front. I had been along it all the way from its southern extremity, in the vicinity of Péronne, to the English Channel.

Just as I was leaving for Paris, I heard of the raid of thirty-five German Gotha airplanes on London. They flew in broad daylight, across the Channel from an airdrome in the vicinity of

Ghent, in V-formation, at an altitude of only thirty-five hundred feet. They dropped their bombs on London, turned around and returned, apparently without losing any planes. The anti-aircraft fire had no effect. The divided control of the air force between the army and navy resulted in a terrible mess. There were no pursuit airplanes organized or properly posted for the defense of London. The navy, which was responsible for defending the air over the water, did not know the Germans were coming and consequently had dispatched no planes to meet them. The army, not having been notified of their coming, had no planes at the coast to fight them off. When the German airplanes started home, the army planes pursued them as far as the water, but no navy planes were there to take up the chase.

The whole thing was absurd and I believed as a result of this raid, the British would create a separate air force. There had long been an agitation along that line; practically every British air officer I talked to favored that organization. The army and navy, however, were jealous of their privileges and authority, and all the old mossbacks of these services had been able to block the move so far.

17

Pershing Arrives in France

June 1917 (Continued)

Back in Paris, I found that General Pershing and his staff were to arrive on June 13th. This was given widespread publicity and elaborate preparations were made for his reception, especially in the way of police precautions to prevent anyone taking a shot at him. People were even posted on the roofs along the line of march to watch for this. Airplanes were instructed to guard against a German raid, as the Germans knew as well as everyone else that General Pershing was coming to Paris. The news was well broadcast; it was supposed to have a dampening effect on the German morale to know that the hero of our American-Mexican frontier had now arrived in Europe to settle the dispute between the French and Germans.

The railroad station, the Gare du Nord, was elaborately decorated with flags of the Allies and with carpets on the floor. A great reception committee, including every kind of person who could get there, was in attendance.

Churchill and I had discussed whether or not we should wear Sam Browne belts and the uniforms we had had made in Europe.

The old blouses or "Mother Hubbards" used by the American army, which stopped a little bit below the waist belt, were popularly known as "Seymours," because you could see more of the seat of a person's trousers than anything else, when they were worn. I determined to wear my new uniform anyway, with a Sam Browne belt, and thus I appeared at the station. Without a Sam Browne belt in France, one was always mistaken for an enlisted man as all European officers wore them.

The train rolled in and there was great cheering as General Pershing, Lieutenant-Colonel James G. Harbord and the rest of his staff dismounted and came into the waiting room of the station, looking a little bewildered. It certainly was good to see them. They were escorted to their automobiles through the tremendous jam by Colonel De Chambrun, the great-grandson of General Lafayette and a brother-in-law of Nick Longworth, and by General Pelletier, a one-armed veteran of the French Army. I rode in automobile No. 8 with a couple of the staff.

As the train of automobiles proceeded toward the Hôtel Crillon, flowers were thrown on them and in their path, and cheer after cheer greeted them. A great program had been arranged for General Pershing and his staff, which had to be gone through with before they could do anything else. Visits had to be made to the President of the Republic, the Minister of War, the Minister of Marine, Marshal Joffre and many others. Everywhere he went, he created a great interest, especially in the Chamber of Deputies. He visited the Senate, the tomb of Lafayette, and then called upon General Pétain.

With General Pershing had come Major Townsend F. Dodd, his aviation officer, an excellent man and one of our oldest flyers. Dodd had been with Pershing in Mexico and had great confidence in his chief. He told me of what was going on in the United States and felt that the great effort being put forth would result in our getting partially trained aviators within a few months, but he was dubious about any efficient airplanes coming for over a year. The Chief Signal Officer's Office, which had charge of aviation in America, he described as a madhouse. Some civilians had been called in who were great industrial organizers and it was hoped something would be forthcoming from them. The army itself, he said, was perfectly helpless to cope with the aviation problem.

I showed Major Dodd everything we had done in Europe, what our plans were and what I thought should be done.

I was a Lieutenant-Colonel by this time and therefore ranked Major Dodd. I had been on duty with the American Embassy but all officers there had been ordered to report to General Pershing. This made me the ranking aviation officer in Europe.

Dodd and I asked General Pershing to talk aviation matters over with us, at which the General asked us to come down to the Crillon after dinner. We found him in his palatial suite and when I remarked that he was very well housed, he replied that unless he moved to some other place he would have to borrow money which he could not pay back for the next ten years, because things were so expensive.

I told General Pershing what I had learned of conditions in Europe and described the data I had prepared for our participation in the war, which could be used by his staff at once. Major Dodd told General Pershing that as I was the ranking air officer in Europe, I should be made aviation officer of the expedition, that is, Chief of the Air Service. I was over there to fight the Germans, I told them, and would just as soon be a pilot in one of the squadrons as anything else. Major Dodd responded that I ranked him and had a more intimate knowledge of the situation than anybody on the ground on account of being on the spot from the beginning of hostilities.

Both of us recommended that aviation be detached from the Signal Corps, of which it still formed a part and made an independent fighting force, as in all other services. Also, that a board of officers be convened, to which all the data we had accumulated could be submitted, with a view to making definite recommendations as to our future organization. General Pershing approved these ideas and a board of officers was immediately convened to investigate aeronautical matters. This was the first time in our military history that aviation was regarded as an independent combatant arm.

The board proposed that the following cable be sent to the United States, which if carried out would have made an independent bureau of aviation for all branches of the service and would at once have coördinated all our activities:

> To harmonize interests and concentrate all efforts I strongly favor establishment of air service department whose head shall be member of executive cabinet charged with all matters pertaining to American Air Service. His assistants to be Chief of the Army Air Service, Chief of the Navy Air Service and a member of the munitions Board or corresponding organization.
>
> PERSHING

It was never sent. If a plan of this kind had been adopted, it would have saved millions of dollars, hundreds of pilots' lives and undoubtedly shortened the war.

The second telegram proposed centralized the control of all aviation matters in Europe, as follows:

> I strongly urge the importance of having all aviation matters in Europe handled only through these Headquarters, both the matters that originate in Europe either in the American service or in the European governments and those matters that originate in the United States and that are handled in Europe either by the American Air Service or by the European governments.
>
> PERSHING

Later this was more or less carried out, but for a long time different aviation offices existed in England, France and Italy, and the navy as well as the army had an organization at each place, neither coördinated with the other. This led to a tremendous waste, which was kept up till the end of the war.

At this time we heard that an American aviation mission was

coming to Europe, under command of Major R. C. Bolling. No previous word or instructions had been received by General Pershing about this mission. It was proceeding directly to Great Britain, presumably to negotiate with them on matters that had to do with the American Expeditionary Forces. Accordingly, Major Dodd was ordered to England to direct the work of this mission.

Officers from the United States began coming in during June. Among others was Major Robert Glendenning, one of the pioneers of aviation in America. He was sent down to Issoudun on June 28th to select the ground for the proposed American aviation school, which later became the greatest in Europe.

The Aeronautical Board adjourned on June 28th, and submitted a definite program for the development of the Air Service in Europe, which was absolutely sound in every respect. This may be regarded as a definite beginning of our great national American aviation, although many of its recommendations were never followed out.

After a conversation with General Pershing on June 16th, in which we talked over the difficulties we were both having in getting any communications from the United States, I proposed that a general officer belonging to the A.E.F. be sent to Washington to act as a representative of General Pershing, and through him all communications should be submitted to the War Department.

We had practically no communications from Washington but information frequently came through to the French government from the French missions and attachés in America, and in this way we were able to keep track of what was being done.

The following telegram for instance, was received by me on June 19th, but had arrived in France on June 14th. It was sent to us by the French Prime Minister's office. One can imagine how the directing officers in France felt, from General Pershing down, when they had to go to a foreign government to obtain information about their own troops.

TELEGRAM

Prime Minister's Office
No. 236
Copies
Secretary of State for
Aeronautics (Cabinet)

d. d. (Service Interallies)   S E C R E T
2 Ministry for War   Washington, no date,
   Army Headquarters, 3rd bureau Received June 14th, 1917.

> Are leaving on the 14th, on the Adriatic, for Liverpool: Major Tulasne, M. Bolling having full powers for industrial questions; Captain Gorrell, of General Squier's staff, and about ten officers and engineers.

Advised ⎫ Lorraine
by   ⎬ Rhone
Letter ⎭ H.S.
Requested repetition
to the S of the
Missions. Meanwhile
telephoned to
Clerget

> Mission of foremen and draughtsmen increased from 75 to 103. Personnel chosen individually with great care. Distribution: 50 LaLorraine factories; 20 Rhone, 20 Clerget, 13 Hispano. Arrange for lodgings in the neighborhood of the factory.

> Successive dates of departure; June 16th, 1st batch, American school, including the material for starting up the school.

Advised ⎫ Ct. Faure
by   ⎬ 2nd Bureau
letter ⎭ Schools

> On same date: 103 foremen and draughtsmen

> On same date, 60 student-pilots without any training, and 15 having had fair training.

> 300 mechanicians will leave within a delay of 10 to 15 days, when the means of transport will allow of it.

> 2nd batch of the American School will leave in the beginning of July.

S E C R E T

After diligent search by the staff, a small building for the headquarters of the American Expeditionary Forces was located at 9 Rue Constantine, diagonally opposite the Invalides, which served quite well for temporary use. It was here that the groundwork for the participation of the A.E.F. was laid, according to the general plans prepared by Major Logan and Major Churchill and aviation plans submitted by myself.

On June 26th, General Pershing and some of his staff went to St. Nazaire to meet the 1st Division, under the command of General Seibert, an engineer officer who assisted in the construction of the Panama Canal. The two brigades were commanded by Generals Bundy and Bullard. The Division went into camp close to St. Nazaire and I am told that the first casualty of the war happened along the docks at that port. The marines were guarding the American property on the wharves, when a man was observed entering one of the buildings, apparently with the object of making off with some of the stores. The sentry challenged him and the man ran away, but later returned, entered the building again and seized something. At the sentry's command to halt, he kept right on running, so the sentry had to shoot him. When they picked him up, they found that he was a Belgian who had done a good deal of stealing around the wharves previously but had escaped every time because the other sentinels could not hit him. So the first person we killed in Europe was one of our Belgian allies.

It was published throughout France that the Americans had come and many more were arriving soon. This certainly had a good effect on the French troops and on the population in general, although many, having already lost all they had, did not care much whether additional troops came or not, thinking that the horror of the conflict would only be prolonged.

Dr. E. L. Gros and I went up to see the Lafayette Squadron, which was stationed near the town of Ham, north of Compiègne and close to where the French and British armies joined. We had to pass through a forest formerly occupied by the Germans and in which they had established offensive works. As we entered this area and crossed a bridge over a little rivulet, we came upon an automobile apparently abandoned there. In a moment however, a lady in a Red Cross uniform appeared, carrying a cup of water. She was trying to fill the radiator of the car with this teacup, carrying the water from the little stream, and as the radiator was entirely empty, this was rather a long process. Just then Mrs. Churchill, wife of our Major Churchill, came up. She had been searching in the German dugouts for souvenirs and had found a good many. She explained they were on their way to a hospital at Noyon and had had a leak in the radiator. We filled it up and saw them on their way.

Arriving in Ham, we found the airdrome near the remains of a large beet-sugar mill which had been destroyed by the Germans in their retirement. The squadron was under the command of the French Captain Georges Thénault. The pilots were lined up to meet us, with Lieutenant Bill Thaw at their head. I was especially glad to see them because a squadron formed principally of American volunteers could assist us greatly as trained leaders.

The equipment showed nothing unusual but everything was comfortable and cheerful. They had two young lions as mascots, called Whiskey and Soda. One had an eye out and I do not think they were very amiable pets.

On the way back we stopped at the hospital of Baroness de Rothschild at Compiègne, in which Miss Morgan and Miss de Wolfe were also interested. Here they treated cases of burns with amberine, which was said to be very successful. This I believe was a preparation of paraffin which was poured over the burned places and acted as a sort of skin under which the membrane was built up until it covered the flesh. Dr. and Mrs. Alexis Carrel also had their hospital in Compiègne, and were said to be doing wonderful work. A number of airplane bombs had been dropped on this town but the hospitals had not been hurt.

The other day General Pershing asked a few of us to accompany him to the Invalides, where we were to visit Napoleon's tomb, see the museum of Napoleonic relics and the collection of old battle flags of the Republic, Kingdom and Empire. We were escorted by some French officers who showed us around this most interesting place and explained everything to us. When we stopped to look at Napoleon's sword, the guardian took it out of its case and held it out to General Pershing, thinking he would take it in his hand; but instead, without touching it, General Pershing bent forward and kissed it. This action made a profound impression on everyone present, on us even more than on the French. It showed that he thoroughly appreciated his responsibilities and felt that until a person had proven himself a great commander in a war such as this, he should be guided by what Napoleon, the greatest of all soldiers, did, rather than attempt to grasp his sceptre and consider himself his equal before proven so.

As a result of this, everyone left in a very happy frame of mind and I do not think that any one of us will ever forget it.

18

First American Troops in Paris

July 1917

Each day I took a flight from the Bourget airdrome, accompanied by Adjutant Fumat, my instructor, who showed me everything about the air game. One day when we were flying near the lines north of Compiègne we were struck by a terrific storm. Between Compiègne and Paris there are a great many forests and we could see trees being blown over by the wind, while the rain poured down in torrents. Our plane had only a 120-horsepower motor and could make no headway so we decided to land. We made for a nearby wheat field, bisected by a road, at one end of which stood a house that seemed to be occupied by French troops. These, we thought, could assist us in case we smashed up or if it was impossible for us to hold the airplane on the ground in the face of the wind. As we neared the ground, I could see an old man and woman driving along in a French cart, holding up their hands as though in supplication to the Almighty that we be saved. It looked like a sure crash.

Fortunately for us, the house on the field was occupied by French artillery troops in repose after their arduous work on the lines, who, when they heard our motor, came rushing out of the building just in time to catch the wings of our plane as we struck the wheat. We rolled no distance at all, and did not break anything about the airplane.

We were soaked to the skin, and the Commanding Officer of the group took us into the house, gave us a good meal and warm drinks, and had our clothing dried out. Everyone wanted to hear about the Americans and we were kept busy answering questions while the storm lasted. It was over in about an hour; we ran up our engine, took off from the road through the field, and arrived safely at Le Bourget.

Fumat and I flew and landed all over northern France. This not only gave me wonderful practice in flying but also a splendid knowledge of the country. No one in the ground army had this advantage of getting over the country so much, and consequently none knew it as well as I.

With the appearance of our troops on the streets of Paris and with the Commander in Chief and his staff established in their headquarters here, we considered that we had formally entered the war. Our air force consisted of one Nieuport airplane which I used myself and that was all.

Major Logan and I continued living together at the Hôtel France et Choiseul. Logan was having his troubles, explaining conditions to the staff. Few of them had ever been to Europe, and most of them were thinking more about rank for themselves than what to do with the troops. They heard that officers were being promoted over them in the United States and this caused a great storm for a day or two. Some affected to look down on the French who had been fighting the war for three and a half years, and although they themselves had never seen a hostile shot fired in Europe, they were full of information as to what should and should not be done.

One day Logan and I were talking of our various friends who had been with us in former campaigns, in Cuba, the Philippines and China. Major Frank R. McCoy's name came up; we wondered what had become of him and if he were still Military

Attaché in Mexico. All our diplomatic representatives and attachés had been ordered to remain at their posts so that our foreign service would not be denuded of personnel. At that moment, a small Boston terrier came bounding into the room, which we instantly recognized as McCoy's dog, that he took with him everywhere. McCoy was close behind him; he had gotten away from Mexico and come straight to Europe, determined to take part in the major conflict. In all our wars and expeditions of the last twenty-five years, it is interesting to note that about the same men have done the fighting, about the same men have sat at the desks and run the paper work and about the same men have stayed in the United States. This war was no exception.

Reserve Major Robert McCormick, one of the owners of the *Chicago Tribune,* was another officer who arrived here well ahead of the others and thoroughly familiarized himself with conditions in Europe. He was anxious to get to the front at the earliest opportunity.

Major Armengaud of the French General Staff and I had worked together more and more since our first meeting in the great Champagne battles in the month of April. The French had tried to assign a full Colonel of aviation to be our aeronautical advisor, but he was the usual sort of person that the political factions running the interior of France tried to palm off on us. He was not a pilot and knew little about aviation. I recommended to General Pershing that he not be assigned to us but that Major Armengaud be given that position.

Dodd, Armengaud and I decided to take a trip in our two Packards through the area to be occupied by the American army and tentatively selected places where our first squadrons would go: one at Amanty near Gondrecourt, and another at Colombey-les-Belles, the latter to be the concentration point for all the equipment issued to the air troops on the line.

We passed through Domremy, the home of Jeanne d'Arc, and I imagine we saw the very house that she came from. Judging from the milkmaids we saw there, she must have been a pretty strong, robust girl. I can well imagine that she could manipulate a two-handed sword with one hand, and that the average man in the south of France was no match for her in physical strength.

We visited Toul, the old fortress town, and inspected the airdrome just outside it, then went over to Nancy where we spent the night. This beautiful city has all the air of a capital; its wonderful old square, its palaces and its gardens are entirely different from anything in France. The city was ordered evacuated on account of the aerial bombardment the Germans were centering on it, and caves had been built along the streets in which passers-by could take refuge in case the airplanes came. We saw many places where hits had been made on buildings, factories and the railroad yards. These bombs had killed a number of people and caused a good many fires.

The following morning we started toward Pont St. Vincent. While ascending the hill, my chauffeur, Flake, had considerable trouble with the car and had to stop two or three times, being unable to fix the trouble. Dodd came up from his car and called his chauffeur to see what he could do. This man took the carburetor off the engine, adjusted the needle valve and had the car running perfectly in ten minutes. It was one of the best and quickest jobs I ever saw. When I asked Dodd where he had found the man, he answered, "I brought him over with me, he is the champion motor driver in the United States." This chauffeur's name was Edward Rickenbacker, and I have never seen a more capable man or one more attentive to duty.

Upon my return to Paris, I found that General Pershing had not yet approved the proceedings of the board of officers which recommended a definite aeronautical organization.

As we heard very little from the United States and did not know if our recommendations were being followed or what was projected, permission was requested to send Captain Harold Fowler to the United States to acquaint the Aircraft Production Board with our needs. Fowler was thoroughly familiar with conditions in Europe, having been with the British service, both with ground troops and aviation. This was approved and he left on his mission.

We were running into more and more trouble with our own staff over aviation matters. It was such a big subject and ignorance about it was so widespread that each member had to be told in detail, from the bottom up, whenever anything new occurred. The staff was being organized on the European model, but instead of working smoothly as the Europeans did, everyone "passed the buck" to the next fellow in true regular-army style. Incoming papers were passed around from one section to another, just as in Washington, with everyone trying to avoid responsibility. They were still trying to handle aviation as an auxiliary of some of the other branches, instead of an independent fighting arm.

Great jealousy was manifested by the staff to those in aviation, because the work was more spectacular, brought more rapid promotion, the aviators got extra pay and were better known throughout their respective countries than those with the ground forces. General Pershing himself thought aviation was full of dynamite and pussyfooted just when we needed the most action. Aviation affairs were pretty badly messed up as it was and if they were turned over to the kind mercies of the General Staff of the A.E.F. we would have had little or no aviation during the war. This would have been a serious thing and might have defeated us, because the French and British, having almost exhausted their supply of pilots, could no longer develop a great air force. Every day I became more convinced that we should put all aviation matters in Europe under the direction of one head, who would be under the Commander in Chief; and not have every Tom, Dick and Harry in the United States, who were neither pilots nor had ever seen an armed German, prescribe what should be done against the enemy.

Pressure was being applied to secure General Pershing's approval for feeding our men into French and English regiments, as individuals, not as organizations. He asked me what I thought of it and I told him that as far as I was concerned, I would serve in an American army or nothing. "What do you mean by that?" he asked. To which I replied that we had come over here to fight as Americans, we were fighting our own war and not that of our associates; that we might need our own army at the end of the war as badly as we did during it, and if we did not develop an army and fighting methods, we would come out of the war as dependents of European nations instead of the victor in the contest as we should be. He smiled and did not say anything, but I knew he was having a hard time with the authorities in Washington in maintaining this very attitude.

Many French officers of Jewish origin were detailed with the English-speaking troops. Owing to their affiliations in trade, they learn more foreign languages than the average Frenchman who actually is a very poor linguist. French army officers were taught German and French naval officers were taught English, so very few of the former spoke English well, or at all. Practically none of them spoke Spanish.

The other day Captain Benedict, one of the French officers on my staff and himself a Hebrew, asked me to dine with one of the prominent Hebrew bankers of France, and I accepted. We went out to the St. Cloud district and to a city block enclosed by a high stone wall, very plain and shabby, as were the heavy doors through which we were admitted by the gatekeeper. But once inside, the appearance of things completely changed, and we found ourselves in a beautiful garden, exquisitely laid out with fountains, flowers and shrubs. In the midst of this was a thoroughly modern house, a magnificent abode, with objets d'art from the four corners of the earth in each room. Our host received us very graciously in the salon and had a company of twelve gentlemen to meet me at dinner, who represented the leaders of practically every department of the French government—in law, politics and even religion. The subjects discussed at dinner were international in aspect and largely related to the financial conditions of the various countries and their prospects for the future.

After dinner, I had a long conversation with our host, who

had spent a great deal of time in the Near East and was quite familiar with conditions in Turkey and Russia, as well as Austria-Hungary, Poland and Germany. His opinion was that Germany would emerge from the war, even though defeated, in better condition economically than the other nations, except America, as no fighting was taking place on German soil. All her factories would be intact, and she would have Russia and Scandinavia to draw on for man power if she found herself short, which was improbable. After the political troubles which would last for a few years at the conclusion of the war, she would again take her place as the leading industrial nation of Europe.

He showed me some of his treasured objets d'art, and some jewels which he took from a safe, the combination of which he alone knew. Among them were some beautiful pearls from Behrin Island in the Persian Gulf.

At the end, he told me that if I ever needed any financial assistance that he could handle it. It was offered in a thoroughly generous way, and I thanked him, but said that I was a plain soldier and not a financier, that I had plenty to feed and clothe myself with and that my wants were few. He told me that all of the officers of his faith who had served with me had reported that I looked after them the same as everyone else, and they wanted to show their appreciation; to which I replied that they had done efficient service and that was what I wanted above everything else.

During my whole evening with him, I was reminded very much of the character of Isaac in *Ivanhoe.* It gave me an insight into one phase of human activity which I would have obtained in no other way, and I appreciated it very much.

19

Organizing the American Army

August 1917

More men were arriving from America and our 1st Division had gone to the town of Gondrecourt just back of that part of the line they would later occupy, and were being instructed in their duties by the French 47th Division of Chasseurs.

If we had been called on to fight alone, I doubt if we could have put up as much resistance with our regular army, steeped as it was in the conservatism of peace-time methods, as with the New York City police force. Think of what General Grant's army of the Potomac, trained as it was in 1864, could do if equipped with modern engines of war and a good air force. At that time we were the leading military power on this planet and had learned this art ourselves in the most difficult theater of war ever fought over.

The staff was still looking for a headquarters behind the zone our armies were to occupy. I was anxious to get out of Paris, where most of the fighting was done around restaurant tables and in political committee rooms, and join our fighting squadrons.

We finally heard that Congress had passed laws creating a great aviation corps, to consist of ten thousand officers and ninety thousand men, and appropriated millions of dollars for material. This was welcome news but with it came the report that the Air Service was to remain a part of the Signal Corps, which meant inefficiency in its worst form, as the Signal Corps had developed into a political organization at the top. Fortunately, amid all this pulling and hauling, General Pershing kept his head, and he was supported by President Wilson, if not in all cases by the War Department and certain of its officers who were anxious to supplant him in command of our forces. He was a very cautious man on account of his long service in the regular army. He had a working knowledge of American politics, with which he undoubtedly was kept in close touch by his father-in-law, Senator Warren of Wyoming, one of the ranking members of the Senate. It seems too bad that in every war the General in command of the armies not only has to fight the public enemy at the front, but his political enemies at home and around him as well, and to an even greater extent.

General Pershing moved slowly about aviation. He knew that it was assuming great political importance in the United States on account of the tremendous sums that were being appropriated for it. He knew that there would be attempts to make a political football of it and that sooner or later, the interests that control the manufacture and supply of the equipment might try to put their own men in charge of the whole thing, both in America and Europe, so as to handle everything in the way they desired.

Officers arriving here confirmed the rumor that our recommendations as to what airplanes should be used had been absolutely disregarded. Instead of the fine and suitable French airplanes specified, they had adopted the English De Havilland as the standard two-seater, to be equipped with a brand-new motor, the Liberty, being made in the United States. There must have been a lot of inside work somewhere by the English manufacturers to put this thing over on the Americans. The DH was designed for the Rolls Royce engine, and of course would not fit the Liberty. It was a fine airplane in its class but it was built for day bombardment work, that is, carrying bombs at a high altitude across the enemy's lines in the daytime. It was not suited for observation work where a long camera had to be used, as the fuselage was not big enough to get a camera into; while the French Salmson that I had recommended met all our requirements at that time for an observation plane.

It was decided to separate the control of the air service in the interior from the combatant air forces, and an order was issued announcing me as Commander of the Air Service of the A.E.F., and Major Bolling as Chief of the Interior Air Service of the A.E.F. Bolling and I drew up in writing what the duties of each of us would be and we had a thorough understanding so as to prevent friction as far as practicable. Of course, this arrangement left no one in supreme command of the air forces but our staff had not yet gotten to the point where they knew enough about handling air forces to approve an up-to-date policy, where one person would be responsible for all air activities.

The French, continuing their operations around Verdun, were beginning another attack in that area, so I again proceeded there, taking Major Churchill with me. He had been doing a good deal of flying, and had become quite conversant with aeronautics, developing an excellent grasp of the relation of aviation to the ground forces.

An excellent pilot was assigned me, and I acted as observer as we flew out over the front again, from the airdrome at Souilly, in a Sopwith airplane, equipped with a French Clerget engine. The plane worked well, the day was very clear and we had an excellent chance to see everything. The lines appeared to be in the same position as when I was there in July, but there was very much more aviation in the sky. Both sides were continually reinforcing and making new squadrons.

The French had their First Bombardment Group up and were attacking St. Juvin, Grandpré and Feleville, concentration points of the enemy. During the day they dropped something over twelve thousand pounds of bombs on these places, from which we could see smoke and fire arising. (That night they dropped about twenty tons of bombs on various railroad stations opposite this area, principally at Longuyon, where a great fire was reported to have taken place. Dun sur Meuse and Spincourt were also attacked by the night bombers.)

The enemy aviation was extremely active. The Germans did not maintain regular patrols, but sent their machines over in a mass, from fifteen to twenty-five in a flight, which were able to go anywhere they desired against the smaller forces of the French. This system did not prevent the French from getting over on the German side but I was convinced it resulted in preventable loss to French aviation, and enabled the Germans to accomplish any mission they set out to do.

During the fighting, an artillery projectile hit the liaison airplane piloted by Sergeant de Hugendorf with Lieutenant Granier as observer. This was from a field gun, not an anti-aircraft cannon. It blew the airplane up, and it crashed to the ground. This was the first time I had heard of such an occurrence; it was remarkable that it did not happen often because the liaison planes flew back and forth within a few hundred feet of the ground and directly in the artillery barrage.

Many French airplanes were lost in aerial combats in this engagement. I saw two aerial combats, both at a short distance. In the first one, the French plane went down in flames, shooting to the earth with a long trail of very black smoke, caused by the ignition of the gasoline. This was a terrible sight. We in the air feared being burned alive more than anything else. There was nothing we could do, as none of the airplanes were equipped with parachutes. They had not yet been applied to use on the front except by the balloonists; but we could just as well have had them on airplanes and many a good man would have been saved.

The great trouble with starting anything new is to break away from the conservative policy of those who have gone before. This was especially true during war, but in the case of our aviation, we had to take chances, because if successful, the results would be so vast; and if not successful, we would only suffer a slight decrease in efficiency. For instance, if we constructed a night bombardment plane capable of going from Verdun to the Rhine and later found it would only go half that distance efficiently, that would still be as good as the airplanes we already had.

I sent Major Churchill up to Chaumont to find a chateau or large detached house for my own quarters and the use of the principal members of my staff, so that we might live together and be brought in more close association. In war, one does not work according to hours, but night and day, and when one finds time to rest, it is necessary to get the most out of it. Quarters on the main roads anywhere in northern France were very noisy, as transport, artillery, automobiles and trucks were passing night and day. Major Churchill reported that he had found a suitable location within a mile of Chaumont, called the Château de Chamarandes, also that he had arranged with Major Bacon for suitable offices in the old French barracks that were to be used by our headquarters. I went up to Chaumont to look over the places he had selected.

I found the chateau to be an extremely interesting place. It had been built by Louis XV as a hunting box in this upper Marne region. Much of the original furniture remained in the house, particularly in the salon, a large room about sixty by thirty feet, called the *Salle des Animaux* or Hall of the Animals. This name was given it from the beautiful paintings of animals that ornamented the walls. The tables, chairs and all the furniture were of the period of Louis XV, as were the chandeliers of heavy crystal. The bedrooms had large comfortable beds and open fireplaces. The garden was beautifully laid out and quite large, and was said to have been planned by the same landscape gardener who constructed the gardens of Versailles. The Marne River branched and ran completely around the chateau, making an island of it.

At the time of the last revolution, the property was sold and passed into the hands of a family named Tisserand. The present male head of the family had surrendered completely to the festive French grape and remained in a more or less intoxicated condition most of the time. His wife, a very energetic woman, handled all the business. After obtaining permission to rent the chateau, we immediately began moving in.

20

American Headquarters in Chaumont

September–October 1917

By now General Pershing's staff had begun to function pretty well. The staff sections, five in number, were called "G" after the English system, "G" meaning General Staff. G-1 handled the administration and personnel; G-2 handled the information, intelligence and espionage; G-3 handled all the war plans; G-4 handled all supply arrangements and transportation; and G-5 handled all military instruction. Ordinarily, a staff was divided into only four sections, but the training of troops was considered of sufficient importance to be assigned to a separate organization. Every question that arose, no matter what its nature, was assigned for action to one of these groups.

The human mind is capable of looking after only about five things at a time. If a man attempts more than this, disaster usually results. Napoleon could handle seven or eight different things at once, but he was a great exception. All generals who know anything of the art of war never divide their organizations into more than four or five principal parts.

Soon after arriving at Chaumont, General Pershing decided that it was necessary to appoint a Chief of the Air Service who would be on his staff and who would coordinate the fighting air force on the line with the service of supply, deal with the representatives of other countries regarding aeronautical matters and communicate with the United States on these subjects. Notwithstanding that this was the fourth change in three months in the organization of the Air Service in France, it was a good one, as it would leave me free to handle the fighting on the line without interference, and Colonel Bolling could go ahead with his supply arrangements in the interior, unhampered by other duties. Accordingly, General W. L. Kenly was appointed Chief of the Air Service and my designation was changed to Commander of the Air Service in the Zone of the Advance; Colonel Bolling was "in charge of the Air Service Line of Communications." Major Thomas DeWitt Milling, one of our ablest and most experienced aviation officers, was appointed Director of Air Service Instruction.

General Kenly, although not a pilot himself, had shown a great deal of interest in aeronautical matters. He attended our aviation school at San Diego, California, and satisfactorily passed the course, such as it was. In France, he had done all he could to learn about the Air Service and had shown himself anxious and willing to do anything in his power to improve this very important branch.

After this, our work became excellently systematized. Being free to go ahead and prepare everything for fighting the Germans, I assembled an excellent body of officers on my staff, all of whom had had as much experience in fighting the enemy in the air as was possible to get. My office completed all arrangements for putting our troops on the line. Manuals were prepared describing the duties of pursuit, observation and bombardment aviation. Bolling worked hard in the interior getting our supplies together, while Kenly represented our needs before the General Staff and coordinated the various elements at headquarters.

Instruction in primary flying for our student aviators was started at Foggia, Italy, and we began sending some flying cadets to the school at Tours, under French instructors. Rickenbacker, who did so well as Dodd's chauffeur, was one of the first students at the latter place; just before we left Paris, he asked to go and I gave him permission.

A board was created by our headquarters to conduct mental and physical examinations for transferring to the United States service all Americans in the French army and at French flying schools. I felt that every plan I had laid out in April and May was being carried out. The principal thing that worried me was getting airplanes, as I was certain from what I heard that very little attention was being paid to our recommendations in the United States.

At every opportunity I sent my officers with the French units on the line to get as much experience as they could. Captain M. F. Harmon, one of our most promising regular officers, and Lieutenant Birdseye Lewis took every opportunity to fly over the battle lines. One evening I sent them in a car up to the French airdrome at Malzeville, near Nancy, to participate in a night air attack against Diedenhoffen. They reached the hill at Pont St. Vincent a little after dark and foolishly kept their automobile lights going. A German airplane observed them and opened fire with machine guns. Before they could put their lights out, several machine-gun bullets had pierced the automobile hood. It taught them a lesson they would never forget and also gave them a great appreciation of what aircraft could do at night. Proceeding to the airdrome, they were taken over the lines by the French. As they approached Diedenhoffen, they noticed how dark all the country was that was occupied by the Germans, but in Luxembourg, everything was lighted up as if for a feast. Luxembourg, it will be remembered, was neutral, and took this way of marking its location at night to prevent the French from bombarding it. Great damage was done to the iron works and German supply depots at Diedenhoffen.

The old Château de Chamarandes proved to be a most interesting place for our headquarters. (I got all my staff to studying French and encouraged them to converse in it as much as possible.) In my spare moments I took every opportunity to hunt with the inhabitants of the valley. All of the upper Marne country still contained a great deal of forest game, especially wild boar which did a great deal of damage to crops. The French were trying in every way to exterminate them, but it seemed impossible. The wild sows had very big litters, from twelve to twenty pigs. They feared nothing except man; no dogs or other animals had a chance with them, and even man was hard put to it sometimes when caught at close quarters. They were covered with heavy fur and had long, sharp, white tusks, were fierce and strong, and gave an appearance of speed and endurance that is difficult to imagine in an animal of that kind.

Many of the hunters were old men of sixty, seventy and even eighty; a few had served in the Franco-Prussian War of 1870–1871. We would take our stand along the trails in the woods to shoot the animals as they came by. There was a bounty of fifty francs on each boar, so whenever I killed one I used the bounty to entertain the old men at luncheon on the days of the hunts.

Early one morning in October I went over to Nancy from Toul, where I had been inspecting airdromes and had spent the night. Entering the Café Stanislas to get some breakfast, I was greeted in a very excited manner by the headwaiter. "Colonel, have you seen the Zeppelin, have you seen the Zeppelin?" he kept repeating. On my answering no, he said that one had passed a short while before with its engines stopped and drifting in the direction of Lunéville.

Without stopping for breakfast, I proceeded toward Lunéville in my car, the fastest one we had; it was said to be the German Mercedes that won the last French road race at Lyons in 1914, just before the war. I could get ninety miles out of it on a clear road, and as this road was fairly open, I made good time. At Lunéville, they told me the Zeppelin had gone in the direction of St. Clement, toward which I headed with all speed. As I neared the town, I saw a great fire, which was the Zeppelin burning, and soon came up to where it had gone down. A group of French soldiers had just arrived to take charge of the debris.

The Zeppelin had been hit at an altitude of sixteen thousand feet by an anti-aircraft projectile and set on fire. Undoubtedly its engines had been frozen, as the atmosphere at that altitude was very cold. None of the crew had been saved; all had hit the ground in the vicinity of the wreck, with arms and legs extended, as is nearly always the case when a man is thrown from an airship or an airplane. (In some places the imprint made by the bodies in the earth was later filled in with concrete, to preserve these gruesome marks for posterity.)

The officer of the guard to whom I spoke told me it was rumored that there were other Zeppelins over France, which had passed during the night, but it was not known whether they were disabled or were proceeding on a raid. After looking over the twisted members of the giant Zeppelin's frame and noticing that there were only three machine guns on board and that she carried bomb dropping equipment, I started back for my headquarters at Chaumont. As I passed through Neufchâteau, another French officer told me that several Zeppelins had passed over France, going from northeast to southwest, and they were all apparently in distress.

At Chaumont, I was immediately informed by my information officer that a Zeppelin, practically intact, had landed at Bourbonne-les-Bains, some thirty miles to the west. After snatching a bite to eat and getting some gas in the car, I took Adjutant Fumat and started, arriving there in less than an hour. I had never actually seen an undamaged Zeppelin before, although I was thoroughly familiar with their construction. The first impression I got from the monster ship was almost indescribable. Approaching it, we rounded a little hill which formed one side of the valley of a small stream. As I looked up, I thought I saw another hill, but on looking again, I saw that instead of a hill, it was the Zeppelin.

The ship, about five hundred and fifty feet long and seventy feet in diameter, had lodged squarely across the valley. Few people were on the scene as the Zeppelin had only been down a

little while. I immediately climbed through it and inspected it
from end to end. It was one of the latest models and was in a
perfect state of preservation, except that all the engines were
frozen. It had been forced down on this account and from loss
of gas, not from the action of French airplanes. Several pilots
from French squadrons in that vicinity had attacked the great
ship on its way down and fired innumerable bullets into its
envelope, many of them incendiary, but with little effect.

I carefully inspected the holes made by these bullets in the
envelope and in the gas bags which they had punctured. Only
.30-caliber guns had been used, and these bullets carried so
little inflammatory substance in them that I think they were put
out by the outer envelope. It would take a great many bullets
from machine guns to cause enough loss of gas to bring one of
these monsters down.

There were some thirteen gas balloons, made of gold-beaters'
skin, in the interior of the ship, each independent of the other.
Some were almost empty. As the ship had landed, two or three
pine trees had pushed their way through the outer casing and
projected into the interior for twenty or thirty feet. The appearance of the inside, with these Christmas trees sticking up
and the partly filled ballonets among the wires and aluminum
framework, was grotesque and strange.

I was much impressed with the wireless equipment, which
was far superior to anything we had. It was said to send and
receive for more than one thousand miles. Only a couple of
machine guns were carried on this ship, which showed how
little they feared airplanes.

I wondered why the crew had not destroyed the ship on
landing, when an old man there, the one who had really saved
the ship, told me his story.

He, with five or six others, had been hunting wild boar in
the valley of the little stream when the Zeppelin came down.
They were all much startled of course but this old fellow kept
his composure and shouted to his companions to rally around
him. The French airplanes swooped over the Zeppelin until it

landed, firing their machine guns incessantly so that the old men were afraid they would be hit; but this one made them stand their ground. As the ship came to rest, one of the crew started to climb up from the front control cabin into the body of the ship. He had a Very pistol in his hand with which to shoot into one of the gas bags and set the whole structure on fire. The old man divined his intention and, covering him with his shot gun, ordered him to get back into the cabin or be killed. The other old fellows covered the rest of the crew, some twenty-one in number, making them descend from the cabins and holding them prisoners until the troops arrived. Very little news or information had been extracted from them.

While there, I was joined by Major Dodd of my staff who had come out to meet me and look over this Zeppelin, the L-49. Dodd had been delayed a little, because he had gone to visit a place where the third Zeppelin, the L-51, had come down. Its front cabin had hit the top of a tree and been torn off, and the Zeppelin, being rid of this weight, had risen again and disappeared. Dodd reported that two men had been found dead in the cabin and an examination of their effects disclosed the orders that had sent the Zeppelins on their mission, together with a complete journal of the trip up to a couple of hours before the accident. We translated these and for the first time knew just what had happened to the Zeppelins.

They had formed part of a squadron that had attacked England; it was the Germans' greatest single Zeppelin raid. Thirteen of these huge ships had been ordered to rendezvous over Belgium and attack certain industrial and shipping centers in Great Britain, including London, Birmingham, Liverpool, Sheffield and others. At the point of rendezvous, two of them had engine trouble and turned back; the other eleven proceeded in a gathering storm to Great Britain and dropped their bombs at the places designated. Then they got together again over the English Channel, but there encountered terrific winds from the northeast and were unable to make sufficient headway against them to keep from being blown into France.

In the morning, they found themselves over French territory, exposed to both air attack and the fire of anti-aircraft artillery. Their orders definitely stated that they should not rise above the hail line, which at that time was about fourteen thousand feet, otherwise they would get into such cold temperatures that their engines would freeze. The hail line is where the moisture in the air turns from a liquid state into ice, its altitude varying according to the sort of storm encountered and the time of year. If this squadron of Zeppelins stayed lower than the hail line, they would certainly be shot down, so their only alternative was to go up high and take the chance of freezing their engines, as there was an attendant possibility that the winds would change and allow them to get back into Germany. This did not happen, however, and one after another of the Zeppelins had their engines frozen and became helpless, no better than free balloons.

The French aeronautical authorities made complete drawings of this ship, which I arranged to have forwarded to the United States. It seemed to me that if the French had brought up a little gas and filled the ballonets of this ship, it could have been flown to the southern part of France, landed and repaired there, and subsequently used against the Germans. This was not done, however.

Around the middle of the month Major Armengaud of the French army informed me that an attack was to take place against the Chemin des Dames, an extremely important part of the line east of Soissons; it would be a good chance to see one of the last large attacks of the autumn. The reason for this attack was that the French feared that the Germans in their spring offensive would try to push through this part of the line. An important ridge and canal ran along the Chemin des Dames which, if the French could capture, would give them a better position for defense.

The morning of October twenty-third dawned drizzly and cloudy, and there was a tremendous amount of mud in the roads;

the airdrome to which we went was very soggy and wet. It contained an observation group, equipped with new Bréguet two-seater planes with Renault 200-horsepower engines, the best airplanes of their kind on the front, either in the Allied or German service. They were the kind I recommended for our air service and I hoped we would get them.

The group commander told me he had the best pilot in the group ready to take me up. He showed me on the map where the French pursuit aviation was to be and what his own airplanes were to do that day. We took the air as early as possible and made a circuit of the lines from one end to the other.

After we had been out a little over two hours I could see the pilot was getting very tired. I signaled him to return to the airdrome. As we approached the landing field, I noticed that the wind had changed about ninety degrees since we had left. The pilot, however, was landing just as though the wind had not changed, and with a good deal of speed. I decided it was better to let him go ahead rather than say anything to him, but I turned around and strapped up my flexible machine guns in the back seat as tightly as I could and prepared for a possible crash. Sure enough, he came in with a straight side wind and with his tail quite high. He set his wheels down hard and the ship bounced about twenty feet. When it came down, it hit a soft place, turned squarely over and smashed to pieces. Although hit in the back of the head by the machine guns, I was able to get out quickly and, on looking forward, saw that the pilot could not extricate himself. I was very much afraid of fire; the Renault engine had an exhaust pipe on the upper part of the motor that always became red hot, and as the airplane was upside down now, the gasoline from the carburetor might drop on it. I pulled the pilot out, however, before any assistance had a chance to arrive. The plane did not catch fire and neither of us was hurt to amount to anything, but the pilot felt terribly about it; he had once taken the Queen of the Belgians up on a flight and now he had crashed with the Commander of the American Air Service. I had given him a pretty hard drubbing and he was exhausted; few people can appreciate how very tired an airman gets in action. I made up my mind, however, that this was the last time any pilot would fly me during the war, unless I was incapacitated.

As October drew to a close, the weather got very cold; the ground was damp and the light shoes the Americans were wearing were no match for the climate. Everyone who knew the country wore very heavy oiled footgear with tremendously thick soles, and some wore wooden clogs around the airdromes to keep their feet dry. With the constant work in the office and the flying and traveling I had done, I had become rather tired and the bad weather brought on a severe cold. The doctor advised me to go to the hospital rather than stay in our cold chateau, as the Spanish influenza, called the "flu," was beginning to make itself felt throughout the army and threatened to lead to serious consequences. So I went up to our hospital in Chaumont which occupied the French army hospital premises, I was given a good room, but for a hospital it was dark and damp, as all buildings in this part of France were. General Kenly came to see me every day, and one afternoon brought the Countess de Salignac-Fenelon and her daughter, the Countess de Castries, whose husband, a Captain, was then a prisoner in Germany. I had only met them once before, at a luncheon, but they insisted on taking me to their chateau at Cirey sur Blaise, about thirty miles from Chaumont, where they looked after my every want and soon had me on the road to recovery. I believe if it had not been for them, I would have had a very severe and protracted illness.

21

Our Air Force Disorganized

November 1917

By the beginning of November, we had established the special schools for pursuit, observation and bombardment aviation, and determined the location for our various squadrons on the line. Just when things had begun to work smoothly, a shipload of aviation officers arrived under Brigadier-General Benjamin Foulois, over one hundred in number, almost none of whom had ever seen an airplane. A more incompetent lot of air warriors had never arrived in the zone of active military operations since the war began. Foulois, I am told, had orders from the President to General Pershing to put him in charge of aviation in Europe, even though he was no longer an active pilot. They say he announced before leaving the United States that he would command not only the American services but in a short time that of all the Allies as well.

The orders to General Pershing left him no discretion, so he had to relieve General Kenly and put General Foulois in charge. While Foulois meant well and had had some experience in aviation in the United States, he was not at all conversant with conditions in Europe. As rapidly as possible, the competent men, who had learned their duties in the face of the enemy, were displaced and their positions taken by these carpetbaggers. Colonel Bolling was relieved of his command in Paris and the contracts he had made with the French for aeronautical material were cancelled. This was serious as it occasioned another long delay in our getting suitable planes.

It was decided that I should remain as Air Commander, Zone of the Advance, until that office was gradually abolished. Since I was seeking nothing except service directly against the enemy, and since none of the ranking officers with Foulois could fly, I was to be given command of the Air Service of the 1st Army Corps as soon as it was formed. In the meantime I assisted as far as possible in attempting to teach the staff officers what the Air Service was all about and how it could be used.

I made frequent visits to the front and on one of these took Colonel Thomas DeWitt Milling with me. We stopped off in the Champagne sector in front of Châlons to see what conditions were during the winter. The country was covered with snow and in many places large boggy areas, caused by rain and snow, had formed between the contending lines. No large operations were being conducted, but trench raids, sometimes involving a whole battalion, were made to capture prisoners for interrogation. Milling and I approached the German lines so closely that we could hear them talking in their trenches. We observed one trench raid made by a battalion of German infantry and, in fact, were mixed up in it. The French had known about it in advance but thought it was to be made in another place. The Germans jumped through and captured several prisoners, then retired.

Trenches were watched everywhere by sharpshooters. Every time we exposed ourselves for an instant, a bullet would sing by. At one place we had to run for it; the camouflage over the top of the trench had been blown off by a shell. Colonel Milling and I crouched down with our backs against the forward parapet in order to escape the fire. He felt a hard lump against his back, and looking around to see what it was, found a skull, which fell out of the earth, at his feet. In many places the parapets were encrusted with human bones; in fact, this whole Champagne area is sown with the bones of soldiers who have died in combat in the wars of hundreds of years. The Gauls fought here, against each other and against the Germanic hordes. Forts are still standing which the Romans used.

The opinion of the French officers at the front was that the Germans would take up the offensive as soon as they could, before the American army was ready to fight. They believed the Germans knew precisely how many Americans were being shipped and how they were coming; also they knew that American ships were landing considerable food supplies in England, which counteracted their submarine blockade to a great extent. There was no indication that the Germans were running short of anything of consequence on the front lines, except, of course, rubber.

When we started back, I said good-bye to Colonel Milling and proceeded to Mailly, where our heavy artillery was being assembled and trained.

After looking over the arrangements, I had dinner with the officers composing the heavy artillery brigade and met their French instructors, then set out to drive through the night to our headquarters in Chaumont. Jones, my chauffeur, and a mechanic were handling the car, a closed high-powered Mercedes, while Captain du Dore of the French air service and I sat in the back. Jones and the mechanic were very tired as they had been driving night and day, so I told them to get inside and I would drive. Captain du Dore sat up in front with me. I took the wheel and we headed in the direction of Arcis-sur-Aube. As we entered the forest area north of the Aube we were making fifty-five or sixty miles an hour. Suddenly I saw in front of me, in the beam of the headlights, one, then two, four, six—a whole herd of wild boars—crossing the road. I pressed down the accelerator to get more speed, in an attempt to kill some of them. Captain du Dore yelled in my ear that if we hit one we would surely go in the ditch, they were so big. I paid no attention but ran squarely into the middle of the herd, hitting some of them pretty hard.

Stopping the car as quickly as possible, I backed up to where we had hit them, and found one boar stone dead. On the other side of the road was another one, stunned and lying there gnashing his teeth. I killed him with one blow of a hammer I got out of the tool box. Another was running around at the edge of the brush, apparently hurt, and I rushed after him, but upon my approach he made off rapidly in the darkness. Anyhow we had two fine young wild boar which I tied to the car, one on each side, and proceeded to Chaumont, reaching there in the early morning.

That night we gave a dinner in the state dining room of the Château de Chamarandes, with the wild boars served in the old French style. It was a splendid feast; the night was cold outside and the guests came in wrapped from head to foot in their furs. We had great wood fires in the large salon and good warm drinks to dispel the cold. Frank Page made a wonderful speech in French, showing that the instruction I had had him take up was having some effect. He wore his fine boots that had been the subject of correspondence between our Ambassador to Great Britain and our Ambassador to France. Quite a while before, he had sent over to London for some boots and his father, Mr. Page, the Ambassador, had sent them to his colleague, Mr. Sharp, the Ambassador to France. In some way they failed to get there and a lengthy correspondence between the two officials, our most important diplomatic representatives, took place, to locate Frank's boots. At last they were found and forwarded to me with a note from the American Ambassador to France, enclosing the correspondence of the American Ambassador to Great Britain, for delivery to Frank Page. I do not believe that any boots were ever delivered to a person in a more distinguished way.

Our first air squadron had now reached the zone of the advance and was sent to Amanty to receive battle instructions, where it would form a nucleus of training for future observation squadrons. Major Ralph Royce had the honor of commanding this unit and the following is the letter which I gave him on November 4, 1917. It was the first order given to an American squadron in the zone of the armies. This was a big job Royce was given, and one which he carried out very well.

AMERICAN EXPEDITIONARY FORCES
HEADQUARTERS AIR SERVICE ZONE OF THE
ADVANCE

November 4, 1917

FROM: A.C.A.
TO: C.O. 1st Air Squadron
SUBJECT: Instruction.

1. You are in command of the 1st U. S. Air Unit in the Zone of Operations and your duties will consequently be difficult and varied. From the very beginning your control will extend beyond your squadron. A desire for the early employment of your squadron at the front must not cause you to lose sight of the fact that its first, and, for the present, primary function will be the organization and training of other squadrons and attached personnel.

2. In chronological order your duties will be:

(1) The supervision of the construction and disposition of all hangars, barracks, works, shops, roads and other construction work pertaining to the Amanty Airdrome. In this connection you will be guided by the plans already drawn up by the Material Department A.S.A. and approved by the A.C.A. and by such other plans as may be subsequently approved.

(2) The proper organization, instruction, equipment, and discipline of your command.

(a) Organization—will be governed by Tables of Organization, A.S.A., now awaiting approval by C. in C.

(b) Instruction—will be given in compliance with duties of an Observation Squadron and with orders published from time to time and in conjunction with the Corps School and Division training.

(c) Equipment—will be provided in accordance with Tables of Organization and regulations to be issued by the Material Department and approved by the A.C.A.

(d) Discipline—The greatest attention will be given to the maintenance of strict discipline. This is especially important due to the nature of the organization and work of the Air Service, and also to the fact that the great majority of the personnel will be without previous military experience.

(e) The establishment and control under the direction of the C.O. Corps School of the Corps Aeronautical School. This school will be responsible for the training, in all but the final stages, of observers for all observation squadrons of the 1st Corps, and for some Army Observation Squadrons. You will be made acquainted with further details of this school at a later date.

(f) The establishment and command of an air park. This will include construction, equipment and operation. This park should be capable of caring for at least three squadrons and will function and be equipped as prescribed in the Tables of Organization, A.S.A., and such orders and tables as are published from time to time.

(5) In addition you are informed that the Air Station at Amanty will be used for the location of squadrons serving with Divisions during the Division training period; certainly for the 1st and 26th Divisions, and probably for some others.

3. At the end of each week you will submit a written report to the A.C.A., showing progress in:

(1) Construction work
(2) Material and equipment
(3) Corps Aeronautical School
(4) Organization
(5) Instruction
(6) Discipline

These reports will be as brief as possible, Nos. 1 and 2 will be addressed to the Chief Material Department through A.C.A.

SGD. Wm. Mitchell,
Col. A.S.S.A.A.C.A.

We were beginning to get a number of well-instructed American pilots, whose flying had been perfected in the interior but who had had no service against the enemy. Major Armengaud and I considered very seriously how these men could be best handled. We had no American airplanes to give them; the only ones we could get at that time were second-class French or British planes, the old French AR and the British Sopwith 1½ Strutter observation ship. We could get no pursuit ships whatever. Taking the matter up with General Pershing, I proposed that half our pilots be sent to the French air service to perfect themselves for duty on the front, with the idea of bringing them back to us as soon as their training was finished. This agreement in no way meant that we should feed our personnel in as replacements into the French or British service, as was proposed when we first came over; but it would provide pilots whom we could use as flight commanders, squadron and group commanders, as soon as our men became sufficiently trained and were provided with airplanes. It took at least a year to develop a squadron commander, and our preparations were so great that by the fall of 1918 or spring, 1919, we would have more pilots coming from America than all the rest of the Allies together.

Our 1st Division was put up into the line during this month, entering the line northeast of Nancy, at a place called Sommervilles. The American regiments were mixed up with the French, as was the artillery. The first American guns were fired at the enemy from the little village of Arracourt. It was reported that the first German prisoner taken by our men was named Hoffman and he was captured by an American soldier named Schneider, a pretty good German name. The Germans retaliated by raiding our trenches and capturing some men from the 46th Infantry. It was in this area that our first soldiers were lost in combat.

22

The Hard Winter

December 1917

It grew chillier as the days went by. The French said it was the coldest winter they had had in many years. Our chateau at Chamarandes was like ice, but we grew used to it, and dressed warmly and ate sustaining food. There were very few steam-heated houses in this part of France; the people claimed they were not healthy. That may be so but they are a great deal more comfortable.

The flu was making great inroads among our troops. More-over, the American shoes issued to them were entirely inade-quate to withstand the climate and conditions. The men called them "hen's skins" and "tango shoes." Marching on the roads with full packs tore them to pieces in a day. I saw a division go by the other day with the men practically barefooted, many leaving blood marks in the snow.

Luckily the armies were practically dug in for the winter. In our country we had been in the habit of pursuing our campaigns in the winter as well as the summer, but in Europe, from time immemorial, the armies have gone into winter quarters. While that was not supposed to be true in this case, it amounted to the same thing. War here seemed to be governed by certain rules, which both sides observed more or less.

In this cold weather, the air forces have had great difficulty in keeping their water-cooled engines from freezing. The water and oil had to be heated in things like movable soup kitchens before being poured into the planes. Considerable air bombing was being done and the poor pilots and observers who had to fly at high altitudes had their noses or entire faces frozen to such a degree that they turned black and the men looked almost like Negroes.

If too much oil is left on the machine guns, they stick when one attempts to work them, as the oil gums up from the cold. The metal itself gets so cold that when it is rapidly heated by the firing of the gun, the seams break. There was a great deal for us to learn about winter flying; for that matter, everything about flying was in its infancy. The war had set it forward many years but a tremendous amount remained to be accomplished. One of my airplanes had a rotary motor which was air cooled and I did not have these troubles with it.

I had some excellent aviation suits made of waterproof gabardine and lined with thick Belgian hare fur, the warmest light material there is. The gabardine broke the wind and the fur furnished the heat. I bought a fine flying cap in Nancy, which fit me perfectly; it was made of mink inside and out and had an attachment which covered all or a part of the face. I wore gloves of fisher fur with large gauntlets and camel's hair lining, that were made in England. I also had mittens to match; and for my feet, I had sheepskin moccasins with the wool turned in. Even these got pretty cold at high altitudes. (The British overcoat that I wore was short, warm and exactly the thing for the trenches. It was lined with camel's hair cloth, which, weight for weight, was just as warm as fur. Strange that an animal used so much in tropical countries should have such warm hair.)

Good aviation clothing is very necessary and important. In June, I requested that clothing of certain characteristics be procured for issue to our troops; the coats to be made of waterproof gabardine lined with Belgian hare and collared with Australian opossum. These could have been obtained in France.

Instead of getting these, the Air Service authorities in America advertised for a coat of certain specifications and gave the contract to some outfit that furnished a coat of heavy duck material lined with dog skin, scarcely cured, that smelled to heaven. Probably everybody's pet dogs in the United States had been stolen and put into these coats. The dye, which was black, rubbed off when the coat was put on over a blouse and left black streaks everywhere, particularly if it was at all wet. The collar, made of billy-goat hair, stuck into your neck and made it so sore you could not turn your head; and sometimes produced boils, as the hair was not at all clean. Thousands of dollars had been spent in the purchase of these coats and they were perfectly worthless.

In Paris I had a talk with Colonel Bolling, who had been relieved of practically all his duties by Foulois. He said that things were going from bad to worse and he doubted very much if, under the circumstances, we could expect any definite number of airplanes from the French, British or Italians, because his arrangements had all been stopped and the airplanes being made in the United States could not possibly arrive in time to be used during the summer of 1918. Bolling had expected to do a great deal in advancing our aviation, and now really seemed quite downhearted. He said that all he wanted now was to get a command on the front. I think he would have done very well there, or any place he was put, for that matter, as he was a brave man and quite a good pilot. He had kept up his flying continually since he had arrived in France and he knew more about the game than most, as he had come during the early part of the show.

I had been boar and stag hunting several times that month, once near Bar-sur-Aube with a French family of a very ancient line, which is said to have held its castle in that area since the time of Henry IV. They were all great hunters but when they approached the age of twenty-five, their eyesight began to fail and all of them became blind before they were thirty. One of the boys was then no longer able to use a gun but could still run with the hounds and participate in the chase. His mother was totally blind but she knew the position of each piece of furniture in her salon so accurately that she could walk about and give the appearance of seeing things perfectly.

I proposed to some of their friends that they ask the family to allow our American doctors to see if they could not stop this terrible condition, which had afflicted their family for generations. They answered that there was no use suggesting such a thing; the family was too proud to call in any physicians and admit that any such affliction existed, so I suppose they will continue in the same way for all the generations to follow.

Back at the Château de Chamarandes, we spent the holidays working hard on our projects and visiting the fronts when opportunity offered. How different this service was from that we had had in Cuba and the Philippines, when we were marching constantly through torrential rains, over mountains and through valleys. Our casualties from the enemy were not so great, but the inroads by disease were tremendous. We had very little food and the facilities for caring for the men were poor and primitive, probably not as good as in our Civil War. Here we had the best food that the world produces, we had permanent habitations, excellent medical attendance and everything that a grateful republic could give its men. Sometimes I think we were pampered and petted too much, particularly the private soldiers. They sometimes seemed to expect more than could be given them. On the other hand, this was not an interesting war for the troops on the ground. There was no marching and maneuvering, no songs, no flying colors and bands playing while going into action. It was just grovelling in dirty mud holes and being killed or maimed by giant projectiles, or permanently incapacitated by gas. The only interest and romance in this war was in the air.

I felt that we had done everything possible during the past year to create an American Air Service worthy of the name and representative of our country. As it was such a new and spectacular branch of the service, it attracted the public fancy, and had been seized upon by the politicians anxious to gain as much out of it as possible. There were just as many politicians in the army as out of it. The men who actually did the work in the air were the younger ones, who had not yet reached the positions they were entitled to in accordance with their ability. So it happened that the upper positions were filled by incompetents from the army and a few from civil life.

I had several talks with General Pershing on this subject, some of them very heated ones. He was very cautious about what he did but he knew pretty well that changes had to be made in the Air Service organization. I believed that when we were ready to go into combat, the incompetents now in charge would be removed and those who understood the use of this fighting arm would be placed in the responsible positions. If this was not done, only the Almighty could take care of the United States Air Service.

The old year 1917 may have been considered a draw between the Germans and the Allies, but the years 1914, '15, '16 certainly were in favor of the Germans, so they had won on points so far. But now a young giant, as exemplified by America, was joining the Allies and the Germans had to crush him in one way or another before he reached his full strength, otherwise they were sure to be defeated.

23

The Yanks Are Coming

January 1918

With the coming of the new year, the Allied armies braced themselves against the attack they knew the Germans would bring. The French and English had tried in 1917, with disastrous results; now it was up to the Germans. It meant the loss of thousands of lives and millions in national resources and treasure, no matter who made the attack. The European nations knew they were reaching the point of exhaustion and that the United States might reap the great benefit from this contest, because we would probably have to use up comparatively little of our national power, and with our resources, manufactories and man power intact at the end of the war, we could step in and get the world's markets.

Another of the kaleidoscopic changes in our Air Service was about to take place. General Foulois came to Chaumont with his staff of non-flyers. It was bad enough having this crowd down in Paris but to bring them up near the line was worse. It reminded me of a story told of old Major Hunter of the cavalry, when General Otis, in command of the Philippines, had taken him to task for not accomplishing more. Major Hunter replied that he had two hundred men who had never seen a horse, two hundred horses that had never seen a man and twenty-five officers who had never seen either. This was the state of the entourage with which General Foulois had surrounded himself.

I was assigned to command the Air Service of the 1st Army Corps, with headquarters at Neufchâteau. I liked this very much because all the troops on the line were to be assigned to this corps and I would have the opportunity of handling them. The other side of the proposition, of course, was that the non-flying members of our Air Service Headquarters were attempting to get rid of all the actual fliers who had superior rank, and this was the scheme in moving me on.

Another thing that made me happy to get to the 1st Army Corps was that General Hunter Liggett was in command of it. He was one of the ablest soldiers I was ever brought in contact with. His appreciation of terrain and the military features of the ground to be used was superior to that of any other man I had known. He could look at a map, which was a flat projection of the ground, and form an exact idea of how it would appear in perspective. When he went to the place, without looking at the map again he could instantly point out each hill, ravine, wood and road with perfect precision. General MacArthur, trained in our Civil War, had this same ability to a marked degree. General Liggett came very near to being sent back to the United States at the same time General Sibert was. Some of the staff officers around General Pershing thought that General Liggett looked too fat. I believe that the order was issued, but another officer was substituted in his place.

The indefatigable Lieutenant L. W. Miller of my staff prepared everything at Neufchâteau for our coming. We had adequate but small offices in one of the houses of the town. I took up my quarters in the house of Madame Garcin. Her father had been Consul General of France in New York during our Civil War and later was appointed Ambassador. He often visited President Lincoln, Madame Garcin told me, and knew him and all his cabinet intimately. Madame Garcin was approaching fourscore years but was just as active physically as ever; she worked around our hospitals constantly. She spoke English perfectly and the French called her the little Yankee. She remembered every detail of her experiences in our Civil War and in Mexico, and all the principal actors in this great drama. To hear her tell of them was like turning back the pages of the book of history for well over half a century. It was strange in this country of Jeanne d'Arc to run across a person so intimately connected with the greatest events in our national history.

And at this time the whole face of this country was covered with the stalwart sons of our America, a people that the makers of history here had never heard or even dreamed of.

February 1918

I made a special study of German aviation during this period. The German pursuit flights were what we called squadrons and were composed of eighteen airplanes. These were divided into three *ketten* (meaning chains) of five or six ships, which corresponded to our flights. They acted together and attacked in echelon, that is, one after the other.

For a while, the Germans used protective flights, assigning a few airplanes to guard a certain locality, but they soon found this was wasteful, because the planes could only stay up an hour and a half and then had to come down for fuel. This gave the other side an opportunity to attack and thus no advantage was gained for a great expenditure of effort. They then began to use their aviation in masses, sending it over all at once into enemy territory, or putting large groups into the air over a locality that they believed would be attacked. A very good system of signaling between these groups and the ground observation posts had been developed, using both visual signals and discharges of anti-aircraft artillery. Whenever a formation of Allied planes went over the front, their numbers, strength and direction were signaled to these Germans groups, who then attacked them.

German airplanes were very good in general, being turned out in production with not nearly the amount of work put into them that the French airplanes had. In the French airplanes, each piece of wood was drawn out from a single piece. It was then planed, sandpapered and even worked down by hand-rubbing. The Germans just sawed off their pieces and left them in the rough. They were just as strong and enduring, and since they were concealed under the fabric covering, I did not see that it made any difference.

At the beginning of 1918 the standard German pursuit plane was the Albatros, which was about equal to the 180-horsepower Spad. The Germans were always experimenting with new types, however, and we could depend upon their having something better than the Albatros soon.

The Germans were particularly good in photography. Their lenses were superior to anything we had, as for years they had produced the best flint and crown glass for this purpose. Their Rumpler plane had the highest ceiling of any photographic airplane on the western front; consequently it was extremely difficult to reach. From the few we had been able to shoot down, we judged that their photographic record of our operations was excellent. A Rumpler came over our American area every day that photographing was possible. The snow on the ground made everything stand out in strong relief, and they must have known exactly what we were doing from the aerial photographs alone.

Their bombardment aviation, which was excellent, operated mostly at night, using twin-motored planes capable of carrying fifteen hundred or two thousand pounds in bombs. From our information, I do not believe they had more than fifty of the larger machines on the front. There were four in each flight; sometimes two or three flights were grouped together for a particular operation. They did very little day bombardment, but sometimes employed the two-seater Rumpler, their photo-graphic machine, for this purpose, using very small bombs of

fifteen or twenty pounds, whereas the night bombers used five-
or six-hundred-pound ones.

The rear of the German army was well covered with good
flying fields and airdromes, connected by telegraph with each
other and with the supply points in their vicinity. Thus their air
forces could be shifted from one side of the line to the other in a
very short time. They had a shorter distance to fly across their
position, which was in the form of a salient, than had the Allies,
who had to fly around the outside of it. They could almost always
concentrate in one place more quickly than the Allies.

Adjutant Fumat brought my airplanes up from Chaumont,
including an excellent new Spad, a single seater. The day after
I got it, a German Rumpler, as usual, started over our area. I
happened to be at the airdrome near Neufchâteau, when it
was sighted at about fifteen thousand feet. I decided to try to
get it. I started off in my Spad with all speed, taxied across the
airdrome, intending to turn it into the wind and then gave her
the gun, without bringing the ship to a full stop. But it began
to swing sideways and I could not stop it. If I cut the throttle and
lost speed, the ship undoubtedly would have turned over (the
wings had already begun to lift) so I gave it all the gas I had
and just as I was leaving the ground, I thought I heard one of
the wheels break. I climbed to about twelve thousand feet but
couldn't find the Rumpler and so returned to the airdrome. I
could see an ambulance on the field, and officers and men
bustling about in a great state of excitement, two or three running around with a wheel in their hands to indicate that mine
was broken. One cannot see his own wheels while flying a Spad.
I landed with great caution, putting the weight on the undamaged right wheel, and felt no particular inconvenience from the
landing except that the ship swung to the left a bit. Everyone
was surprised that I had not turned over. The wheel, instead
of collapsing sideways, had the spokes driven straight through
the tires and in this way gave me considerable support.

On February nineteenth, I took Lieutenant-Colonel Stewart

Heintzleman, Acting Chief of Staff of the 1st Army Corps, with me in my two-seater airplane and flew over the position of our 1st Division at Menil la Tours, and out over the German positions, showing him Montsec and other important points. This was the first time that any American General Staff officer had flown over the enemy lines, and also the first time an airplane bearing the American insignia had been piloted by an American over the lines. To be sure, the plane was French but it carried our colors, the concentric circles of red, white and blue, with white center. It is a coincidence that Heintzleman's grandfather, General Heintzleman, was the first officer to go up in Professor Lowe's balloon at Yorktown, while a member of General McClellan's army in 1862. Court Zeppelin, then a Lieutenant of the Prussian cavalry, was a military observer at the same place.

Our divisions were now beginning to go up on the line. The 42nd Division, called the Rainbow because it had troops from several states, was near Lunéville, and on February 21st, I went to visit it, with an old friend of mine, Colonel Winship, our Judge Advocate. We met General Charles T. Menoher, the Commanding Officer, and his Chief of Staff, Colonel Douglas MacArthur, whom I had known since I was a small boy. MacArthur's father was in my father's regiment in the Civil War. The Division impressed me as splendid.

Winship and I had supper in Nancy and on the way home our motor car caught fire in the engine, due to a broken exhaust pipe. We took our tin hats, filled them with water at a nearby hydrant and tried to put the fire out in that way, rather a foolish proceeding. Jones, my chauffeur, with much greater presence of mind, threw his coat and blanket over the engine and put the fire out before any damage was done.

My office in Neufchâteau was at 10 rue de la Comédie, which I think was a good name for it, considering the state of our air organization on the front. General Foulois at Chaumont was attempting to exercise direct control over everything at the front and rear. He had a non-flying officer at Colombey-les-Belles who was trying to do the same thing. I was supposed to have command of the air units on the line, and Royce, at Amanty with our first American squadron, did not know who his boss was. He got his supplies wherever he could find them. I helped him out as much as I could but really had no authority to do so.

On February 26th, Company B, 2nd Balloon Squadron, arrived on the line, the first American air unit to enter into active hostilities against the Germans. I felt that our active participation was not far off, as our first airplane squadron was ready to come up. I took General Liggett out to see our balloon company. They maneuvered the balloon, handled the telephone from the car to the ground, had their operations office up with the maps, showing the enemy positions and exhibited their complete equipment. They cut loose a parachute with a sand bag attached from an altitude of two thousand feet; the sandbag was not well fastened to the parachute and broke loose, hitting the ground about twenty feet from General Liggett, with great force. Had it hit him, the 1st Army Corps would have been minus a commander.

24

The Germans Destroy the Fifth British Army

March 1918

On March 5th, I went out to Villacoublay to look over the new French airplanes. The first Liberty motor had just arrived and was about to be mounted in a Bréguet plane. It was a good-looking engine, quite similar to the Lorraine-Dietrich, but with twelve cylinders instead of eight. It was on the stand and I saw it turned up to seventeen hundred revolutions. There were many things about it, however, which would have to be attended to before we could take it to the front.

I also learned that the 1st Squadron was to be equipped with the two-seater Spad with Hispano engine, a dangerous airplane that had been discarded by the French. I had recommended the Salmson for us but for some reason, General Foulois had agreed to take these Spads. He was no longer able to fly himself and did not know the danger of this aircraft. The more I saw of the way non-flying officers were conducting our Air Service, the surer I was of many rocks ahead.

On March 6th, I took Lieutenant Blair Thaw, William Thaw's brother, out to Le Bourget with me, to show him what planes were desired. This airdrome was the general reserve for all aircraft in the French service, and contained line after line of hangars, all very close together and filled with planes. It offered a wonder target for bombardment. The Germans, I thought, would not be long in hitting it. I arranged to have the 1st Squadron get their planes at Le Bourget and fly them to the front, and left Lieutenant Thaw to attend to the details. He was an excellent pilot and well versed in the technical end of the business.

On March 14th, at 11:00 A.M., I received a telegram that had been following me about for some time, inviting me to attend a meeting of the French Senate at 2:15 P.M. the same day, in honor of the French aviators, Roland Garros and Pierre Antoine Marchal, who had just escaped from Germany. Garros was one of the most distinguished pilots living. He was the first man to loop the loop and brought down a Zeppelin in the first part of the war, but was taken prisoner shortly afterward. I wondered how these old-timers would do on the front now; things had changed so much during the last two years.

There was only one way to get to Paris on time and that was by airplane. The days had been getting warm and bright, but there was still a good deal of haze and the visibility was not good. However, I took my single-seater Spad and started out. Soon I ran into considerable fog and thicker haze, and my compass began to whirl so it was difficult to tell which was north. I passed over several rivers and went down close to the water once, within about twenty feet of it, to determine which way the current was flowing, but could not tell. Then I tried to ascend above the haze, with no better success. Finally, I decided to take a compass bearing in the direction in which I thought Paris lay and hold it for awhile. I was beginning to run short of gas, after two hours in the air, when suddenly a city loomed up beneath me which I recognized as Soissons from its church steeples, one of which had been partly shot off. I was headed directly into Germany, with about five minutes gas left in my main tanks. Soon I would have had to land and would have found myself in German territory. Turning, I flew until my gas gave out, then turned on the emergency tank, and landed in a field about twenty kilometers from Paris, at Clavesouilly. There I obtained a military automobile and rushed into Paris, but did not reach there until 4:30 P.M., too late to participate in the exercises.

I took every opportunity to get to various parts of the front, to see what was transpiring. In the interior, our schools were working well and our pilots showing up better than any on the front. Rickenbacker, our former chauffeur, was distinguishing himself in the schools, along with many others. After studying the situation at the front, I could see no reason why we could not assemble a large mass of aerial maneuver and strike, one day opposite the British front and the next day opposite Verdun, or clear into Germany as far as the Rhine.

On March 24th, hearing that the Germans had attacked the Fifth British Army, opposite the Amiens sector, I decided to visit the scene of operations. I flew first to Ville Neuve, the airdrome back of Épernay in the Champagne, where out first pursuit group was being formed. Major Ménard, the great pursuit commander of the French, had his group there alongside of our new one. He was very much pleased with our pilots; Raoul Lufbery had joined the group. They were equipped with the Nieuport 160-horsepower plane with rotary engine, which, although it had many admirable characteristics, had been rejected by the French as being too weak. It seemed too bad we had to take second-class stuff.

From Ville Neuve I proceeded to Le Bourget where everyone was agog over the great battle that was taking place in the north. Next morning it was cold, dark and cloudy, with flakes of snow in the air, but toward afternoon the wind from the north cleared things up a little and I got into the air in my single seater, going straight north over Senlis and Compiègne toward Noyon.

A tremendous contest was taking place for the possession of this town. Nothing remained of the British Fifth Army. The French aviation had cleared the air of the Germans, who were taking this opportunity to recuperate their air forces after the terrific fighting they had had against the British for over a week, so I was able to fly where I pleased and see what I wanted to.

In some places I flew only a few hundred feet over the Germans, who were approaching in columns from everywhere in the direction of Noyon. Almost every other man seemed to be dragging a machine gun. Further on, I could see the fighting going on equally strongly for Morest and Chauny. German reserves were echeloned deeply behind St. Quentin.

The wind was blowing at sixty-eight kilometers an hour, at three thousand meters up, from the German toward the French lines, so if my motor stopped, the wind would carry me with a dead stick a long way into French territory. It was so cold and damp that ice began to form on my wings and along the wires.

While I watched, the German infantry apparently cleared the city of Noyon. Fortunately, for the Allied cause, General Fayolle finally arrived from Italy with his troops, which were thrown against the German flank in the vicinity of Noyon. The German infantry seemed to me to be irresistible, but their motor trucks with steel wheels could not go across no-man's land to follow up the troops. If they had had a more powerful air force that could have been thrown ahead of them, followed up by a few divisions of cavalry, the war might have been over. I have never seen a battlefield so denuded of troops as this one was of the British.

I returned to the airdrome at Le Bourget at 6:30 P.M. From what I can learn of this whole affair, what happened was this: The Germans decided to put the British out of commission for the rest of the summer, preparatory to an attack on the French. The British Fifth Army under General Gough, which held the right of the British line, was selected as the point of attack. The Germans used an entirely new system: bringing their troops up under cover of darkness, they formed the attacking echelons into columns, with orders to go right over the trenches held by the British and attack the reserves behind them, knowing that the moment the alarm was sounded, the British reserves would be put in motion to the threatened points. Behind these columns, the Germans formed their troops in line for the purpose of occupying the British trenches, capturing the troops and holding them in case of a counterattack. The movement was a great surprise. At the moment of assault, a short, well-timed artillery preparation took place which drove the British into the trenches and cut many of the entanglements and obstacles. The assaulting columns quickly crossed the positions, and before the British knew it, the Germans had reached their reserves that were marching along the roads in column, thinking themselves safe, and absolutely destroyed them. The second wave of Germans occupied the British trenches, turned them around and prepared them for defense.

The British Fifth Army was a thing of the past, a running mass of fugitives, and a great gaping hole existed in the line.

General Foch had apparently anticipated an attack somewhere in this area and it was he who ordered up the troops from Italy and threw them in yesterday where I saw them. As a result of these operations, General Foch was made supreme commander of all the Allied forces in northern France.

On my flight back to Neufchâteau, I saw that the roads everywhere were filled with transport, artillery and troops moving to the scene of the fray. I reported my estimate of the situation to General Liggett, who was itching to get into the fight and thought that four of our divisions could do good work, and I believed they could.

On the 31st, I went down to Chaumont and saw General Harbord who told me that General Pershing had offered to put any or all of our troops into the line in this great crisis. We must have then had half a million men in France. While untrained, many of them never having even fired a rifle, they certainly could do a great deal if given a chance.

It is strange how quickly the French people sensed what was going on. Word traveled like wildfire through northern France. Although no news was allowed to be published in the papers of what was happening to the British army, every inhabitant of the upper Marne knew that the great crisis was at hand. Everybody knew that as soon as the attacks against the British subsided a little, the French army would be jumped on and thousands would pay the price of their defense.

25

First American Air Forces
Enter the Combat

April 1918

The Germans were beginning to hit Paris with their long-range cannon which shot seventy-two miles. Many people at first thought that the projectiles had been dropped by airplanes. They did not believe a gun could be constructed to shoot that far. A measurement of the curvature of some fragments of the projectile told the size of the gun, and from the angle at which the shots fell, it could be told about where the gun was located. Airplanes were sent over to locate and destroy it, but the gun's real position was so well concealed and so cleverly camouflaged by dummy positions constructed around it, that they were not successful in their mission.

The object of this long-range bombardment was to congest the lines of communication around Paris so as to make it difficult for the French to move supplies rapidly through this area to their troops. It was also intended to frighten the ammunition workers, government employees and other citizens so that they would evacuate the city. There was quite an exodus from Paris. Continued airplane raids were made by the Germans at this same time and the city was darkened every night. Numbers of additional anti-aircraft cannon with their crews were withdrawn from the French army and stationed around the city but they did little good. At night searchlights and balloon barrages were placed at appropriate points, the latter being a series of small balloons holding up wires at a height of five or six thousand feet. Some were even put in the center of the city, on the Champs-Élysées. The routes that the Germans were supposed to follow in coming down from the north were covered at certain points by these balloon barrages; but I believe the Germans knew where they were and avoided them, just as we knew where the German barrages were located.

In spite of the terrible mess which our Air Service had gotten into as a result of so many non-flying officers being at the top, some order began to come out of it. The 1st Observation Squadron, with Major Ralph Royce commanding, made its first patrol over the line on April 11th. Our 94th Pursuit Squadron moved to Toul on April 8th, and the 91st Army Observation Squadron came up also. All these squadrons were now definitely assigned to my command and we worked hard on their battle training, at the same time forming the nucleus of our bombardment aviation.

Whenever we could get them, men who had had experience with the French and British services and in whom the pilots had confidence were put into the key positions. Among them was Major Raoul Lufbery, who was then leading the Americans in the number of enemy planes shot down. Lufbery's father was an American citizen and his mother a French peasant woman. Lufbery was quite a wanderer and his first experience in aviation was as a mechanic with a French aviator who was touring India. Later, he went into the French Foreign Legion and served as a mechanic in the air forces. He then took flying instructions and with great difficulty learned to fly. At first a very poor pilot, he developed into one of the greatest experts in individual combat and pursuit work on the western front.

All eyes were on our men. They were wonderful pilots, as far as the flying itself went, but they had never been exposed to actual combat with the enemy, so it was a question as to what would happen. Our first air squadron on the line, the 94th, adopted a catchy insignia for its ships, Uncle Sam's hat with a ring around it, to signify that the United States had entered the ring in the European war.

We of course were still under French command but I arranged with the Commander of French Aviation of the Eighth French Army to give us a definite sector to defend. We were assigned the area between the Meuse and Moselle rivers, with our left at St. Mihiel and our right at Pont-à-Mousson, the first definite sector assigned to an American flying organization.

We were favored with a bit of rare good fortune on our very first day of independent operations on the front, which I believe had a more important effect on American fighting aviation than any other single occurrence. It gave our men a confidence that could have been obtained in no other way. It must be remembered that our inexperienced men were entering the lists against fighting airmen who were as good as any the world had yet seen. The German aviators had splendid airplanes, machine guns and ammunition, excellent instruction in their duties and a fine organization behind them.

The eventful day was the 14th of April. Orders had been issued for a patrol, consisting of Captain David Peterson, Lieutenant Edward Rickenbacker and Lieutenant Reid Chambers, to go up to five thousand meters and intercept any enemy airplanes that crossed the line. I wanted to stop all the German photographic machines from taking pictures of our back areas where the troops were being assembled. Lieutenants Douglas Campbell, Alan Winslow and James Meissner were ordered to stand by on the alert at the airdrome, ready to take the air at a moment's notice.

The morning of the 14th dawned rather cold and foggy, but our patrol nevertheless proceeded over the front, where it was discovered by German lookouts and anti-aircraft artillery posts. Our men became separated in the fog but fortunately all returned to the field at Toul without mishap. Shortly after their return, our anti-aircraft artillery stationed at the top of Mont St. Michel just outside Toul signaled that German airplanes were approaching the city above the fog, at which our alert was ordered to take the air. The whir of the German motors could be heard by the citizens of Toul and also the roar of the American engines as they took off. Meissner could not start his ship and therefore remained on the ground.

Hundreds in the city and vicinity looked out to see what would happen. A remarkable picture met their gaze. The German machines were concealed by the fog, but just as the two American ships approached the cloud ceiling, the German planes came out of it and were instantly attacked by Alan Winslow and Douglas Campbell. Winslow shot the first plane down and Campbell the second.

Both German airplanes had been brought down and our pilots were back on the airdrome within four and one-half minutes after they left it. It was the most remarkable exhibition ever given on the Western front and occurred in full view of all the soldiers and citizens residing in that part of the country.

Neither of the German pilots was killed. One of them was a very capable officer, the other also a good man. They reported that they had been ordered to attack two enemy machines that were crossing the lines between St. Mihiel and Pont-à-Mousson, undoubtedly those of Rickenbacker and Chambers who had become lost in the fog.

I have always thought that another thing was intended. The Germans knew full well that our air units had just reached the line and that in all probability our men, new at the game, would not be as alert or as competent in their work as at a later date. Not long before this, some German machines had come right down onto the French airdrome at Toul, set fire to several airplanes on the ground with their flaming bullets and shot up the whole place, killing several people.

If they could have done this to the Americans right off the handle, it would have had a dampening effect on our morale and would have greatly improved that of the German aviators.

(I have always wondered if these German airplanes, taking advantage of the fog, were not attempting to do this very thing.)

The remains of the enemy airplanes were taken into the square at Toul by order of the French Commanding Officer and the mayor of the city, and the enthusiasm of the citizens was tremendous. I lost no time in publishing these facts all over the army and to our aviation in particular. I brought General Liggett to pay a visit to the squadron a day or so afterward and he, with his usual affability, congratulated the officers and told them of his sincere appreciation for what they had done.

By the end of the month we were in full action on the front and each day our men showed up to better and better advantage —Rickenbacker, Chambers, Meissner and others. We had our losses too, which I shall not mention in this chronicle. The burning of a pilot in the air as his ship catches fire from the hostile flaming bullets is a terrible thing. He is there alone, suspended in space, with no companion to share his misery, no man at his elbow to support him, as in the infantry on the ground. When he is wounded and falls, it is for thousands of feet, instead of two or three, as a man on the ground does. We were inflicting a loss of at least three to one on the enemy, though, which was remarkable for a new outfit. Our men were full of dash and exceptionally cool in combat.

Some amusing things also happen. One day one of our hospital units with a number of good-looking nurses moved into the French hospital at Sebastapol, about a mile from the airdrome of the 1st Pursuit Group. Our men were overjoyed to meet these nice American girls and every evening they could get off or sneak off, they went over to the hospital to see them.

The Commanding Officer there, one of our regular surgeons and an old friend of mine, complained to me one day that the work of his hospital was being very much interfered with by our young men. He had no objections, he said, to their coming to see the nurses, but they stayed up so late at night that the nurses were good for nothing the next day, and he wished I would instruct the pilots to bring them in earlier. Accordingly,

I sent word to this effect to Major John Huffer. I heard nothing more about it for some days, and then the Commanding Officer came in to see me again. This time he seemed quite put out. He told me that although most of our pilots had complied with the order I had issued, some of them had disregarded it and he had found it necessary to issue orders to the nurses, just the day before, that none of them should go out with or see our pilots. That morning, he reported, several of our airplanes in formation had flown over the hospital and bombarded it with long rolls of toilet paper, which was then covering the tops of the buildings and hanging in festoons from the telegraph wires. This performance greatly interfered with the discipline of his whole organization and he wished some drastic action taken.

I went out to the hospital to see what had happened and it was quite a sight. The paper had been dropped in rolls, which unraveled on the way down and it was all over everything—the funniest sight I had seen in a long time. Of course I knew who had done it but took no action beyond telling them to cut out all foolishness in the future.

The thing we most greatly lacked was superior commanders for our larger air units. There were practically no officers of the regular army who were competent. None of them had had experience in war and with very few exceptions, none of them were good enough pilots. On the other hand, there were many temporary officers who were perfectly capable of handling organizations of any size. I found that for quick perception and power of initiative, ability to assume responsibility and to act at once on their convictions, the temporary officers were far ahead of the officers of the regular army.

The non-flying aggregation who were all-powerful in aviation, attempted to put non-fliers into the upper positions so as to get the rank. How many of our pilots were killed as a result of this seemed to be a secondary consideration with them.

Still another change had taken place in our air organization. General Foulois had his headquarters in Tours, but spent most of his time in Paris, where Colonel Halsey Dunwoody, now in charge of aeronautical supply, was really doing good work. There was no Air Service liaison officer at Chaumont. The General Staff was trying to run the Air Service with just as much knowledge about it as a hog has about skating. It was terrible to have to fight with an organization of this kind, instead of devoting all our attention to the powerful enemy on our front.

I had many talks with General Pershing on this subject, some of them very heated, with much pounding on the table with fists on both sides of the argument. One time he told me that if I did not stop insisting that the organization of the Air Service be changed, that he would send me home. I answered that if he did, he could soon come after me. This made him laugh and our talk ended amicably.

One evening, when I motored over to Nancy for dinner, I noticed that a bright moon was shining and knew it would not be long before the German bombers would be around. I left my car at the door of the Café Walter, ready to leave quickly in case the alarm sounded. No lights appeared in the city, but in the bright moonlight it must have been as plain as day from the air. Sure enough, the alarm soon rang out and I left the café, driving rapidly to a hill near Pont St. Vincent, from where I could see exactly what happened.

We could hear the engines of the German planes and from their sound identified them as Gothas, which meant they were carrying big bombs. The anti-aircraft fire was incessant and searchlights swept back and forth over the sky, revealing nothing as usual. Suddenly I heard three loud reports, one after the other, and saw the great flashes on the ground as of great shells exploding. Then everything was quiet.

Still the droning of the Gothas kept up, so I continued to watch. Three more deafening explosions rent the air, and after the last one a great fire sprang up in the center of the town, apparently spreading to various buildings. We could hear the fire engines as they went through the streets. The sound of the Gothas died away and I returned to Nancy to see what had happened.

The first three shots had been directed at an ammunition factory. One had hit across the street from it but the other two had gone straight through the roof and entirely destroyed the factory. It would not make any more shells during the war. The second three shots had been directed at the railroad station. One of them had gone through the roof of the station, doing a good deal of damage which could be repaired very quickly however. The second fell among the railroad tracks and just blew a big hole, but the third one hit a train loaded with gasoline and set it on fire. It was still burning furiously and the blaze had spread to several houses nearby. Two German airplanes had done this.

Just think of what two hundred would have done if they had had them to send over! That is, provided they had wanted to destroy the city, which I doubted very much. Nancy had been evacuated almost completely of its civil population on account of the air attacks, and there were few troops quartered there. If there were more, the Germans would undoubtedly have bombed it to a greater extent.

About a month before, Harbord and De Chambrun had an experience with bombs in Nancy, which gave Harbord a very good insight into what airplanes could do. I think Harbord had the idea, as most ground officers had, that bombs were not particularly effective. In this instance, he was in his room in the hotel when the alarm sounded and instead of getting into the cave under the hotel at once for protection, he foolishly stayed in his room in the sixth story. A bomb hit in the street directly opposite his room, demolished the whole side of the hotel and I believe blew him into the bath tub with a window casing around his neck for a necklace. If a few more of our general staff officers could have had this same experience without its hurting them any more than it did Harbord, it would have been an excellent thing.

I also, out of bravado, had remained above ground in my first airplane raid a year before and learned that it was the wrong thing to do if one expected to stay among the living. An experience like that demonstrated that if we had had sufficient bombardment aviation, we could have brought the war to a close by carrying it to the vital points in the interior of Germany and making the people sue for peace. This would have been much less costly in lives than the old way of conducting the war.

In the area behind us, the British were building up an independent air force, the first force of this kind to be gotten together. It was designed to attack the interior cities of Germany. The British had very sensibly combined all their air power under a separate ministry which was co-equal with the army and navy. This is what we should have done.

Our navy was trying to have an air service, the way the British navy did at the beginning of the war. They hadn't any airplanes to supply their men but had many pilots. I had some French airplanes but not enough pilots. The navy was going to conduct an air war of their own somewhere, nobody knew where exactly. This performance just meant a tremendous waste of money, men and energy. All of our aeronautical resources should have been put with my organization and have fought as one great American unit, that would have the combined punch where it was needed.

I continued to fly over the lines almost every day, keeping track of each organization, each commanding officer and almost every pilot. How much more fun it would have been to be a pilot in one of the squadrons. During the Spanish-American War, when I joined the 1st Wisconsin Infantry as a private, I had more fun than at any other time and wanted to remain where I was; but my father, then in the United States Senate, made me accept a discharge and later a commission, which, of course, was a good thing but not as pleasant as being with my old friends from our home town, in our local company.

CHAPTER

26

Heavy Casualties

May 1918

We now had an actual observation group acting, composed of two squadrons, the 1st and 12th. We had a pursuit group consisting of the 94th, 95th, 27th and 194th Squadrons, with an air park, under command of Major Atkinson. We had an army observation squadron, the 91st, and a bombardment squadron was almost ready to come up to the front. Our force began to grow rapidly.

We were now not only using our squadrons on the front, but were having maneuvers and aerial instruction with the ground troops at the schools and in the training areas. Our infantry divisions were beginning to come up, one after another. We had all the equipment that money could buy, but lacked what money could not buy—experience and a good corps of officers. Both of these would come with work on the front, but at a tremendous cost in lives.

The headquarters of the French Eighth Army desired to present the Croix de guerre to our officers who had distinguished themselves, and accordingly, on May 15th, a formation took place at the Toul airdrome. There were French troops, as well as Americans from the 26th Division, accompanied by their bands. The ceremony was attended by General Passagat, commanding the 32nd French Army Corps, General Liggett, commanding the 1st American Army Corps and General Edwards, commanding the 26th American Division. General Gerard, commanding the Eighth French Army, and I made the presentations.

We had lost two good men who were on the list for citations: Charles W. Chapman, killed in action, and James Norman Hall, whom we thought at that time was dead. They received the decorations posthumously. Peterson, Rickenbacker and Meissner were decorated.

The end of May proved to be a very sad period for me. To begin with, Major Lufbery was killed on May 19th. Lufbery was our leading pilot, and a great source of strength on account of the confidence our men had in him, and because of his great ability to impart details of air fighting to them.

I was sitting in my office in Toul on May 19th when the alarm was sounded that a German airplane was near. I looked out the window and saw the anti-aircraft artillery filling the air with projectiles. The German airplane, a two-seater Albatros, was so close to the ground that I thought it was going to land, but suddenly it rose again. I dashed for my automobile to get to the Toul airdrome, telling Hall, my operations officer, to notify the French aviation at Nancy that a German airplane was headed in their direction.

As I left in my automobile, I could see one of our airplanes engage the German ship but in an utterly futile way. The pilot did not close up but expended all his ammunition uselessly in the air. (For this performance I sent the pilot to the rear.)

I hurried for the airdrome but was stopped by a foolish sentinel on the way in, who asked where my pass was. As I arrived on the field, an airplane cut across to head off the German ship. This I was told was Lufbery. As we had several patrols out over the front that morning, there was nobody else ready to go after the German machine at the time. It was too late for me to get in the air, so I returned to the office and went to work.

In a few minutes, my telephone rang and I was informed that Major Lufbery had been killed. His plane had fallen at a little place about six miles from Toul on the Moselle River. A detail from the 1st Pursuit Group under the commanding officer had gone to get the remains, and I went over to find out what I could about his last fight.

The little village was on a high bank which gradually slopes off to the Moselle. At this time of the year it was covered with flowers and fruit trees in bloom. Lufbery's body had fallen out of his plane into the back yard of an old shoemaker's house.

This back yard was a typical French back yard of that class of people. There were little boxes for rabbits, a place for a cow and chickens. A long white picket fence separated the yard from others. Along the fence on both sides was a fringe of flowers. It was on this picket fence that Lufbery had fallen. One of the pickets pierced his left leg and unquestionably greatly broke the fall. He hit the ground and lay on his back, dead.

The shoemaker's daughter rushed to Lufbery's body and opening his flying suit, saw his decorations and recognized him immediately. Lufbery was a great hero among the French peasants, because his mother was a peasant. The girl immediately covered the body with flowers and waited for others to come and carry it to the town hall, where our men received it.

The old shoemaker's description of the combat was the best that anybody gave me. He said that all of a sudden the alarm was sounded for an approaching German plane. The people ran for the cellars, but immediately afterward the roar of an American airplane could be heard, and the people yelled to each other: "The Americans are coming—we will be saved." Many then came out of the cellars.

The large German plane was close to the ground and the pilot and observer could be plainly seen. At the same time, coming from the direction of Toul with an unbelievable speed, a single small American airplane approached the German. He came straight up on to the tail, and it looked as if the two airplanes touched each other. Four or five shots were fired by the American, but the German did not reply. The American turned quickly, climbed in the air, and came straight for the German, again under his tail. Again the airplanes looked as if they were touching; again shots were fired by the American. The German replied with only four or five.

The American airplane drew off gradually, turned upside down and it looked as if a sack filled with something fell out of it. It was the pilot, Lufbery. Smoke then began coming out of the plane. It caught fire and glided several hundred yards, then crashed and burned up.

There was no mark on Lufbery's body except one bullet shot through the left hand. It appeared very probable that either his controls were cut, causing the airplane to turn over, and he fell out, or that he jumped out because it was on fire. I doubt very much if an old pilot like Lufbery would have jumped on account of fire. All the eyewitnesses I talked to said Lufbery fell out before the plane caught fire. I think it quite probable that Lufbery, in his hurry to get after the German plane, failed to tie himself in the plane with his belt; that the German shots cut his controls, his airplane turned over and he fell out. Just think —if he had had a parachute he could easily have been saved!

Lufbery had never shot an airplane down on our side of the line. All his combats had been in enemy territory, and he was terribly anxious to shoot one down where we could get at the wreck, both on his own account and to show our new pilots how it was done.

The German plane proceeded on its way and was attacked by pilots from the French pursuit group at Malzeville, under Captain Jean Derode. The German shot down the leading ace of Derode's group but later was forced to land, and the pilot and observer were captured.

This German crew had been sent over to distract attention from another airplane flying at a high altitude for the purpose of taking photographs.

The Germans at first had sent over several airplanes at high altitude. Our men shot them down. They were followed by pairs of airplanes. Again our men shot them down (our Nieuports were now able to go as high as the German Rumplers). Finding that this scheme did not work, the Germans sent over an airplane at high altitude and one at low altitude, knowing full well that the one at low altitude would probably not return.

The bravery and devotion of this German crew can be imagined. They were held in great respect for their daring fight, although they had killed two of our best men, one in the French service and one in ours. There was more chivalry left among our airmen than was the case with the ground troops.

In this war the ground troops seldom met their adversary face to face. They operated out of dirty, wet ditches, covered by dust, smoke, mud, fragments of shells and machine-gun bullets or by gas clouds. All this talk about closing up with the bayonet is largely a myth. When troops got close enough for that, one side or the other broke and ran away. War on the ground resolved itself into an attack of masses that employed missile-throwing weapons to keep the adversary as far off as possible.

In the air, the action was entirely individual as far as combat was concerned. A man singled out his adversary and they engaged in mortal combat. Already we had received notes from the Germans, dropped on our airdromes, as to what had become of the pilots we had lost, and with a request for information as to their pilots whom we had shot down.

On May 20th, we buried Lufbery in a little cemetery beyond the Sebastapol Hospital, in the corner of a wood. Already several of our airmen were in it, some killed by the enemy and some killed by the poor machines that we had to equip our men with. We all assembled and went out to the cemetery with Lufbery's casket piled high with flowers. General Gerard, General Edwards and I made short addresses, during which the airplanes of our 1st Pursuit Group flew over, led by Rickenbacker. They came low down and dropped flowers over the grave as the casket was lowered.

The hard work and losses they were sustaining were beginning to tell on our pilots a little. I heard that Miss Elsie Janis, the actress, was to be in our area, so I sent over to see if she could come and give an entertainment for our 1st Pursuit Group. Although she had given three performances that day, she came to the Toul Airdrome.

Our men fixed up a stage of boards, held up by gasoline trucks, in an old prewar hangar on the flying field, which was lighted by electricity generated by one of our machine-shop trucks. All the windows were shaded so that the lights could not be seen outside and draw fire from a German bomber. Miss Janis gave a remarkable performance which was thoroughly appreciated by our men.

I was having lunch on May 27th at the Café Bosquet in Toul when my adjutant, Captain Kelleher, came to me with a very perturbed look on his face. I could see as he approached me that something serious had occurred. He called me to one side and said: "I have some bad news for you. Your brother has crashed in an airplane." I asked him if he was dead and he said that he was. The accident had occurred at our air depot at Colombey-les-Belles.

He had flown down to Chaumont in the morning to attend to some matters of equipment for the air troops. He had had one forced landing on the way down, due to oil trouble in his engine, but had landed, repaired it, and proceeded on his journey. Coming back, he attempted to land at Colombey-les-Belles. The airdrome at this place is quite bad.

As he came in to land he had too much speed. His wheels hit hard and he bounced. He lowered the tail of his ship. The next time the wheels and the tail skid hit hard and again he bounced. Apparently he decided to make another turn of the field, so he gunned his motor and started to make a circle. When he started to make the turn, the longerons or beams in the back part of the fuselage broke and the ship fell to earth, and he was instantly killed. It was a weak ship.

Thus died my only brother, a splendid young man of twenty-three years of age. He had everything in him that a brother should have. He was greatly thought of and respected by everyone with whom he came in contact. Major Frank Page took charge of the body and all the arrangements for the funeral, which we held next day in a manner similar to Lufbery's.

This was his first campaign, and it seemed to me that if either of us had to be killed I should have been the one, because I had been in several campaigns before. While primarily his death was due to a weak airplane, I think that his eyes were not as good as they should have been and that he stretched matters in his physical examination to get by the doctors, in his anxiety to be in the Air Service and near me.

My mind was made up more than ever to rely on the judgment of the doctors as to a man's fitness for flight. Our doctors proved their value more and more every day. I also determined to continue trying every kind of airplane myself that our men had to use, before adopting it for our service.

It is a tradition in our family that every male who is able goes to war immediately on the outbreak of hostilities. My mother had both her sons and four sons-in-law in the services. She had contributed every male member that she could. She was getting old now and I was afraid that my brother's death would have a very bad effect on her, although she would never complain.

The death of Lufbery and my brother had been a great spur to the pilots in the 1st Pursuit Group. They immediately began to put forward redoubled efforts to shoot down the Germans. On the afternoon of my brother's funeral, I got in my airplane and inspected all of the aviation that we had on the front, including the work of the pilots over the line.

Douglas Campbell and my brother had been among the first ten flying cadets to come to Europe in August, 1917, and were close friends. He made up his mind to shoot down several German airplanes to make up for John's loss. On the last day of May, he shot down a two-seater in single combat, which crashed just north of the headquarters of our 1st Division at Menil-la-Tour. In this combat, the German observer exhausted all his ammunition. Campbell considered letting him go, but on second thought he knew the German aviator had secured valuable photographs of our area, and he shot him down.

Campbell reported that as he approached for the last shot, the German observer stood in the back seat with his arms folded, looking him squarely in the face. His empty cartridge belt was dangling over the side of the airplane from his machine gun. He was waiting bravely for the death which he knew was sure to come. Both the pilot and observer were officers of the Prussian Army and were given a suitable military burial.

Another change had taken place in the Air Service. General Mason Patrick, an engineer officer, had been made Chief of the Air Service. General Patrick had always been an efficient engineer officer, and had recently been in charge of what we call utilities in the service of supply. Of course he had no real knowledge of the Air Service, but things had become such a mess in the interior that it was necessary to put somebody in charge of things there in whom General Pershing had confidence.

Patrick was in Pershing's class at the Military Academy at West Point and had always done good work. He would get along pretty well if he kept his hands off the air units that were actually fighting. If not, he would get into trouble, because the time had arrived when we were actually fighting hard against the Germans and interference by non-fliers would be disastrous.

Our 1st Army Corps, under General Liggett, was to be put into the line as an organization just as soon as possible. All the active air units on the front were to be assigned to it, and I was to retain command of them. General Foulois was to be assigned as Chief of the Air Service of the First Army. As there were no air units in the First Army and would not be until the First Army was formed, he would not have very much to do.

Milling was coming up to the front to take command of a wing. Every two or three months we changed the title of our office, but fortunately we were left fighting the enemy all the time. The only actual change that took place was that we got a new rubber stamp with which to mark the correspondence. I had a good working staff, and the air units that we had on the line could be rapidly expanded as our men came up.

The English were badly smashed up and were trying to replace their losses in men and equipment. In the meantime, they were putting up what amounted to a last stand, as was shown by the order issued by General Sir Douglas Haig, commanding the British army:

> Every position must be held to the last man. There must be no retirement. With our backs to the wall, and believing in the justice of our cause, each one of us must fight to the end. The safety of our homes and the freedom of mankind depend alike upon the conduct of each one of us at this critical moment.

The French knew that they were to be attacked next and that the British would be unable to render much help for a while.

". . . a German machine had come down with the pilot badly wounded . . . and on the side in large letters was painted the word *Vera.* . . . This, the French pilots told me, was the name of the German pilot's sweetheart. I suggested that *Vera* be sent to America for inspection."

"After lunch at the mess, we started for the lines; I carried my helmet, gas mask and field glasses. I asked Captain Raulin to take me where an attack was going on, so I could see what was necessary in this kind of warfare."

"One flight over the lines gave me a much clearer impression of how
the armies were laid out than any amount of traveling around on the ground."
Mitchell (left) beside two-seater Spad. Probably with Adjutant Fumat.

"In my spare moments I took every opportunity to hunt with the inhabitants of the valley. . . . Many of the hunters were old men of sixty, seventy and even eighty; a few served in the Franco-Prussian War of 1870–1871."

Lieutenant-Colonel A. J. Paegelow,
who was in charge of balloons.

". . . a Zeppelin, practically intact, had landed at
Bourbonnes-les-Bains. . . . Several pilots from French squadrons
in that vicinity had attacked the great ship on its way down
and fired innumerable bullets into its envelope, many of them
incendiary, but with little effect." October 1917.

Brigadier-General
Benjamin D. Foulois,
Chief of Air Service.

Brigadier-General Benjamin D. Foulois and officers discussing new
Liberty photo and observation plane. Colombey-les-Belles, France. July 28, 1918.

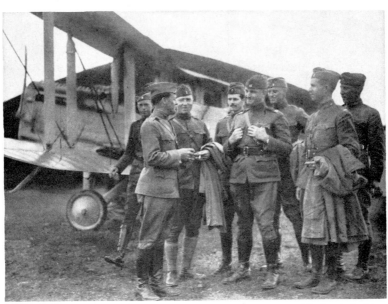

"We arrived at my headquarters, where the foreign offices and our own were assembled for orders. General Pershing gave them a very nice talk, telling them how much he appreciated the work they had done at St. Mihiel and that he relied on the Air Service to be the eyes of the army and to lead us forward to victory again in the Argonne."

Colonel Halsey Dunwoody.

Colonel T. D. Milling,
General Mitchell,
and Major Paul Armengaud.

"Our 94th Squadron was then occupying the former German bombardment airdrome just outside Longuyon; and Rickenbacker, Douglas Campbell, Meissner and several others had come up on a rubbernecking expedition, called a tour of observation." Left to right: Lieutenant Joseph Eastman, Captain James Meissner, Lieutenant Edward Rickenbacker, Lieutenant Reed Chamber, Lieutenant Thorne Taylor.

27

Last Grand Attack of the German Army

June 1918

The Germans attacked the French Army in force. The blow came along the Chemin des Dames. The Germans used very much the same strategy and tactics against the French in this area as they did against the Fifth British Army, in March. Their advance toward the Marne was so fast that the French army units that stood in their path were entirely destroyed, and even the French airdromes were taken, with the airplanes in them —some two hundred planes being lost in this way by the French.

Again there was a tremendous hole in the line.

The only real reserves were our new American divisions; and these, I learned, General Foch ordered to the vicinity of Château-Thierry to try to stop the German advances. Of course, what the Germans were trying to do was to seize the line of the Marne and occupy the Mountain of Reims, the key point in that area. If they were successful in this, they would be able to bring up their troops and supplies behind the curtain of the Marne.

The French were terribly afraid of this great German stroke. It was reported that the Germans had shut down all their munitions factories because they had enough ammunition to last them until the end of the war, no matter if it took two or three years.

They had taken all the available men from the factories and from the interior of Germany and put them in the ranks for this great attack. German troops had been brought up from Italy, and reserves and second-line troops from the Russian frontier. Now was the time for us to get into it, whether we were ready or not.

Up to the middle of the month we worked out the manner in which we should take our air forces to the Château-Thierry area. We decided to form them into a brigade under my command. Colonel Milling was to have direct command of a wing at Toul, to which all the squadrons coming up from the interior were to be assigned for battle training.

As soon as this was decided, I went to Château-Thierry to the headquarters of the Commander of the Third French Army, General Jean Degoutte, who instructed me to coordinate our work with his chief of air service, Major Gerard.

I have never seen a more stunned group of people than the officers at the Third French Army Headquarters, and for that matter, the troops as well. They acted as though they had been hit hard in the head with clubs. They had been under a constant attack for nearly a month; they had lost miles of territory, thousands of men and hundreds of airplanes. There were no reserves to relieve them, they just had to hold the ground or die.

I organized the movement of our air units from Toul to the Château-Thierry district into three echelons, a part from each group going ahead to the airdromes to which the planes were to fly, to prepare for their coming. The airplanes were then flown directly to their destinations, where the squadrons found arrangements already made for them and most of their mechanical personnel on the ground.

The third echelon, called the rear party, remained at the old airdrome, cranked up the machines as they departed, picked up everything that was left, then proceeded in motor trucks to their new station.

This was the first movement of our air service from one part of the front to another, and was accomplished most successfully. The 1st Pursuit Group flew as a unit with some seventy planes and arrived with only two ships absent, which had landed on account of motor trouble but rejoined the next day. Our observation squadrons did equally well, although equipped with inferior airplanes.

Belleau Wood, an important position near Château-Thierry, had been held by the 2nd Division for almost a month. On the 1st of July, they were ordered to attack the village of Vaux. The 12th Observation Squadron adjusted the fire of the artillery, protected by the 1st Pursuit Group. Major Brereton piloted the plane, with Lieutenant Hazlett as observer, that started the fight. Due to their excellent observation work, the city of Vaux was taken, with five hundred prisoners, and completely destroyed by the artillery.

We were now engaged in daily and constant fighting. Major Gerard desired that we put patrols along the front, to act defensively against the German observation planes that were coming over to reconnoiter. This I considered poor strategy and told him so; but we put it into effect.

Of course the Germans merely waited until they saw our small patrols of five or six airplanes and then jumped on them with vastly superior numbers.

The best groups of the German aviation were in front of us. Jagdstaffel One, the famous red-nosed pursuit group formerly commanded by Baron von Richthofen, was against us. Jagdstaffel Two, equally as good, occupied the airdrome at Coincy. Jagdstaffel Three operated from airdromes in the vicinity of St. Quentin. The commander of each of these groups had from twenty-five to fifty Allied machines to his credit. The pilots composing the flights were the most expert the Germans had on the western front.

The Germans employed formations of from twenty to thirty machines and it was merely suicide for us to continue to act as we did in small patrols. In a few days we lost Quentin Roosevelt and many other good men.

I now had assigned to me the fastest airplanes on the western front. Each day I flew along the front, alone and without protection, because if I took several planes along with me, we would be slowed up, easily noticed and certainly brought to combat. This would have interfered with my work of watching everything and preparing ahead of time for what we should do. My only fear was a surprise attack from the direction of the sun. I had become quite expert at seeing enemy planes, and our own also for that matter. I also had tremendous confidence in Adjutant Fumat's French mechanics, who spent day and night looking after my planes. So far I had never had a motor stoppage in the air.

Our pursuit group still had the Nieuport No. 28 planes but they were wearing out and we could get no replacements for them. The German aviation had been completely equipped with the Fokker D-VII airplane, probably the best pursuit ship on the front. When I insisted that we get 220-horsepower Spads for this group at once, I was answered by the usual talk of the non-fliers that our mechanics were not used to fixed motors and only understood the rotary motor in the Nieuports. I told them that our mechanics could handle anything and that I was the judge of what airplanes we wanted.

They had a lot of British Sopwith Camel planes with Clerget engines that they wanted us to take. I was not familiar with this ship so flew up to our air reserve depot at Orly to try one. A very heavy wind was blowing and the ceiling was low. I asked the Commanding Officer, Colonel Baldwin, to get me out some Camels as quickly as possible. They informed me that these were very tricky machines, that the day before one of the best pilots had been killed in one. However, on my insistence they rolled them out; I got into one, taxied down the field, turned it into the wind and took off. I had risen only a few feet from the ground when the engine suddenly stopped; but I felt it ahead of time, poked the ship's nose down quickly and landed between two hangars without breaking a wire. I had choked the Clerget engine by giving it too much gas suddenly. This is the way the pilot had been killed the day before, I think.

I got into another one and took it up about three thousand feet to maneuver it about. I found it very quick on the ailerons; it climbed well but had a very slow speed, probably not over 110 to 115 miles an hour, and dived very slowly.

I think the German Fokkers made about 125 or 130 miles an hour, and they dived with great rapidity. The Sopwith Camel was no match for them in the kind of fighting we were having at Château-Thierry, so I told the Commanding Officer that he had better send them to the schools as we could not use them at the front.

Dunwoody then put forward his utmost efforts to get us Spads and we immediately began to obtain them from the French.

My reconnaissance across the front convinced me that the Germans had a great supply point at Fère-en-Tardenois. Every time I had flown over it there had been a tremendous movement of German teams, temporary railroads, motor trucks and all kinds of transport in that vicinity. The town had several large woods near it, which I believed were filled with supplies and ammunition.

We were pushing aerial night reconnaissance into that area, as were the French. Major Armengaud of the French aviation was with General Foch at the Château Bombon, immediately behind us. He and I kept constantly in touch with each other. Armengaud noted all the reconnaissance made over the front by both the French and American aviation, keeping a record of it each day. In addition, he posted up a map for each day, which showed where we considered the center of the German movement to be. This, Armengaud called his cinema. It was perfectly accurate. He estimated the Germans would attack somewhere around the middle of the month and when the attack came it would be the greatest ever seen. Marshal Foch knew all about our air reconnaissance and was shown Armengaud's "cinema" every day.

As our patrols were being so badly chewed up and we were losing so many men, both in the pursuit and observation aviation, I went to Major Gerard and told him I believed our present

tactics led to nothing and were destroying all our aviation, because we were spreading it out in a thin layer across the front,
while the Germans acted in large groups and could puncture
our thin line of patrols anywhere. I asked him to request bombardment aviation and proposed that with this we attack the
German supply points at Fère-en-Tardenois. By massing the
bombardment and all our pursuit aviation together, we could
deliver a united attack against a key point in the area, which the
Germans would have to defend, otherwise their main ammunition dumps would be blown up and their supplies burned.

He agreed to this and asked his General Headquarters for
bombardment aviation. They replied that they had none which
could be spared at the time, but forwarded the request to General Foch's headquarters. Foch immediately asked the British
if they had any bombardment aviation which they could spare.
The British replied by sending a brigade of their air force to
our support at once; three squadrons of bombardment, equipped
with DH-9 airplanes with 180-horsepower Beardmore engines,
and four squadrons of pursuit, two of SE-5's and two of Sopwith
Camels. It was a formidable and efficient force and came
through the air with an aviation general as commander of it.
They landed at the airdrome near that of our 1st Pursuit Group
at Saintes.

The following day we made a combined air attack on Fère-
en-Tardenois. The British bombardment attacked with tremendous valor. They came down in broad daylight to within a few
hundred feet of the ground, blowing up several ammunition
dumps which could be plainly seen by our ground troops. The
Germans were taken completely by surprise and now had to
stand on the defensive in the air, as this was their key point. If
we blew up all their ammunition there and wrecked their supplies, their movement into the Château-Thierry area would be
brought to a standstill. We had no such keypoint behind our
front and could therefore afford to denude our side of offensive
aviation and push everything into the attack.

Unfortunately the British lost twelve bombardment airplanes in this attack, as the Germans were concentrated over all sides. But our observation airplanes were not interfered with after this, as the German pursuit had to keep in the air constantly to defend the Fère-en-Tardenois area. We had found the Achilles heel of the German position north of the Marne and had seized the initiative in the air.

It was the first case on record where we, with an inferior air force, were able to put the superior air force on the defensive and attack whenever we pleased, without the danger of the Germans sending great masses of the pursuit aviation over to our side of the line. What we could have done if we had had one thousand good airplanes instead of a measly two hundred and fifty!

Some wonderful reconnaissances were made by our observation aviation, usually operating in pairs. In spite of the losses, the morale and nerve of our men remained unshaken. It was a joy to see how quickly the replacements coming up from the interior went into the fight.

One of our pilots who had just come up became separated from his squadron and engaged in a free-lance patrol, when he met a German directly over our infantry lines. Our man attacked with such vigor that he soon forced his opponent down, out of control. The German landed and was seized by our infantry troops and our pilot landed in an adjoining field. The German saw the ship come down and expressed a desire to meet the American. Our pilot hurried over to get a glimpse of his prisoner, as it was his first day on the front. When the German heard that he had been shot down by a novice, on the line for the first time, he flew into a rage. He himself had nineteen official victories to his credit. As he was hustled back to the rear, he bitterly complained of his hard luck in being downed by a *kind* (child).

Hardly a plane of our observation aviation returned without having entered into combat. I was on the observation airdrome at Franceville one day when a pilot, with Harwood as observer, landed from a reconnaissance flight. Harwood had seven or eight bullet holes through his flying suit, several slight wounds on his body and the tip of his nose was shot off. In spite of all this, he made an excellent report of his mission and observed, "The only thing that bothered me was the way the German incendiary bullets made the fur in my flying suit smell when they went through it!"

28

The Battle of Château-Thierry

July 1918

I established my headquarters at a little place south of Coulommiers, at a country estate called Haute Feuille, belonging to a family named Becker, who owned large department stores in Paris. It was a shooting box and the estate was filled with pheasants and hares.

On July 9th I sent the following letter to General Foulois:

HEADQUARTERS AIR SERVICE
FIRST BRIGADE

July 9, 1918.

MEMORANDUM FOR   Chief of Air Service, 1st Army.

1. The air service of the First Corps is now operating in a manner which I believe will meet the present conditions of warfare and will serve as a model on which to build in the future. The Chief of the Air Service of the Corps is at Corps Headquarters with his staff, transportation and transportation for couriers. He is connected by telephone with an advanced landing field, which is about four kilometers from him, on which he has airplanes on the alert and also courier airplanes. (Courier airplanes will be used both day and night as soon as we can get night flyers trained.) (Advanced landing field at Ferme de

Moras.) The observation airdrome is at Francheville, which now has three squadrons on it—Salmson No. 1, Salmson No. 12 and Sopwith No. 88. The Group Headquarters, Group operations Officer, Group G-2 and French liaison officers are on duty at that place. This airdrome is connected by telephone to the C.A.S., 1st Army Corps, with the 1st Pursuit Group, with the Headquarters, 1st Brigade Air Service and with the French Sixth Army.

2. The whole question of liaison is rendered very difficult and we are extending the use of radio, courier airplanes and motorcycles.

3. In order to get an officer of experience to handle this group, it was found necessary to place Major Hall in command. This officer is very familiar with observation work. He is not yet a pilot and will probably require about three hours more before he becomes such. It will be remembered that sometime ago Major Davidson was asked for this place.

4. I hope to begin night flying this week at the airdrome at Vaudoy. Although I am not prepared to make a definite recommendation, I believe that each corps will require one squadron for night work alone; army squadrons will have to be organized in the same proportion.

5. The Pursuit Group, which is now the only one with the Sixth Army, has been moved from the field at Ormeaux to the field at Saintes, which was formerly occupied by the 1st Corps Observation Group. This move was made quickly and very efficiently, and it interfered in no way with its operations. I believe this group can be considered as thoroughly efficient and it is hoped to begin to reconstitute them with Spad airplanes beginning next week. This Group operates for the main purpose of preventing hostile pursuit incursions into our territory. It receives the alert information by radio from the anti-aircraft artillery. The front is divided into a system of squares about seven kilometers on a side. The anti-aircraft artillery give the co-ordinates of this section when enemy aircraft appear over them, etc. The messages are sent in cipher. The squadron is capable of putting out four patrols of one squadron each. These are echeloned in flights of five airplanes each. Ordinarily there are two flights for duty in each squadron. The work has been very heavy.

6. A park is now being installed at Courtalin. It will be several days before it begins functioning.

7. We have been having a great deal of trouble with the American Lewis guns. I sent two trucks to Colombey-les-Belles today to obtain the old French Lewis guns which had formerly been turned in by the squadron. This is very important and I request that there be no delay in turning these guns over to the trucks sent.

8. The supply system in general leaves a great deal to be desired, but everything possible is being done by those in charge of supply at the present time.

9. The method by which transportation is being handled, that is, with the motor transport service through G-4, instead of it being handled by the air service, will not and cannot work in the Air Service for reasons too numerous to mention. It is requested that strong and insistent recommendations be made to G.H.Q. that this condition be remedied at once. In a service which has to change its methods, equipment and ways of working almost daily, such as the Air Service, great elasticity must be permitted; and on account of the distance encountered between elements of the air service itself and the rapid moves which have to be made from one field of operations to another, a relatively large amount of transportation has to be kept constantly on hand.

10. A telegram from the C.A.S., 1st Army, relating to detail of future squadron commanders has been received today and measures taken accordingly. I think the selections made are very good.

11. This office is asking for replacements in personnel direct to Tours. So far no answers to the requests have been received.

12. The staff of the First Brigade now consists of the following:

Captain N. P. Kelleher, Adjutant and Commanding Detachment
Captain P. J. Roosevelt, Operations Officer
1st Lieut. J. B. Dupuy, Assistant Operations Officer
1st Lieut. Laurence W. Miller, Equipment Officer

This staff will have to be built up, which will be done gradually. It has not been possible to get out operations reports consistently heretofore for your office but I hope that they will begin regularly tomorrow, and in addition, a daily telegram will be sent containing any important information. The courier system seems to work pretty well.

13. I believe in the development of the Air Service that the greatest difficulty will be encountered in obtaining group and higher commanders. I will be in a position here to begin instructions of two or three group commanders and wing commanders at a time in the very near future. It is requested that consideration be given to this. I believe it is of great importance that the 2nd Pursuit Group, a day bombardment squadron, the Army Observation Squadron and the full complement of balloons for the 1st Army Corps be sent here as soon as practicable. The places are all ready for their installation.

14. The attack of the Germans is awaited daily and during this attack we will be subjected to a great deal of pressure because the German aviation in attacking the Fifth Army will work out of the salient opposite us so as to hit them in the rear and this will result in heavy work for all our aviation here, both observation and pursuit.

> WM. MITCHELL
> Colonel, A.S.S.C.
> Comdg. 1st Brigade Air Service.

On the same day I wrote Foulois, there was a meeting of the corps commanders of the Sixth French Army, commanded by General Degoutte, at his headquarters. The corps commanders, their chiefs of staff, Major Gerard and I attended. General Degoutte explained the dispositions he wished made to defend the area against the Germans in the attack which we knew was coming soon. He then asked each corps commander to explain what his dispositions were to carry out these orders. Each one in turn arose and explained what he had done to meet the orders. When it came General Liggett's turn, he arose and in a straightforward manner, clearly and concisely stated the manner in which he had carried out his part of the program. I never felt more proud of one of our commanders, as it was the first time a great body of American troops under its own command had entered into this combat. General Liggett with his fine, strong face and his six-feet-two of good American bone and muscle, stood up there among the warriors of the old world as an example of the power and potentialities of our own great country. I think that all those present were impressed as I was. I am intensely proud to be associated with him.

We were living in daily expectation of an attack and I was doing everything in my power to get up the new airplanes with which to equip our pilots. Every day I became more convinced that our flying men, with the excellent training they were receiving in the schools in the interior, and under the leaders that we had developed on the front, would be superior to any other airmen in the world, and it was only a question of time before we would have the ascendancy over the Germans. But as things stood on this part of the front during the first half of July, I thought we were outnumbered in the air almost five to one.

On the afternoon of July 14th, I hurried into Paris to get more action about our new airplanes. Masses of German troops had been moved down to their attacking positions. We did not know exactly where they would attack, but we felt sure it would be against the Mountain of Reims.

That night I was getting a late dinner preparatory to starting back to my headquarters, when Donald Brown of the Red Cross came in and sat down with me. At precisely 12:10 A.M. (July 15, 1918) we heard the reverberation of guns to the north and, looking in that direction, could see tremendous flashes in the sky. I was certain that the main attack of the Germans was being launched. I told Brown that if he wanted to see the greatest battle in history he could come with me. We started in my fastest automobile for my headquarters at Haute Feuille, which we reached a little before 3:00 P.M.

The whole sky was lighted up by the flash of the artillery on both sides. Rockets and signals were appearing everywhere; searchlight beams were sweeping the sky; the buzz of airplanes going and coming, and the noise of their bombs dropping, covered the whole of the line. As yet we were uncertain where the main attack was being made.

I called up our pursuit group and observations groups on the telephone and ordered them to have everything ready to operate by daylight. Just as I finished this, Major Gerard, with Lieutenant Lafont, who had first taken me over the line in April, 1917, reached my headquarters.

Gerard was greatly perturbed. He informed me that the main German attack was on; that they were pressing the front of the Third French Army, of which we were a part; and that a great attack was being made against the Fourth French Army under General Gouraud in the Champagne. He did not know what success the Germans had had so far, but he did know that our troops were making terrific resistance at every point so as to prevent the Germans from crossing the Marne.

He told me that the orders for the aviation, for the following morning, had miscarried and the word had not reached the French Air Division in sufficient time for them to prepare for an early morning attack. The only air troops left for this part of the front, he said, were our pursuit group, our observation squadrons and the British Brigade.

We discussed the advisability of putting up a barrage or curtain patrol along the front at daylight. This I would not approve of as it would merely lead to unnecessary losses and give us no advantage. I proposed that we hold all our air forces in readiness to act a little before daylight; that we send out night reconnaissance at once to cover the whole front of the army, find out what the enemy was doing and act accordingly. This he agreed to and went back to his headquarters.

I snatched a few minutes' sleep, then, accompanied by Donald Brown, went to the airdrome of the 1st Pursuit Group at Saintes, where I took an airplane and flew straight north until I reached la Ferté-sous-Jouarre, and then north of this to where our lines began. The ceiling was quite low in places, but I saw no German airplanes whatever nor any movement of troops on the ground, except a general artillery fire all along the front.

I turned to the right and flew up the Marne. Not a German airplane made its appearance. The ceiling was now from three hundred to twelve hundred feet; I was running through light clouds and haze and then out again into more open spaces. As I approached Jaulgonne, I met a few Fokker airplanes, who either did not see me, or if they did, paid no attention to me.

There are high banks along the Marne at this place. I was flying around them as I had to fly so low on account of the fog and clouds that I could not see across them for any great distance. Suddenly as I rounded a turn of the river east of Dormans, I saw a great mass of artillery fire hitting the south bank, and, spanning the river, five bridges filled with German troops marching over. I looked everywhere for German airplanes but there were none in the sky at that time. I received no anti-aircraft fire and apparently no attention was paid to me, although I flew within five hundred feet of the bridges. Looking down on the men, marching so splendidly, I thought to myself, what a shame to spoil such fine infantry.

I went a little further up the river, then turned up toward Reims. A terrific battle was going on in that vicinity and the air was full of German planes, so I turned around and came back to the bridges. By that time, a terrible combat was taking place on top of the hill just south of the bridges. The opposing troops were almost together. This was the nearest to a hand-to-hand combat than anything I had seen so far. I thought they were Americans, and later found that it was our 3rd Division. They were the ones who stopped the advance of the Germans at that point. I do not think they had any artillery, as I could see none.

There were now a good many German planes in the air, and I had to be careful. I reached the airdrome of our 1st Pursuit Group safely and we immediately ordered the whole group to Dormans to attack the bridges and the German troops on the ground, and to clear the air over the combat between the Germans and our troops. The French Air Division was informed where the bridges were, and, although they had to come a great distance from their airdromes, back of the Champagne front, they succeeded in hitting them.

I immediately proceeded to General Liggett's headquarters at la Ferté-sous-Jouarre and reported to him and Craig, his Chief of Staff, what I had seen and my estimate of the situation. I sent in a report to the headquarters of the Third French Army and Major Gerard, and communicated with Armengaud at General Foch's headquarters. This was the first definite information that was obtained that morning about the location of the bridges and the movement of the Germans.

It was now apparent in my mind that the Germans were aiming for the Mountain of Reims, that the movement across the Marne at Dormans was for protecting the right flank of this attack and that their attack against the Fourth French Army in the Champagne was to protect the left flank. We heard that General Gouraud had retired from all his front lines, allowed the Germans to occupy them without resistance and was now counterattacking them with his whole army and making headway.

I went down to see Armengaud at General Foch's headquarters, and we went over the situation. It was quite evident that, as the Germans were attacking at the head of the salient of which the base was formed by Soissons on one side and Reims on the other, if we could get in from either side of the base, we could turn the whole German position, and if successful, attack them in the rear and perhaps destroy their whole army. It was the best chance that presented itself during the war and Marshal Foch was not slow to avail himself of it.

Obviously the place to attack was near Soissons. Our reconnaissance showed that it was not heavily held by the Germans, although why they had made such a mistake, I could not tell.

The following day we were instructed to prevent German reconnaissance over our area at all costs, so we pushed our attacks again in the direction of Fère-en-Tardenois.

We were informed that our 1st and 2nd Divisions, accompanied by the Moroccan Division, were to move north that night, the 15th, to the vicinity of Soissons and attack as soon as the movement was completed. During the day, troops from various parts of the line were moved south along the roads from the vicinity of Soissons, so as to make the Germans think that reinforcements were being sent to the right of the French Third Army and to the left of the Fourth, near Reims. That night, when the American and Moroccan Divisions moved up to Soissons, no lights were shown and great secrecy was observed, in contrast to the usual procedure of heralding far and wide every move of the American troops.

It was an operation fraught with the greatest importance for the Allies. If it succeeded, the Germans would have to retire from the Château-Thierry salient, and before they could recover sufficiently to break through again, the American military forces would have brought such an accession of strength to the Allied cause that it would be impossible for the Germans to gain the mastery.

On July 16th, we counterattacked the Germans opposite the left flank of the Fifth French Army. Zero hour was at 12 noon and our aviation participated in it. We had some violent combats, but held our own in fine shape. We attacked in echelon by flights of five airplanes each, one after the other. The Germans fly in a group of five airplanes, a fan formation, as they call it, which, when it hits one of our flights, spreads out on both flanks and attempts to get over, under and on each side of it. This seems all very well theoretically, but a spirited attack of one flight of five ships of our pursuit throws it into confusion. The succeeding flights, still holding their formation, come in one after another and the last formed organization wins the fight. I looked for the Germans to change to our tactics in a few days.

29

The Americans Attack at Soissons

July 1918 (Continued)

The attack at Soissons was to take place on July 18th. German aviation, I knew, was concentrated over their main attack centering at Reims. I had kept any great amount of aerial activity away from the vicinity of Soissons. On the night of the 17th, I went to bed thinking that our orders for the morrow were set, and that the British Brigade at Ormeux and our 1st Pursuit Group would be available for the fight.

At 3:30 A.M. I was awakened by Major Gerard, who in great agitation told me that the orders had been all mixed up and the British air brigade had been directed to attack in the Reims area. This left our 1st Pursuit Group as the only air organization to cover the front on the day of our most important attack. I told Gerard that we could handle the matter, but that the whole group would have to act together and in addition we would put in all our observation aviation, to lend what assistance they could.

He agreed to this entirely and when dawn broke, off went every airplane we had to clear the air over our comrades on the ground in the most important operation during our participation in the European War, if not in the whole war since the beginning. Fortunately, the Germans were taken by surprise and we kept the sky clear while our splendid division, the 1st and 2nd, with the Moroccans between them, broke the German line west of Soissons.

(It may seem strange to some that a great soldier like General Ludendorff had denuded that most important part of his line. It is one of the rudiments of military strategy, when one is acting out from the point of a salient, to hold the base of the salient strongly, because if that is broken the enemy may get behind you and attack from reverse, which is fatal. I have been told that General Ludendorff, the German Chief of Staff, counted his troops in certain areas according to the number of battalions. A battalion normally contains about one thousand men, of which five hundred or six hundred can be depended on to fight on the line. The German battalions in many cases, however, were reduced to a strength of one or two hundred men, so that no more than fifty or a hundred men were available for duty. Thus while it appeared from the number of battalions in the area that enough troops were on hand to defend it, in reality only a handful of men were there. They put up a terrific resistance and died in their tracks, but there were no reserves to back them up.)

I flew over the area during the attack, in the afternoon. The Germans began to get a few airplanes over, but it was too late. The next day I noticed a great deal of German movement throughout the salient, and was sure a German retreat was to be made. In the next few days, fires appeared at various places in the German area, and we believed they were burning some of their supplies. The attacks kept up at Soissons. I went up to see the condition of the 1st and 2nd Divisions as they came out of the line. Although very tired, they showed all the characteristics of good troops. They held their formations; there was little straggling. Their equipment was in fair condition; their officers carried themselves in a splendid manner.

Our balloons under Major Paegelow were doing especially good work. While the troops on the ground did not know much about using them, Paegelow always had them ready and always up with the troops, and we got a good deal of information from them. As our aviation was so far outnumbered by the Germans, I knew that we would have lots of balloons shot down, so I had Paegelow provide two spare balloons immediately behind each one that was on the line.

One of our balloon companies had an observer jump five times in a parachute in one day; three times out of his burning balloon and twice when it looked as if his balloon would surely be burned. I shall recommend him for the D.S.C.

We had been issued only two anti-aircraft machine guns for the balloon companies. Later I obtained four, but now I wanted to get as many as I could. I told Paegelow that he did not have enough machine guns with his balloon companies. He asked me where he should get them and I told him I did not care where he got them, that I wanted them there by the next day. Imagine my surprise when I visited one of the balloon companies the next day and counted thirty-two machine guns which could put up a terrific barrage. Upon looking at them, I saw they were German Maxims, really better guns than we have, with corrector sights for anti-aircraft fire. Old Paegelow had found and captured a machine-gun depot and had immediately appropriated all that he could possibly carry away in every kind of a vehicle obtainable.

I went down to Bombon, General Foch's Headquarters. Armengaud was elated. All of the data that we had gathered from the air had proved to be correct. The point of attack as shown by our aerial reconnaissance was exact and we had been able to tell within a few hours when the attack would come.

We were now sure that the Germans were on the run. They escaped our trap at Soissons because we could not get into the salient fast enough. I consider the Battle of Soissons one of the decisive battles of the war. The first was the Battle of the Marne, in which it was determined that the French Republic could not be conquered during the first onslaught; second was the Battle of Tannenberg, in which the Germans destroyed the Russian military power. And now the Battle of Soissons, which has thrown back the German advance at the most critical time of the war. From now on there is no question but that we can build up sufficient military strength to crush the Central Empires.

In the midst of all this I learned of poor Bolling's death and how it occurred. When he had been stripped of all his authority in Paris, he applied for service on the front. We had determined that as soon as he became familiar enough with the work, he would be made Chief of Air Service of the 2nd Army Corps. To perfect himself, Bolling kept up his flying eagerly, and obtained permission to go to the British front. He proceeded there with a small Fiat car and a chauffeur.

During the March offensive, when the Fifth British Army was destroyed, Bolling hurried out to the front to see what was going on. The British Air Force alone was holding up the German advance along the sector by attacking the German troops on the ground as they came forward, which gave a respite to the fugitives of the British Fifth Army in their retreat.

Hurrying toward what he supposed to be the line still held by the British troops, he ran squarely into an outpost of Germans. They called on him to surrender but rather than do this, he jumped into a shell hole beside the road and defended himself with his pistol. The chauffeur was overpowered and captured. Bolling refused to give himself up, and after shooting several Germans, was himself killed.

I felt his loss very keenly. Bolling was a fine officer and a splendid type of American. We had been in hopes that Bolling was captured because we could establish nothing definite as to what had become of him. Now we knew that he was gone.

There were constant mixups of all sorts in our Air Service administration. This was due largely to ignorance of proper methods on the part of the officers concerned, but there were also petty bickerings and jockeyings for position. I wrote the following letter to General Foulois on July 19th, setting forth the condition of some of our outfits.

HEADQUARTERS AIR SERVICE
FIRST BRIGADE

July 19, 1918.

My dear Foulois—

I am writing you this note in order to bring to your attention the necessity for exercising care in our methods of control over our units in order to avoid unnecessary complications which lead to misunderstanding with other troops, uncertainty in the minds of our own Air Service commanders, and a general interference with discipline in the command. I refer particularly to direct dealings with subordinate commanders and subordinate units by various headquarters without reference to the superior commanders of such units.

To begin with, I have just received, by roundabout methods, information that the 88th Squadron has been assigned to the 3rd Army Corps. I have not received any order and know nothing about it. This squadron at present has six Sopwiths (1½ Strutters) available for duty. It has no independent photographic outfit. It has no radio truck and in many ways is not organized to operate by itself. Suppose that it goes and reports to the Commanding General of the 3rd Army Corps. As they have never had direct control over observation units heretofore, they probably will not know what to do with it. Next, it will have to be moved to a new airdrome and the matter will have to be taken up with the French. Third, the squadron will have to be completely re-equipped and supplied with both personnel and material, and a replacement will have to be arranged for. You can very easily see the complications that will arise if it is not handled as a part of this Brigade. If orders had been sent to these Headquarters for the 88th Squadron to be attached to the 3rd Corps, I believe that I could have had this squadron in shape to do so by this time; and without any further instructions, or knowing anything about it, I am going this afternoon to the 6th French Army, find out what they have heard, then to the Headquarters of our 3rd Army Corps to learn what disposition they wish made of it and what work is required of it.

It is quite interesting to note that there is a British Brigade right along side of me here—the 9th. It has just about the same strength as this brigade. A British army corps is being brought into practically the same area as our 3rd Corps is, and is being supplied with observation aviation by the Royal Air Force. Now, according to our method, that is to say, what we have done before, the squadron commander would get direct orders to report to the Commanding General of this corps. He would not know anything about conditions of any kind existing there. The result has always been a mixup. What is actually happening in the British force is that the observation squadron reports to the Royal Air Force Commander. The Brigade Commander makes complete arrangements for its installation, supply and work. It is then reported to the Army Corps Commander and assigned its tactical mission by it. The French army has a similar method, as have also the Germans. Now the point I wish to make in this respect is that I should be notified of changes of this kind so that all arrangements could be made accordingly.

The inconvenience which your office was put to as to questions of jurisdiction between this Brigade and the Corps Air Service of the 1st Corps, was entirely due to the fact that Major Royce raised these points with the Chief of Staff, which had no bearing on the general situation in this theater and which were directly contrary to the verbal orders given Major Royce by me, which were to come down here and make it his business first to get the observation group for the 1st Corps itself ready to function before anything else was done. He did not do this but obtained letters from the Chief of Staff, 1st Corps, to Commander of Aviation of the 6th French Army, to the effect that he was in charge of all aviation in this area, that there should be no control over corps air troops except through the Corps Commander, and a lot of things of this kind. You have seen the mixup which it causes in supply, general tactical direction and coordination, which, incidentally involve the questions of the relief of officers in this command, squadron commanders for new squadrons, etc.

I believe it very important that you consider the necessity for regarding the judgment of commanding officers of units on the ground as distinguished from the judgment on a certain thing formed at a distance. For instance, I refer to the way in which orders were issued for the change of command in the 1st Obser-

vation Group from Major Hall to Major McNarney. Major Hall
was put in command of this group because he was the only officer available at that time who had the experience and ability to
handle the group under the conditions which existed. He is not a
pilot but has done a great deal of flying, has been in the war
practically since the start, and as an actual matter of fact, knows
more about observation aviation than any regular officer that we
have in the army today, I believe. The policy is a wrong one as a
matter of principle to put in a man that is not a pilot in command of a unit of that kind, but I believe that when he should
have been relieved and how he should have been relieved should
have been left to the superior commander on the ground. Without disparaging the ability of the officer who relieved him, this
man has had no experience practically in commanding a group.
As you know, he was relieved from command of a squadron at
Chatillon and sent away for cause, and he was directly put into
command of this group in the middle of a battle without consultation with the commanders on the ground. This is against all
military teaching that we have ever had. As a matter of fact,
things are going along pretty well in the group because we are
keeping it under very close supervision. This very eventuality
was foreseen and an officer asked for nearly a month ago for this
group.

It often becomes necessary to relieve officers on duty with units
peremptorily on account of the way they act or handle their units
in the face of the enemy. There is no time for boards or peace-
time methods in such cases. For instance, right now the Commander of the Pursuit Group has officially requested the relief
of a Squadron Commander and an Adjutant. His reasons are
sound and I shall relieve them and send them to the rear. However, it is not a comfortable feeling on the part of commanding
officers if each one of these cases is going to be made a point of
by superior authority and a lot of fuss made over it. Not that
we object to the fuss particularly, except that it takes a lot of
time, as we are sure of our premises before acting. I do not know
of any arm or any other branch of our service that has a board
sitting on whether officers are handling their units properly in
the face of the enemy during a battle.

Another case is your telegram with respect to the relief of

Captain Roosevelt and sending him back to the First Pursuit Group for duty upon a request of the Group Commander. This is a direct case of a Group Commander taking this matter up with superior authority without my permission, and it is making a Group Commander's judgment on the situation here superior to that of the Brigade Commander, which I do not believe is your intention to have done. It is also against the spirit of the telegram received from you the other day when a certain individual was asked for for a specific duty and I was informed to take personnel for this purpose from units under my command.

Correspondence for squadrons and groups should always be sent through Group Commanders. The necessity for this is quite evident not only from a standpoint of discipline, but from a standpoint of simplicity of administration, etc. We must be very careful, particularly with troops acting on the line, not to allow junior officers to go running around among them talking with pilots, Flight Commanders, Squadron Commanders, and even Group Commanders, who know little or nothing about the general situation or even about their specific work except about that which concerns themselves, and have these junior officers go to higher authority without consultation with the superior commanders of these units on such situations. I have particularly in mind reports made by Major Royce and Colonel Gorrell regarding different things.

This note is written in the spirit of help and not as a complaint, and it is exactly the same condition that I assisted you with when we were in G.H.Q., on the subject of having people called up under your command. If the methods such as I have indicated above are not used, when the Air Service gets to be any size, and it is practically that now, no coordination or united effort will be possible.

Sincerely,
WILLIAM MITCHELL

On July 25th, General Foulois sent me the following letter, which rather surprised me. Foulois certainly was trying hard at this time to do everything that he could, and we were supporting him from our end.

France, July 25, 1918.

From: Chief of Air Service, 1st Army.
To: Commander in Chief, American E.F.
Subject: Assignment of Colonel William Mitchell as Chief of Air Service, 1st. Army.

1. I recommend that Colonel William Mitchell, Air Service, be assigned to duty as Chief of Air Service, 1st. Army.

2. In connection with this recommendation, I wish to bring to your attention the most efficient service of Colonel Mitchell during the past month, in the organization, battle training, general supervision and guidance of the Air Service units which have been operating with the Franco-American troops in the Château-Thierry area.

These units had had but a limited amount of tactical training in the quiet sector of the Toul area, when they were ordered to the Château-Thierry area. The unit commanders, although excellent officers, and eager and willing to learn, had had no experience in major tactical offensive operations, such as were encountered immediately upon their arrival in the Château-Thierry area.

Colonel Mitchell, as Commanding Officer of the 1st Air Brigade, and as the representative of the Chief of Air Service, 1st Army, was directed to exercise technical supervision over these units, and, if necessary, in emergencies to exercise tactical supervision in order to absolutely insure efficient results. I am glad to say that the technical and tactical supervision exercised over these units by Colonel Mitchell has resulted in a minimum loss of life, a maximum effective use of material available and a high fighting spirit of morale which will be most beneficial in establishing the standard of efficiency for all new Air Service units now organizing and to be organized in the future.

B. D. Foulois,
Brigadier General, S. C.

Copy to Colonel Mitchell
Copy also sent to Inspector
    General, A.E.F.
Spoke to the C. in C. personally re the work you had done and he was highly pleased. Also told him what I thought of the G.S. In-

terference and he stated that no tactical changes would be made without my approval. Also discussed general tactical development of A.S. as we agreed on and he approved. Hope to be up again in few days.

Foulois

On July 27th, I was formally notified of my appointment as Chief of the Air Service of the First Army, and instructed to take command of the air troops. I was ready for this because for over a year I had been working on just what we would do in that eventuality. I moved my headquarters up to la Ferté-sous-Jouarre. The last days of July were spent in making arrangements for organizing the Air Service of the First Army.

Although there were many things left to be desired, I felt that our work at Château-Thierry had been remarkable.

30

The Great Attack on St. Mihiel

August–September 1918

I estimated that within three days after we attacked, the Germans could concentrate very nearly two thousand airplanes against us. I therefore decided to assemble a force of two thousand to cover our initial attack, no matter where it might be. I immediately took up the matter with the French, through Armengaud, to find out what they could spare. General Foch approved everything in principle that we put forward, and our work went rapidly on.

I now began to get together the old staff officers whom I had trained, with Colonel T. D. Milling as Chief of Staff, the best one I have seen in any service. Different commanding officers use their Chiefs of Staff in different ways. I always had mine coordinate the various staff sections and see that the machine functioned properly.

When commanding, I always drew up my own orders for the military operations of the fighting units, and personally checked the sending and receipt by the unit commander of their special orders. When orders were not obeyed, it was usually the commanding officer who was at fault. Either the orders had not been delivered or they were so written that nobody could understand them. I always kept an officer at my headquarters, whose name I shall not mention, whom I had read all the orders. If he could understand them, anybody could. He was not particularly bright but he was one of the most valuable officers I had.

I now prepared and completed the details of our exact method of operation during the proposed attack, the summary of which I had given General Pershing on Aug. 20th, as follows:

HEADQUARTERS AIR SERVICE
FIRST ARMY

SECRET

August 20, 1918.

MEMORANDUM FOR   Commanding General, 1st Army.

The employment of aviation in the proposed attack is divided into four phases:

I. Preparation.

II. Night preceding the attack.

III. Day of the attack.

IV. Exploitation.

I. *PREPARATION:*

    (a) In order that the attack be made by surprise, it is important that the attitude of the sector be not changed.

    (b) The general mission of aviation (in I.) is to—

        (1) Absolutely prevent access to our lines by enemy reconnaissance aviation;

        (2) Secure complete information about hostile formations by means of photo missions and night reconnaissances without arousing the suspicion of the enemy.

    (c) Mission of pursuit aviation in I.—

        (1) Constant patrol on our lines in order to produce an absolute barrage;

        (2) Usual offensive patrols in order to maintain the normal activity of the sector.

    (d) Mission of bombardment aviation:

        Normal work of the sector.

(e) Mission of observation aviation—
    (1) Maximum photographic reconnaissances;
    (2) Night reconnaissances when enemy movements
    are suspected.

II. *NIGHT PRECEDING THE ATTACK:*

(a) Mission of bombardment aviation; during the whole
night preceding the attack.
    (1) Attack by high-explosive bombs (English Avia-
tion) of the strategical objectives, i.e., airdromes,
stations, railroad crossings, bridges, ammunition
dumps; (confirmed by photos)
    (2) General attack by bombs on personnel (French
Aviation) of camps, enemy cantonments and airdrome.

III. *DAY OF THE ATTACK:*

(a) Mission of pursuit aviation—
    (1) Offensive mission—High patrols deep to the rear
of the enemy lines to break up enemy aerial formations and help the bombardment aviation in
its mission of bombarding enemy airdromes, and
scattering enemy columns on the road.
    (2) Protective mission—If the infantry signaling is
efficient, *and in this case only,* an attack may be
made by machine guns on the enemy's reserves
which are in formation for counterattack. To prevent enemy infantry planes from entering the
battle zone. To help the advance of the tanks.
(b) Mission of bombardment aviation—
Protected by pursuit aviation to attack and destroy
enemy airdromes, break up trains and convoys on
the roads, and carry on the same work as that of the
night bombardment aviation in destroying stations,
bridges, railroad crossings, ammunition dumps, cantonments, etc.
(c) Mission of observation aviation—
Surveillance, artillery adjustment, liaison and reconnaissance.

IV. *EXPLOITATION:*

The squadrons move forward to the new advanced fields which were previously prepared, extend their zone of action and execute the same missions as the day before. However as a retreating army is in open ground, the airplanes will operate as low as possible in order to seek the obligatory points of passage of the enemy's columns and to destroy them with bombs and machine guns at such places.

The high-explosive bombardment aviation (English Aviation) will be specially detailed to destroy railway crossings and important bridges located in the zone far from the battlefield.

> WM. MITCHELL
> Colonel, A.S.S.C.,
> C.A.S., 1st Army.

We worked hard on every branch of our aviation and I took particular pains to have the observers in the observation flights carefully instructed as to what they should do with their ground troops.

I moved my headquarters up to Ligny-en-Barrois on August 27th. Lieutenant Miller had prepared for the movement. He had a fine mess organized for us, run by a wine merchant, his wife and daughters. We took over a public school building as our headquarters. Each staff section had its appropriate location and I had a splendid big room, on one side of which was Milling and on the other, Armengaud.

I had an amazing relief map of the whole St. Mihiel salient where we were about to attack. It had been made up by the French balloon companies operating in the area, and was the work of several years. I had procured the various pieces and put them together, and the whole thing occupied a floor space of about twelve by twelve feet. Each hill, woods, road, detached house, large building, railroad yards, ravine—in fact, every incident of the terrain—was remarkably depicted. This map, combined with my intimate knowledge of the country derived from studying it for many years and from flying over it, made me feel that I knew this part of the world as well as any man living, better probably than any Frenchman.

General Pershing was now in high spirits; we were getting our American army together and our air people, who for a long time had felt that Pershing did not know, or care to know, very much about aviation, were beginning to change their minds as he was helping us in every way possible. I guess he could not swallow the whole hog to begin with, had to take it easy, but it had put us back a good many months. One had to expect that in the organization of a new outfit, and from now on I hoped he would do better. I was sure he would if we delivered the goods.

Our old air units were now becoming well organized, and, although they had only been on the front two or three months, they were going like clockwork. The closing days of August saw my staff splendidly organized under Milling as Chief of Staff. No better working organization ever existed in the American armed services.

We were assembling the greatest army the United States had ever seen, to do battle on European soil. Thousands upon thousands of men filled every road, while all means of transport were bringing up the tremendous amount of supplies they required.

September 1918

The first of September saw my headquarters permanently organized and a force of 1,476 airplanes and twenty balloons, under my command, concentrating to join battle with the Germans.

Thirty thousand officers and men handled the airplanes. They were disposed on fourteen main flying fields and a great many substations, while three large supply points handled the material for the Americans, French, British and Italians. It was the greatest concentration of air power that had ever taken place and the first time in history in which an air force, cooperating with an army, was to act according to a broad strategical plan which contemplated not only facilitating the advance of the ground troops but spreading fear and consternation into the enemy's line of communications, his replacement system and the cities behind them which supplied our foe with the sinews of war.

In addition to the American, French and British units, I had some squadrons of Italian bombardment aviation, who did all they could in their sphere. Here we were, a force of four nations, acting together with no discord, misunderstanding, jealousy or attempt to shirk or escape the maximum duty or losses which may be required. Such a thing could not have occurred with ground troops. I say this because the game on the ground is such an old one, and the element of novelty and development has ceased to exist in it. In aviation, there is an entirely different feeling between the persons engaged in it. It is an extremely dangerous and hazardous occupation and every man who is a real pilot is looked up to and appreciated by his fellows.

Most of the officers on our general staff, with a few marked exceptions, had no appreciation of what this great air force meant. Not a single one, however, except Major Bowditch, had shown any inclination to go up in the air and see what was going on. Just think of such a thing! Here was a great military operation about to be undertaken, the success or failure of which meant everything to American arms. A tour in the air by the Commanding General or the Chief of Staff would have given them an insight into the positions and locations of the enemy and our own troops which could have been obtained in no other way. I could have taken them myself and protected them so that there would have been ninety-nine chances out of a hundred of their getting back unscathed (even if they did get killed, there were plenty of people to step into their shoes); but out of all this group only one chose to go up in the air.

There are a great many points of difference between the management of an air force and that of an army or navy. An air force operates in a new medium, the air, which offers a wider scope for action than either land or water. They must be communicated with through the air, that is, by radio or visual signals. When air forces are committed to a combat they cannot be withdrawn and redisposed ordinarily, but must come back to the airdromes to refuel and replenish before renewing the fight. Air forces cannot dig holes in the air and get into them where the enemy will not see them, and where they may sit in safety and comfort. The premium of successful combat is shooting down the enemy and the forfeit when unsuccessful is to go hurtling to earth in a flaming coffin. Air forces are the eyes of the army, and without their accurate reports, ground forces cannot operate.

We had three tasks to accomplish: one, to provide accurate information for the infantry and adjustment of fire for the artillery of the ground troops; second, to hold off the enemy air forces from interfering with either our air or ground troops; and third, to bomb the back areas so as to stop the supplies for the enemy and hold up any movement along his roads.

The shape of the St. Mihiel salient furnished an interesting situation. It projected into our line in the shape of a horseshoe, rather a sharp one at the toe, the point of which was located at the city of St. Mihiel. The Germans pushed in here in 1915 and occupied it in an attempt to surround Verdun.

It must be remembered that the most direct line of advance from Germany into France is through Koblenz, Treves, Verdun, Nancy and then straight toward Lyons, where the centers of population and factories of France are located. Conversely, if we could advance into Germany by way of Treves and Koblenz, we would have the shortest line through this great gateway into the country of the Teutons. Now our American army, acting under its own chiefs and holding its own sector of the line, was charged with the duty of advancing into the Treves Gap, and by pushing on, to threaten this great open portal into Germany.

Our line at most places was more or less straight and the Air Service acted out from it more or less homogeneously all along the front. Now we were attacking a salient, so I intended to change the ordinary procedure and employ massed air attacks against the vital points in the enemy's rear. In this case, we could hit first from one side of the salient, then from the other, just as a boxer gives a right hook and a left hook successively to his opponent.

In the present case, I would have a preponderance in the air for at least two days before the Germans could concentrate. I had therefore issued orders to the French Air Division that they would attack entirely by brigades, nothing smaller. There were two brigades of about four hundred airplanes each in the Division. One brigade would habitually attack twice a day on the right of the salient, entering it from west of Pont-à-Mousson. The bombardment would attack Vigneulles, Conflans and Briey.

At the time their gas was beginning to run out, the second brigade of the Air Division would attack the same places from the left of the salient, crossing the lines in the vicinity of Genicourt and Fort Haudainville. In this way, while the Germans were resisting and fighting one of our brigades, I would catch them in the rear with the other brigade. I would time it so there would be sufficient gas left in the airplanes of the 1st Brigade for them to continue the combat for about thirty minutes after the second arrived.

Nothing like this had ever been tried before. It marked the beginning of the great strategical air operations away from the troops.

Our own observation squadrons were assigned definitely to the troops on the ground. For their local protection at low altitude, we had our own American 1st Pursuit Group, under Major Harold E. Hartney. I considered this group the peer of any fighting organization on the front.

Our bombardment wing, consisting of the 2nd and 3rd Pursuit Groups, with the bombardment group, would act out from the head of the salient and attack Vigneulles. We had done everything we could with this new bombardment organization but they had not yet had the experience required to make them proficient.

Our bombardment group was not in good condition. It was

poorly commanded, the morale was weak and it would take some time to get it on its feet. This was largely due to the fact that when I was away in Château-Thierry, the 96th Squadron was left behind in the Toul area. The Major who was then in command of the 96th flew over into Germany with what ships he had available for duty. He lost his way in the fog and landed in Germany with every ship intact. Not one single ship was burned or destroyed and the Germans captured the whole outfit complete. This was the most glaring exhibition of worthlessness we had had on the front. The Germans sent back a humorous message which was dropped on one of our airdromes. It said, "We thank you for the fine airplanes and equipment which you have sent us, but what shall we do with the Major?"

I know of no other performance in any air force in the war that was as reprehensible as this. Needless to say, we did not reply about the Major, as he was better off in Germany at that time than he would have been with us.

The day for the attack drew near. Major I. B. Joralemon had done wonderful work in locating our great air host, preparing its airdromes and getting its supplies. Colonel DeWitt, G-4 of the General Staff, had helped us to the limit. On September 7th, the French Air Division reported and took its place.

We moved the air forces into their airdromes with the greatest secrecy possible so as not to let the Germans know how many airplanes we were assembling. We were careful not to make too great a display over the front; but on the other hand, we kept our pursuit patrols working up as high as they could go, about twenty thousand feet, so as to prevent German reconnaissance.

In our advance airdromes for the observation groups, such as at Souilly, I had camouflage or fake hangars constructed with fake airplanes in front, so that if the Germans took pictures of them, it would look as if a certain number of aircraft were there. Each day I had the position of these camouflage airplanes changed so as to make it look as if the place were active.

I issued orders to the 88th Squadron, among others, which was commanded by Major Christy, to occupy the airdrome at Souilly. They were to come up from Luxeuil, near Belfort, and arrive just before dark, so as to put their airplanes into the hangars immediately and in this way escape observation from the enemy. During the night of September 9th, I had real hangars put up exactly where the camouflage hangars had been. This same system had been followed on the other airdromes. In every other case, the organizations, flying low, arrived just before dark and immediately hid themselves. Christy, however, apparently did not get the spirit of the order. He arrived with his squadron in broad daylight, leading it himself, lined it up on the airdrome, then took his own ship with the best observer and actually made a reconnaissance away over Metz and got away with it. He was lucky not to have been killed but it disclosed our whole position at Souilly. The enemy then knew exactly what was there. It was a very brave act but absolutely the wrong thing to do. I told Christy what I thought of it. (Christy never did anything like that again; in fact, he developed into one of the best commanders that we had on the front.)

September 12th had been decided upon as the day of our grand attack. It was the greatest army ever assembled under the American flag; four hundred thousand men with over three thousand cannon were facing the enemy. Our air force consisted of nearly fifteen hundred airplanes.

Of course the Germans knew that we were going to attack them in the St. Mihiel salient. Their power of offensive and initiative passed after the battle at Soissons. St. Mihiel was a dangerous place for them to hold; in fact, they could not; all they could do was to delay our operations. They therefore had no intention of holding it and had put in, in addition to a few of their first-line organizations, a lot of second-line troops and Austrians, in which were included many *Honvéd* or Hungarian regiments.

In my personal reconnaissance with Major Armengaud over the lines on September 10th, I had noticed considerable movement to the rear which indicated that the Germans were withdrawing from the St. Mihiel salient. To my surprise and consternation I found at the meeting of General Pershing's staff on the evening before the attack that our Chief Engineer recommended that we delay the attack because there had been considerable rain. This, he said, held up our light railways used for getting up artillery ammunition. The question of adequate water for some of the troops would be difficult and a thousand and one things which could not be done were mentioned. I was surprised to see that several of the old fossils there agreed with this foolish view. You can always trust an Engineer Officer to go on the defensive whenever it is possible. I was the junior member of the staff and when it got to me for my opinion, I told them very plainly that I knew the Germans were withdrawing from the St. Mihiel salient as I had seen them personally, that our troops were now in position for the attack and were keyed up to it; furthermore, I said, there was not going to be much of a battle at St. Mihiel anyway, and our troops might be better off without artillery, as they would probably shoot a good many of our own men anyway; and all we had to do was to jump on the Germans, and the quicker we did it, the better.

General Pershing smiled, and ordered that we attack.

On September 11th I assembled the officers from every major organization of the Air Service within our great force—British, French, Italians and Americans. I read them the orders myself and asked each one individually what he could do to comply with them. Each one went back to his organization thoroughly conversant with what he was to do for each day of the attack.

The morning of September 12th dawned dark and cloudy, with intermittent rain. Clouds hung low and the visibility was very poor. Nevertheless, our Air Service with that of the Allies went over the lines, and I was much pleased with the fact that virtually no German airplanes got over our ground troops.

We forced the German airmen to fight away back of Vigneulles and Conflans, thirty miles away from our ground troops. We had many combats at these places during the day.

On the 13th, we could see that the enemy was concentrating all his available air power against us because he was losing too many prisoners. The Germans did not care whether we took the St. Mihiel salient or not, as they knew they were incapable of taking the offensive in the Verdun and Metz areas, but they did not want to lose a lot of prisoners and equipment. Our air force, however, by attacking their transportation trains, railroads and columns on the roads, piled them up with debris so that it was impossible for many of their troops to get away quickly, resulting in their capture by our infantry. We had forced them to measure strength with us in the air with their main forces, and if they did not come and attack us, we intended to destroy Metz, Conflans, Diedenhoffen and even Treves.

The British, under General Trenchard, tore into their airdromes, smashed up their hangars and forced them to fight at all points. An airman may stay on the ground if he wants to and let the other fellow go ahead, but if the other fellow starts blowing up everything, he will have to get up in the air and fight him, or allow complete destruction. We were constantly forcing them to fight in the air; of course, it was a walkover on the ground for the army.

By the 14th, the German air service began to appear in great numbers and we had a tremendous number of combats. There was one fight which I wish to mention particularly, because it illustrates the terrific destructive power of pursuit aviation when acting against bombardment aviation.

On September 14th, one of our bombardment squadrons, belonging to a French group, failed to meet the pursuit aviation detailed to protect it, on account of poor visibility in cloudy weather. Nevertheless it proceeded in the direction ordered, to bombard the objective. There were eighteen airplanes in the squadron, fifteen being two-seaters and three being three-seaters. The three-seaters were equipped with six guns each, and, as far as volume of gunfire was concerned, were the most powerful airplanes on the western front. They were unable to maneuver as rapidly as the single-seaters, however, and therefore did not fulfil the ideas of their originators who thought that through volume of fire alone they could defend themselves against small, highly maneuverable single-seaters. The three-seaters were supposed to be for the protection of the two-seaters; that is, these powerfully gunned airplanes were expected to fight off the enemy pursuit while the bombers concentrated their whole attention on dropping their bombs on the targets.

The squadron flew in a V-formation, like a flock of ducks. One of the great three-seaters was on each flank and one in the opening behind. When this squadron crossed the line on the way to its objective, it was passed by a patrol of twelve German pursuit airplanes flying one behind the other, about five hundred meters above it. The German patrol deployed in line formation behind the bombardment squadron. Four of the enemy planes attacked the three-seater which was behind and sent it down in flames. The other eight kept up a long-range fire at the squadron so as to derange its aim while dropping its bombs on the city of Conflans. At the same time, anti-aircraft artillery opened fire at the vanguard of the squadron while the German pursuit ships attacked the rear. While anti-aircraft guns failed to hit any of the airplanes, their bursting shells allowed the German pursuit organizations, which were now concentrating for an attack on the squadron, to see where they were. During this time, the Commander of the Bombardment Squadron noticed German airplanes rising from Mars-la-Tour, the airdrome close to Conflans.

All the bombs were dropped on the objective and the return flight was started to our lines. Just as the turn was made, a fresh enemy pursuit squadron joined the former, immediately deployed and attacked the rearmost plane and shot the observer through the leg. He continued to battle, however, and hit one enemy plane which fell in flames. The formation was now well on its way back when a third enemy squadron attacked ours in front and to the left. The bombing squadron was now being attacked in three dimensions, from underneath, above and on the same level.

The great lumbering bombing machines huddled together as a flight of geese might when attacked by falcons. The pursuit planes dived at them from all directions, firing their machine guns, then zooming up in the air or turning over on their backs at a speed of about two hundred miles an hour, taking an erratic course to avoid the fire of the big ships and then resuming their position for attack again.

By this time the big three-seater protection plane on the left had been shot in one of its engines and started slipping down. Immediately when it left the formation, it was jumped on by three German machines. In a moment, it was shot to pieces and disappeared in flames. The fighting had now become terrific. More German machines were constantly joining their comrades. The signals made by the artillery projectiles bursting in the air and the radio on the ground told the German aviators that our bombardment squadron had no pursuit protection and was an easy victim. The attacks of the German pursuit ships were carried on up to within fifty feet of the bombardment planes.

The next airplane to be hit was No. 13; a two-seater, which caught fire and dropped its movable gasoline tank. It dived at a sharp angle, turned over on its back about two hundred meters below the squadron, lost its left wing and then crashed to the ground.

At this same moment a German pursuit ship was shot down, on fire. No. 2 bombardment airplane was hit in the gasoline tank in the upper wing and caught fire; but the machine, flaming like a torch, kept its position in the formation. The machine gunner was magnificent in his courage, fighting the hostile airplanes while the flames slowly crept up around him. The plane continued to fly for about two hundred meters, leaving behind it a trail of fire about twice as long as the ship itself. Pilot and observer by this time were consumed and the airplane dived to its doom.

At about that time a German Fokker plane, diving vertically with its engine full on, lost both its wings. Now the whole right wing of the squadron had been shot down and a rearrangement of formation was made so as to get the remaining machines into V-formation again. Machines Nos. 9 and 14 were then both hit at the same time, No. 14 catching fire. The pilot of No. 14 stretched out his arms toward the sky, and, waving his hand and saying farewell to the remainder of the squadron, went to eternity. No. 9 machine disappeared and, as it did, an additional German pursuit machine retired from the combat crippled. No. 15 machine was now having a hard time keeping up with the formation. Its gasoline tank had been perforated by bullets, its aileron control cut and its rudder hit. However, it kept up.

By this time the squadron had come back to our lines and was joined and protected by our pursuit aviation. The combat in its intensity lasted for forty minutes, and of eighteen airplanes which had constituted the squadron, only five remained. Most of the crews were wounded and their planes perforated in all parts by bullets. They had never once broken their formation or failed to obey the orders of their leader. They furnished an example of military precision and bravery which is required of all airmen.

31

America's Greatest Battle Begins

September 1918 (Continued)

The battle of St. Mihiel was really over on the first day, and every objective had been accomplished. I was glad to see that our tanks did so well, because I am convinced that in the future the tank will be the only means of advancing on the ground against a well-intrenched and determined enemy. George Patton rode into St. Mihiel on the back of one of his tanks, away ahead of any other ground troops in the vicinity.

We won a great victory at St. Mihiel. But we actually advanced only two or three miles on the ground. We had not had to move any of our airdromes or to change any of our air arrangements. The army might fight for a month and not get too far away from the support of our present aircraft locations. This was not getting to the interior of Germany. What did it amount to, except killing thousands of our men and the enemy's?

General Pershing was tremendously pleased with our operations at St. Mihiel. He told me that we had been the eyes of the army and led it on to victory. He wrote me the following letter:

AMERICAN EXPEDITIONARY FORCES
Office of the Commander-in-Chief
France, Sept. 1, 1918.

Colonel William Mitchell,
    Chief of Air Service, First Army, A.E.F., France.

My dear Colonel—

Please accept my sincere congratulations on the successful and very important part taken by the Air Force under your command in the first offensive of the First American Army. The organization and control of the tremendous concentration of Air forces, including American, French, British and Italian units, which has enabled the Air Service of the First Army to carry out so successfully its dangerous and important mission, is as fine a tribute to you personally as is the courage and nerve shown by your officers a signal proof of the high morale which permeates the service under your command.

Please convey to your command my heartfelt appreciation of their work. I am proud of you all.

Sincerely yours,
JOHN J. PERSHING

On September 15th, I began arrangements to move into the Argonne area, and locations were selected for all of our air force.

Although the American squadrons under my command were being rapidly increased, the French needed their Air Division for use in the center of their line. We, therefore, had arranged that if I was too badly put to it by the enemy, in our part of the sector, I could call on the French and if the military exigencies permitted, they would come to my assistance. Of course, this was not as satisfactory as it might have been but it was the best we could do; and it was very good of the French even to agree to this, because they were being hard pushed in the Champagne. It would be a great advantage to have all air forces—American, British, French and Italian—under one command, as thus we could put the mass of our aviation where it was most needed at once, instead of having to bicker about it for days. The Germans had now organized their whole air force in the center of their position in France, and were acting *en masse,* which was the proper way. They were able to throw it to the west against the British, to the east against us and to the center against the French.

Our troops were moving to the Verdun area with precision and accuracy, again due to Colonel DeWitt, who had organized the routes we go along.

Our balloons did very well in the St. Mihiel battle. Although not used to the extent that they should have been by the ground troops, they rendered splendid service under Paegelow. The observers in the baskets showed great bravery in remaining aloft under all conditions, night and day, and in some cases, where their balloons were burned by hostile attack, jumped from their baskets in parachutes.

The enemy balloons, although they did little actual good to their troops, were a source of constant irritation to our ground troops. If a soldier on the ground saw any hostile aircraft in the air, no matter how impotent it might be, he at once conceived the idea that everything he did was seen and immediately reported, and that as a result the enemy could direct his artillery fire against the reserves that were coming up from behind to help him. Aircraft really exerted an uncanny influence—on new troops particularly, and even on old ones—and quite rightly, because many of these things were true. The balloons, however, could see much less than airplanes.

The casualties and losses during the offensive may be summarized as follows:

Sept. 12 Balloon No. 10—Balloon was driven into the trees by a high wind and so torn as to render it unserviceable; 1st Lt. David G. Boyd had his leg broken and back sprained when the basket was thrown against the ground.
Balloon No. 12—The cable of the balloon was snapped by a strong wind when the balloon was close to the ground. One parachute was smashed by being crashed against the ground. The balloon was last seen

at an altitude of 3000 meters, traveling toward the enemy lines. 1st. Lt. G. S. Hinman, A.S., U.S.A. and 1st. Lt. Roland S. Tait, A.S., U.S.A. remained in the basket.

Sept. 13   Balloon No. 20 (French)—Balloon was punctured by diving into a tree.

Sept. 14   Balloon No. 5—Balloon was burned by an enemy plane. Balloon No. 2—An American plane (Salmson) collided with the cable of Balloon No. 2, wrecking the plane and killing the pilot and observer in the plane, but causing no appreciable damage to the balloon.

Sept. 15   Balloon No. 1—Balloon was burned by an enemy plane. Balloon No. 2—Balloon was burned by an enemy plane.

Sept. 16   Balloon No. 9—Balloon was deflated by enemy shrapnel.

Our 1st Pursuit Group, detailed to act in close cooperation with our ground troops, not only protected them wonderfully from enemy air attack but smashed up German formations on some roads to such an extent that our pursuing ground troops were able to capture several thousand prisoners.

While General Trenchard of the British Air Force was visiting my headquarters one day, several officers commanding ground troops dropped in and one of them mentioned that his troops were much bothered by the hostile balloons; none of the others had any comment to make about the cooperation of the air service, but each one said that he had never seen the air so clear of enemy aircraft as at St. Mihiel. Of course, the air is a big place. It was almost as hard to keep hostile airplanes out of the air as it was to keep hostile projectiles away, but at St. Mihiel we had cleaned up the air pretty well.

Trenchard said to me, "This is the most remarkable exhibition I have seen; in my own service, after we had been in the war for about six months, none of the Generals of the ground troops would even speak to me because they thought I was personally responsible for the enemy airplanes going over their troops." He was much pleased with all our arrangements.

In view of the comment about the German balloons bothering our ground troops so much, I called up Major Hartney, Commander of our 1st Pursuit Group, and had him come to my headquarters. I told him that the orthodox way of attacking balloons, by approaching them in various directions and then pushing the attack under cover of the sun or of the forest, or some other method of obscuring the approach of the actual attacking airplane, was pretty well understood by the Germans. I mentioned to him that at night the balloons were pulled down to the ground and remained in their nests, and that they arose early in the morning with their envelopes damp and therefore would not burn readily when hit by our small .30-caliber flaming bullets. In the afternoon, as the sun was in the west, we had to go pretty far into the enemy's country to approach the balloons under its protection.

I told Hartney to go back and figure out a new way of destroying the balloons; I did not care how he did it. Hartney, who was an enthusiastic and able man, would keep cocking his head from one side to the other, saying, "Precisely, precisely," as I gave him the instructions; but all of the time he was thinking how it would be possible to devise methods which had not been tried in the last three years.

The next morning, September 18th, Hartney told me that he had a solution. Upon returning to his group, he had gone and looked at the position of various balloons and had also sent some selected pilots to do the same thing. They also had discovered the nests of several German balloons. Hartney's solution to the problem was to send out only two pilots, one to stay above to protect the lower one. The lower one was to fly along close to the ground and shoot the balloon in its nest, just at dusk or even after dark.

Accordingly, Hartney equipped the airplanes of Lieutenants Joseph Wehner and Frank Luke with 11-mm. or .45-caliber machine guns, which fired a large flaming bullet. He told me that he would attack that evening at dusk and for me to look over toward the place where the German balloon was. If I saw a large fire, it would indicate that the balloon had been successfully attacked and was burning. I did so, and exactly at the time appointed, the fire occurred. Later another one occurred.

That evening Hartney called me up and said that Luke and Wehner had destroyed two balloons, and in addition Luke had shot down an enemy airplane just south of Verdun. He had come down close to the ground where the airplane fell so as to make sure of the capture of the pilot. This was indeed wonderful work.

I told Hartney to continue to destroy all the German balloons, and he responded, "Yes, sir, there won't be one left on the front in a few days."

This proved to be almost correct. The Germans moved all their balloons back and put dummy balloons up, with nobody in them except a straw figure, to try and divert our attention. These they surrounded with great numbers of machine guns on the ground, which they hoped would shoot down our planes, lured to the dummy balloons. The Germans did not pull the dummies down to the earth when we came near them but left them in the air, hoping in this way to fool our people.

Unfortunately, Wehner was killed shortly after this. Luke, now acting alone without Wehner, was shot down in enemy territory and unfortunately was killed while defending himself with his pistol. He had obtained more victories [nineteen] than any other pilot during the time he was on the front.

I moved my headquarters to Souilly on September 22nd, and established it a short distance from General Pershing's. We now made ready for the battle of the Argonne.

Our problem in the Argonne was quite different from what it was at St. Mihiel. There we had a salient which projected into our lines. Here we had a more or less straight front, except on our right flank at Verdun, which was refused or sloped back and to the right. This gave an excellent opportunity for the German aviation to attack us in flank in the air. This nearly always led to a rear attack. It was even more serious in the air than was a similar attack on the ground. During the Battle of Verdun in August, 1917, I saw the German aviation come in from the right of Verdun and shoot down the French balloons without mercy, and also cover the French lines with their reconnaissance planes everywhere. I knew that this same thing would happen to us when once the battle started. Therefore, as far as enemy reconnaissance and work over our own ground troops by German planes was concerned, I had to watch our right flank.

I decided to mass our offensive aviation on the center axis of advance of the whole army. This line ran from Epinonville to Romagne to Bantheville. This was the area through which the high roads that supplied the German army came from the north, both from the valley of the Meuse River and also from the direction of Buzancy. Our object in doing this was to destroy the German stores of ammunition and supplies in the area behind the army; to attack any infantry reserves coming up, and also to force the air fighting well into German territory.

Our whole front on the ground was about fifty miles long, with its windings and sinuosities. Our straight-line distance in the air, however, was a little over thirty miles from one side to the other. This was a tremendous battle front, however, for a single attack. Our army had ready to put into the line more than half a million troops and forty-two hundred pieces of artillery, the greatest mass of artillery ever brought together under one single direction for a battle.

The ground in front of us was very bad, chopped up with hills, woods, brush and streams. The French had been able to make practically no headway against the Germans in this area since the beginning of the war. The Germans had it remarkably well organized, with trenches and machine-gun nests. They had always held this part of the front with comparatively few men so as to release more men for operations elsewhere.

In addition to our own aviation, I was getting considerable assistance from the French, two Italian bombardment squadrons and General Trenchard, whose British independent air force cooperated with us in bombarding the German airdromes and supply points.

General Pershing decided that the initial attack should take place on September 26th. Accordingly I assembled the officers of the various aviation units, on the afternoon of September 24th, to give them their instructions. I had previously asked General Pershing if he would come up to meet the air officers when they were assembled and he told me that he would be very glad to. I went down to his headquarters to get him; he immediately dropped the work he was doing and accompanied me, with his aide, Major Peter Bowditch, up the little street of Souilly.

As we walked up the street, General Pershing was congratulating me on having kept out the hostile airplanes to so great an extent, and I was explaining to him how we did it. While engaged in this conversation, I looked to the northeast and saw one puff, two puffs, three puffs of smoke and then a rapid anti-aircraft fire, taken up by one battery after another. I knew that a German Rumpler airplane was coming over us, and soon it appeared, perfectly silhouetted against the clear sky. It paid no attention whatever to the anti-aircraft fire, but came straight on over us. I said nothing to the General about it; he glanced up and said nothing to me. The airplane had avoided our high patrols up twenty thousand feet on our right flank. It had entered behind Verdun and was going right across the angle formed by our lines, to the northeast. Patrols of the 1st Pursuit Group were up in that direction with orders to intercept any high flying German airplanes, and I hoped they would be successful.

We arrived at my headquarters, where the foreign officers and our own were assembled for orders. General Pershing gave them a very nice talk, telling them how much he appreciated the work they had done at St. Mihiel and that he relied on the Air Service to be the eyes of the army and to lead us forward to victory again in the Argonne. He listened while I gave the orders and instructions, then I walked back with him to his headquarters, and quickly returned to my own.

I had hardly sat down before Colonel Dodd, my information officer, came in with a report that a German Rumpler two-seater had been detected crossing from the direction of Verdun toward the northwest, 21,000 feet up, and had been shot down in our own territory by a patrol from the 1st Pursuit Group. This was the plane that had passed over us when I brought General Pershing up. Some of the photographic plates had been captured intact, and when developed, revealed a perfect picture of Souilly, with the motor cars grouped around my headquarters, and all exposed formations plainly showing.

Our attack was launched in the early morning of September 26th. The artillery bombardment was terrific. How much good it did, I do not know—I don't think very much. I had put a small advance airdrome just outside Verdun, which was only about three and one-half miles from the front lines, and had placed a flight of our planes there to be constantly on the alert to attack any German low flying planes that came in opposite our right flank. It was commanded by Lieutenant Jerry Vasconcelles.

When the artillery preparation opened in the early morning, the cannonade was so terrific and the physical reverberation in the air was so great that the metal gasoline tanks on the Spad airplanes of Vasconcelles' flight were sprung and made to leak. This was the only instance of the kind I had ever heard of. Of course the discharge of explosives constantly broke windows and smashed other things at a distance, but to have artillery fire loosen the seams in gasoline tanks in an airplane was an unusual occurrence.

There was a little mist on the morning of the 26th, but the rest of the day proved fair and rather warmer than the day before. The visibility was quite good. Our airplanes left the ground before the break of day and were well out on the German side when the battle got in full swing.

Again we dominated the air but not to the extent we had at St. Mihiel. Not only had the Germans more airplanes in the vicinity, but the shape of the front was such that it was extremely difficult to keep the German planes out from one flank or the other. Our bombardment aviation, acting well into the enemy's country, kept them pretty busy and although many incursions were made on our side of the line, we kept the air fighting, generally speaking, well away from our ground troops.

Late in the afternoon of the day of the attack, when flying over the central part of our line, I noticed a terrible congestion of motor traffic at Avocourt. Columns of our transportation stood several miles long on three roads running into Avocourt, where they all came together. Not a wheel could be turned, either to the front or to the rear, because the trucks were in no-man's land and if they did not stick to the roads they would immediately mire down for good. Never have I seen such a congestion on a European battlefield. It was a terrible example of inefficiency on the part of the staff of our center corps. If the German aviation had been able to attack this column, it certainly would have destroyed it. This would have put the whole central army corps, the 5th, out of ammunition and supplies. A counterattack then by a small organization of Germans would have broken a hole right straight through the center of our line and nothing could have stopped it, because we could not have moved troops up along the roads to help the 5th Corps.

We had received many reports that the German aviation had received armored airplanes that could resist machine-gun fire. Here, in this great congestion of motor trucks, was the target for which they had been waiting.

I immediately concentrated all our bombardment aviation against Romagne and Dun-sur-Meuse, so as to keep the fighting in the back areas and make the German pursuit aviation remain twenty or thirty kilometers away from the line, to defend these important places.

I assigned the 1st Pursuit Group under Hartney to keep up a constant patrol at an altitude of only about three hundred feet —in fact, almost down among the infantry—to prevent the hostile airplanes from getting in there. Had we not done this instantly, I believe that this whole mass of transportation would have been destroyed and burned.

As we were pushing in the air so strongly—fifteen or twenty miles the other side of the infantry—the Germans could send no pursuit airplanes with their battle flights, as they called them, to protect them. The result was that our pursuit airplanes shot down great numbers of the enemy's attack aviation which was attempting to destroy our truck trains.

Reports came in from the front lines at this time that the German aviators kept constantly over them and that our planes would not attack them. Accordingly I sent Colonel Dodd, my information officer, up there on the ground. He went as far as he could in a motorcycle, then got out and walked for miles around the stalled transport. He reported to me that the transport could not move for three days, as all the trucks of three divisions had been routed through the one center of Avocourt, and it would take three days for the engineers to make roads for them to move on.

Dodd also reported that he saw no German aircraft over our front at low altitude and that he observed six combats on the enemy's side of the line. He met the General of our forces who had complained that German airplanes were constantly near them. When Dodd asked him how he knew they were German planes, he replied "When we fire machine guns at them, they retire into Germany"—that is, on the German side of the line. As a matter of fact, they were the airplanes of Hartney's pursuit group, flying low and watching every part of the line, to guard against the low flying enemy attack, and our troops not only did not know them but kept shooting at them.

The Germans had painted their airplanes so that they looked just like the ground when seen from above. The German airmen would get down to within one hundred feet or so of the earth, or even lower at times, fly up ravines or behind forests and pounce on infantry columns or wagon trains and surprise them before they could conceal themselves. We had a couple of engineer companies lined up for mess that were attacked in this way by a flight of German attack aviation. They killed eighty-seven men and wounded a couple of hundred before the engineers could get to cover.

Fortunately, by the last day of the month this terrible mess of motor trucks in the center of our line was straightened out. The Commanding General of the Corps was relieved and another one put in command of it.

Our troops kept attacking the German position and the losses were terrific, from a comparatively small number of Germans, in proportion to the ground we gained. All of the ground in front of the German position was very well organized and defended by German machine-gun troops, excellently trained and well protected.

The Argonne Battle was not a particularly interesting one from an air standpoint. The infantry on the ground just knocked its head against a stone wall. It was terrible for us to look down from the air and see the uncoördinated, not to say disorganized, nature of the combat which resulted from not using the airplanes sufficiently for reconnaissance. At one place, infantry attacked all alone without artillery helping them. A little way off, an entirely separate combat was taking place, then again a little further on there was no fighting. In another place, the artillery was firing with terrific speed against nothing, and the infantry was awaiting word to occupy the ground supposed to be held by the enemy, when really there was no enemy within a long way of it.

The troops nearly always completely lost contact with the enemy, then when they did come up, they were surprised by the German machine-gun nests in prepared positions, and suffered terrific casualties. There was one thing to be said, however, and that was, in spite of the losses, General Pershing never faltered in pushing the offensive once he started it.

The way our whole position appeared from the air was about as follows: Our right rested on the Meuse River; further to our right or to the east, there was very little action. From there to the west, there was a series of more or less detached combats, with tremendous masses of Americans huddled up in some places and spread out in others, until the Argonne Forest was reached, about thirty miles to the west. The Argonne Forest then stretched its mass of trees and dark shadows, where practically no action was taking place, for about ten or fifteen miles; then from there to Reims, about thirty more miles, there was a great battle going on, which increased in intensity as the days went by. If the Germans had had the power of offense they had possessed earlier in the year, they would have cut our ground troops to pieces, but now they had not "got the punch" and were maintaining a passive defense, which was lucky for our army.

We were experiencing a great deal of trouble with the ground troops in making them answer the signals from the air and properly maintain their radio stations for communicating with our airplanes. Our pilots had to fly right down and almost shake hands with the infantry on the ground to find out where they were. Many of the infantry and artillery officers left the handling of the wireless stations to the first sergeants of their company. The sergeants said that they got tired of seeing wireless-operators sitting in a hole in the ground, doing nothing and safe from the enemy's fire, so they assigned them to kitchen police or some other duty of that kind. As a result there were no communications at a critical time.

It was practically impossible to impress the men in the ranks, through their own officers, as to the value of aviation. They did not even know what the insignia on our planes was, in many cases. They had been taught in the United States that our airplane insignia was a star on the under surface of the plane; whereas, the insignia of all Allied aviators was round concentric circles, with the colors of the country they belonged to. Wherever possible, we took the infantry battalions back of the line to our airdromes and took the noncommissioned officers and other soldiers up in the air. This impressed them with the necessity of coöperating with the airmen as much as possible, and they transmitted it on to the privates. I had Colonel Dodd prepare the following, which we threw down from our airplanes to all the infantry positions where we went:

FROM THE AMERICAN SCRAPPERS IN THE AIR TO THE AMERICAN SCRAPPERS ON THE GROUND

DOUGHBOYS—

While you are giving the Boche hell on the ground, we are helping you to the limit in the air.

The artillery are behind you anxious to help with their shells.

Headquarters is trying through us to keep in close touch with you and to render aid whenever you are checked or outnumbered.

Keep us posted at all times as to where your front lines are, either with Bengal lights, panels, or—if nothing else is available —wave a white towel or any white cloth.

Your signals enable us:

To take news of your location to the rear.

To report if the attack is successful.

To call for help if needed.

To enable the artillery to put their shells over your head into the enemy.

We prevent the enemy planes from telling the enemy artillery where you are; we bomb and machine-gun enemy troops whenever the chance offers.

If you are out of ammunition, and tell us, we will report it and have it sent up.

If you are surrounded, we will deliver the ammunition by airplane.

We do not hike through the mud with you, but there are discomforts in our work as bad as mud, but we won't let rain, storms, Archies nor Boche planes prevent our getting there with the goods.

Do not think that we are not on the job when you cannot see us—most of our planes work so far in front that they cannot be seen from the lines.

Some enemy planes may break through our airplane barrage in front of you, and may sometimes bomb and machine-gun you, but in the last month we have dropped ten tons of bombs for every one the Boche has dropped. For every Boche plane that you see over you, the Boche sees ten Allied planes over him. For every balloon that he burns, we burn eight.

Our losses of aviators correspond to your losses, but for every one that we lose, the Boche has to pay with heavy interest.

Whenever a Boche plane is brought down in your sector, do not collect souvenirs from it; you may remove an article or marking that would have given valuable information to us. If Boche aviators are not dead when they land, wait ten minutes before approaching within one hundred feet of the plane after they have left it; sometimes they start a time bomb. DO NOT TOUCH ANY-THING IN A BOCHE PLANE—they sometimes carry innocent looking infernal machines.

Use us to the limit, show your panels, burn the signal lights, wave a cloth; anything to tell us where you are and what you need.

After reading this, pass it on to your Buddie, and remember to show your signals.

YOUR AVIATOR.

32

Over the Argonne

October 1918

A good many visitors came up during the month of October. Colonel Arthur Woods of New York visited me and I took him up for a flight over the front. I also took up John T. McCutcheon of Chicago, the eminent cartoonist and writer. Mr. John D. Ryan, the Assistant Secretary of War, in charge of aviation, in company with General James W. McAndrew, the very able Chief of Staff of the A.E.F., were here. We had a conference in my battle headquarters at Souilly, at which I explained to them the situation of the air forces in Europe. Ryan seemed to understand what was going on better than any other of the department heads I have seen.

The organization of our Second American Army is now being pushed. This army is to be located in the Toul area, to act on the right of the First American Army and to attack the great city of Metz, fortified by the Germans to the limit of their ability. It has therefore been decided that we should assign a certain amount of aviation to each army and then assemble all of the pursuit and bombardment aviation that we could and mass it into a great force with which to strike deep into Germany. General Pershing has informed me that I am to command the whole air force, that is, the aviation of both the armies and the general reserve of aviation which will be assigned to the group of armies.

The days wore on with constant hammering by the infantry against the German positions. The flying in support of the First Army had become more or less a routine matter. There was one day, however, the 9th of October, when the enemy had assembled a considerable force of infantry and artillery on the east bank of the Meuse, opposite the right flank of our 3rd Corps, commanded by General Robert L. Bullard. These German troops were being concentrated in the woods, near a place called Damvillers. If they could creep in against our right flank and make a surprise attack, they would cause a great deal of damage. If we could smash up their concentration, blow up their ammunition dumps and burn their supplies by an attack from the air, the whole German maneuver might be stopped.

Accordingly, I asked the French Air Division if they could assist me in such an operation. They replied immediately by sending three hundred and twenty-two airplanes in a single formation, carrying thirty-nine tons of bombs to attack this place. Our aviation redoubled its efforts along the front of our troops and against the German supply points that we had been attacking before. The great air formation flew right over our whole army on this beautiful clear day of the 9th of October. I had had to act so quickly that I had no time to inform General Pershing or the staff of this attack, so when it approached, I ran over to the General's headquarters and showed him and his staff officers this marvelous picture as the airplanes passed over. I then went back to the airdrome, got in my airplane to see the effect of the air attack against Damvillers and also to look over the position of our own air forces along our front.

A view of this attack is impossible to describe. Squadron after squadron of Bréguet bombers, flying in V-formation at about twelve thousand feet, went straight to their objective. On each side of them and above and below, hovered small single-seater airplanes for their protection. It looked very much like a succession of flocks of swans and teal ducks; the swans being the bombardment ships and the teal ducks the pursuit ships. As they arrived over the target the leading squadron of from fifteen to eighteen airplanes dropped all their bombs at once. As each plane carried ten bombs, this meant one hundred and fifty bombs to each discharge. As the bombs struck the ground, terrific explosions and detonations took place which we could easily hear up in the air.

Within a minute after the first squadron attacked, the second one attacked and so on until twelve squadrons had delivered their bombs. While this was going on, sixty German pursuit planes were attempting in every way to get at the bombers. They came down from the direction of the sun in a succession of groups of from ten to fifteen airplanes each; the French pursuit aviation handled them beautifully. Whenever they came within reach, they were set upon by about three French airplanes to each German. Individual combats were taking place all around the bombardment ships, but not one single bombardment plane was shot down, nor was a single pursuit plane lost on the enemy side of the line; whereas we received official credit for twelve enemy planes shot down.

Just think what it will be in the future when we attack with one, two or three thousand airplanes at one time; the effect will be decisive.

During the night of the 9th, the British aviation threw down forty-two tons of bombs, which gave a grand total of eighty-one tons of bombs thrown down within twenty-four hours, on the enemy's side of the line—the greatest amount ever put over in a single day during the war.

All of this hammering was having a great effect on the Germans. Reports were coming in from prisoners which showed that we were destroying numbers of their airplanes and making such holes in their airdromes that they constantly had to make new ones. After each of our attacks, the German machines returning at night would find holes big enough to smash their planes directly in the middle of their supposedly good flying fields.

Whenever I had the opportunity, I visited the infantry lines and checked up on the service the troops were getting from their observation squadrons. One day I wandered into General Bullard's headquarters. He was very busy as usual.

He said, "Mitchell, there is an enemy balloon right opposite me which sees everything we are doing and I wish you would shoot it down." I replied that I would do so at once.

As a matter of fact, I had already ordered an attack on this balloon some hours before, and I knew that the airplanes would be there within a few minutes. I called up the 1st Pursuit Group and asked Hartney when the attack would begin, and he said that they were about to start. An attack against a balloon required considerable preparation and could not be done on the spur of the moment. The balloon had to be located, had to be approached from different directions, several feints had to be made so as to draw off the hostile pursuit aviation and then the main attack was launched from an unexpected direction so as to surprise them.

I did not tell General Bullard about these preparations, but I did tell him to watch in the direction of the balloon in about one-half hour and he would see a big column of smoke appear. I left his headquarters and had hardly gone back a mile along the road when over us came the flights of the 1st Pursuit Group on the balloon mission. Within a few minutes afterward, the German balloon was in flames and a great column of smoke was ascending into the sky. I had hardly reached my headquarters when General Bullard called me up and congratulated me. I told my staff and the 1st Pursuit Group about what had happened and we laughed heartily over it. General Bullard to this day thinks that we organized the attack and shot down the balloon after he requested it.

I had a long conference with General Pershing on October 17th. We discussed the formation of aviation of the group of armies. I also proposed to him that in the spring of 1919, when I would have a great force of bombardment airplanes, he should assign one of the infantry divisions permanently to the Air Service, preferably the 1st Division; that we should arm the men with a great number of machine guns and train them to go over the front in our large airplanes, which would carry ten or fifteen of these soldiers. We could equip each man with a parachute, so that when we desired to make a rear attack on the enemy, we could carry these men over the lines and drop them off in parachutes behind the German position. They could assemble at a prearranged strong point, fortify it and we could supply them by aircraft with food and ammunition. Our low flying attack aviation would then cover every road in their vicinity, both day and night, so as to prevent the Germans falling on them before they could thoroughly organize the position. Then we could attack the Germans from the rear, aided by an attack from our army on the front and support the whole maneuver with our great air force. This was a perfectly feasible proposition. The Germans were already using parachutes for their pilots. Many a good man of theirs had been saved from an untimely death by this device.

Tanks had proved themselves to be the instrument *par excellence* of advancing over the ground, and I wanted to see just as great a development of this army as possible. From the air we could see what the tanks were doing better than from anywhere on the ground. I thoroughly believed that tanks could be handled in fleets and be supplied by other tanks. If we could get well to the rear of the enemy with our air forces and have tanks jump on him in front, we would come pretty near to destroying the German army.

One of the battalions of the 77th Division became detached from it, and was surrounded by Germans in the Argonne Forest. It was commanded by Major Whittlesey. I ordered chocolate and concentrated food and ammunition dropped off to it. Our pilots thought they had located it from the panels that it showed, and dropped off considerable supplies. The battalion held out and rejoined its command, but I later found that they had received none of the supplies we had dropped off. The Germans had made up a panel like theirs and our men had calmly dropped off the nice food to the Germans, who undoubtedly ate it with great satisfaction.

One day our bombardment attacked the railroad station at Longuyon; they missed the station by two and one-half miles but hit in the middle of a German division at drill, killed and wounded over two thousand men, including some of the members of the commanding general's staff. Another time our bombers hit at night an ammunition train, drawn up in the railroad station at Longuyon. On one side of it was an incoming train filled with troops and on the other a railroad train of men on leave, going to the rear. Five hundred and fifty men were killed outright and over two thousand wounded.

One of the pilots in our day bombardment put a bomb straight through the top of the round house at Longuyon, destroyed eight or ten locomotives in it and blew up the whole place. We have photographs to show this, in addition to the reports of prisoners and spies.

We lost many a good man and, of course, would continue to lose more. Many of these had been taken prisoner, and as our aviators knew so much more about the general situation and the position of all the troops than any other officers of corresponding rank, we had to be very careful to instruct them as to what they should do in case of capture. The following is a list of "don'ts" each aviator was supposed to know:

DON'TS FOR FLYERS WHO LAND IN ENEMY TERRITORY

It is important to impress upon pilots and observers and any others whose duty may take them in an airplane across the lines, the following points with regard to minimizing the amount of information which the enemy would be able to obtain should the machine and occupants fall into their hands:

(1) Don't carry any papers, official or private, whilst in an airplane. In order that this should become a habit, it is not sufficient to empty one's pockets only when a flight east of the lines is undertaken. Envelopes containing private correspondence give away the identification of the prisoner's unit.

(2) Don't mark airdromes and other information concerning our own side of the line on maps which are taken up into the air. The smallest mark is sufficient to indicate an airdrome to the enemy should the map be captured.

(3) Don't, if captured, trust anyone, whether in German uniform or uniform of any of the Allies. Speak as little as possible and don't enter into conversation. Friendliness shown by the enemy should at once cause suspicion.

(4) Don't forget that a clever interrogator will obtain information from you in the course of a casual conversation, therefore, again speak as little as possible.

(5) Don't address letters, which the enemy says he will drop for you across the lines, to your Squadron Wing or Brigade; address letters to the headquarters of your Air Service and they will be sent from there to their right destination.

(6) Don't forget that the Germans want to know, not only about aviation in general, but more particularly American aviation. They will make unrelenting efforts to obtain this.

(7) The Germans use listening apparatus in prisoner-of-war cages and other places where prisoners are located, so that conversation with other prisoners is overheard. Therefore don't discuss military or aviation matters of any sort or description with anyone, even your best friend, as your conversation will be overheard by the enemy by means of listening apparatus.

(8) German interrogators will dress up as Allied officers or soldiers and will be placed in the same room as you with the object of learning your information; therefore again suspect anyone whom you do not actually know.

(9) Don't be misled by the kindness which will be shown to you when first captured. Champagne dinners and such like things will be provided for you in order to get you to talk.

(10) Don't ever be put off your guard.

Advanced Headquarters,
Royal Flying Corps,
26th August 1917.

WARNING TO BRITISH AVIATORS

The following instructions in the form of a warning have been given to British aviators. American officers and aviators should note them and appreciate their importance:

If you are unfortunate enough to be compelled to land behind the German lines, you may be agreeably surprised by the apparent hospitality and generosity of your welcome there. The German officers will probably have you to stay with them as their guest for a few days at one of their squadrons, and will make you most comfortable. You will probably be extremely well entertained with the very best of everything they can offer. An abundance of good champagne from France will oil the wheels of conversation between the officers of the German Flying Corps, and one whom they will probably term a brother officer of the English Flying Corps. They will appear to be very good fellows, straightforward, cheerful and keep on the scientific side of flying, apart from their ordinary work with which they may say you are quite fed up. They will probably lead you to talk about the possibilities of aviation after the war, and profess little interest in aviation as actually applied to war. It may not take much wine to gladden your heart and to induce you to lay aside your suspicions and reserve and forget the guile which lies behind their artless questions.

And so unaccustomed as you are to this form of deceit, you may fall another victim to this clever combination of cunning and hospitality. But though they may succeed for the moment in making a favorable impression you will afterwards have every reason to remember during this war the Germans have proved themselves to be a cruel and unscrupulous enemy, but they are sound financiers, and have an eye to good investment. It does not cost them much to entertain you well, and even if it did, they expect to get an adequate return for their money in the form of information unwittingly imparted by you.

That is why they give you all the delights of the Carlton and Savoy, with none of the regrets of an overdraft at Cox's, and that is why you will be treated as a highly honored guest, instead of being half-starved in one of their now notorious prison camps, a treatment which is in fact only postponed until they have squeezed every ounce of useful information out of you.

The work is done by experienced men. Quite unknown to yourself, one or more of the seemingly irresponsible flying men are highly trained intelligence officers who will sift bits of useful information from your most brilliant bon mot, received with the keenest amusement and gratification.

On the other hand, different methods may be employed, though these are not so common with prisoners of the Flying Corps as with others. You may be browbeaten and ordered to disclose information under pain of suffering severe penalties if you refuse. Remember that this is only a ruse and that they will not carry out their threats. It is more probable that they will respect you for your patriotism and discretion.

It is quite possible that you may be placed in a hut with an officer alleged to be an English prisoner, speaking English fluently, and knowing many people in England well, and wishing to have news of everyone and everything, or perhaps he will ask no questions, relying only on your confidences. It will be difficult for you to believe that he is not a companion in misfortune, but this is a common trick of all intelligence services and a very profitable one.

Therefore be on your guard and remember that in a show like this it is impossible for any individual not at the head of affairs to say what is of use to the enemy and what is not. Remember that any information you may inadvertently give may lengthen the war and keep you longer in Germany, may cost the lives of many Englishmen, may strain the country's resources even more than they are being strained at present. Don't think this is all imagination and needless caution. The need of it has been brought out by experience. No careless or irresponsible feelings ought to weigh with us against anything we can do to hasten the conclusion of the war.

—Air Service Special Bulletin No. 3.

We continued, of course, to receive many complaints from the ground troops about not getting enough airplanes to them and that the observers did not see them or repeat their signals at the time that they were required.

To make sure that each observer and pilot was certain of having everything ready on his side, I had the following instructions published for their guidance:

PREPARATION FOR AN INFANTRY MISSION

The few cautions to observers and pilots printed below were issued to Divisional Squadrons before one of our recent offensives.

INFANTRY PLANE
Observer.

Have the exact time.
Have all maps required.
Have you your code?
Is your wireless ready?
Have you the proper pencils?
Going to the lines, spot your Corps-Division-Brigade P.Cs.
Get a general view of the situation.
Then study the line, point by point.
Make sure about each point and then pass on to the others.
Ask for the line only if you can't get it.
Try to understand the battle—get interested in it.
Watch the grenade fights: small round puffs of clear smoke.
Try to find Boche machine guns.
You'll find four (4) or five (5) men around these.
Send all your information at once by wireless.
Send it clearly and repeat it.
If the advance looks checked, try to understand why.
Try to spot the resistance centers.
Go down and drop a message to the Battalion or Regimental commander, giving him the probable importance of the German resistance, the position of the German machine guns, his own position, and the situation of his flanks.
All this information is to be sent also by wireless.
Then fire on the Germans with your own machine guns.
Watch its effect.
Never omit to send the "Understood" fire when you have seen the Bengal flares or panels.
Never omit to send the "Understood" fire when you have seen a Battalion or Regimental panel.

Watch carefully the ground fires; you will get good information from them; repeat the demands by wireless.

Try to look—get used at once to the battle and think only of your job.

Write your weighted messages carefully.

PILOT

Try to understand the situation as well as your observer.

Be an aid to him and not a nuisance.

Put him on a certain point, and—

Hold that along the line.

Watch for alien machines.

When going down for weighted messages, take care of your motor, your temperature and batteries.

When firing on Boches, aid your observer by firing with your Vickers.

COUNTERATTACK PLANE
Observer.

Watch all probable area given by G-2.

Watch all cover—woods, small woods, hedges, villages.

Make sure before sending information.

German uniforms look dark.

Movements are always slow.

Watch for anti-aircraft gun flashes—send at once information by wireless and then attack with your machine gun fire.

Control the fugitive target group fire.

Fly low and watch also our first line from time to time.

Send as much information as you can and all German activities; fuses, planes, flashes—if you can't see men moving.

Drop, if necessary, messages on the batteries if they don't seem to receive your wireless in case of strong counter-attack imminent.

Drop messages telling all your information to the Division and Corps P.Cs.

As time went on, we obtained better coöperation from the infantry, particularly the 1st, 2nd and 42nd Divisions, which constantly improved in their liaison with the air.

We were beginning to get pretty straight reports from the interior of Germany, of political uprisings and trouble, most of which seemed to have originated in the navy at Kiel, particularly with the marines stationed there. Also, the older German reservists who had been garrisoning the Russian frontier seemed to have combined with the workmen in the interior to foment revolution. There were rumors that they had formed such a strong revolutionary organization that they might overthrow the German Empire. We heard about mutinies, the refusal to transport munitions and food to the troops on the front and the refusal of men to serve. I was inclined to think these things were true as we got indications of them from the prisoners we captured. While the German troops on our front were fighting as bravely as ever, I believed they were running short of some important necessities for continuing the combat.

On October 21st, I assumed command of the aviation of the Group of Armies, which gave me command of the entire Air Service of the A.E.F. fighting against the enemy. In relinquishing command of the Air Service of the First Army, I published an order to all those concerned as follows:

HEADQUARTERS AIR SERVICE, FIRST ARMY
AMERICAN EXPEDITIONARY FORCES

GENERAL ORDER France, October 21, 1918.
No. 19.

1. Special Order No. 287, dated G.H.Q., A.E.F., France, October 14, 1918, appoints me as Chief of Air Service, Group of Armies.

2. Colonel T. DeWitt Milling is appointed Chief of Air Service, 1st Army, by the same order and is hereby announced as such.

3. In relinquishing command of the air troops of the 1st Army, I desire to express my admiration and appreciation for the manner in which their duty has been performed by the whole command. You came into full battle a new and untried organization. You served shoulder to shoulder with our French, British and Italian Allies. You have shot down and destroyed two hundred sixty-one airplanes and thirty balloons. You have covered the army while it has been attacking, marching and holding its

positions. Your reconnaissance has extended over the enemy's whole position to a great depth, both night and day, and you have worked smoothly and energetically with our Allies, and have met the best air troops the enemy possesses, and destroyed them.

4. There is no record superior to yours in aviation. That it is thoroughly appreciated by our Commander-in-Chief is shown by the following letter written at the end of the battle of St. Mihiel:

AMERICAN EXPEDITIONARY FORCES
Office of the Commander-in-Chief.

Colonel William Mitchell,   France, September 16, 1918.
Chief of Air Service,
  First Army, A.E.F.,
    F R A N C E.

My dear Colonel:

Please accept my sincere congratulations on the successful and very important part taken by the Air Forces under your command in the first offensive of the 1st American Army. The organization and control of the tremendous concentration of Air Forces, including American, French, British and Italian units, which has enabled the Air Service of the 1st Army to carry out so successfully its dangerous and important mission, is as fine a tribute to you personally as is the courage and nerve shown by your officers a signal proof of the high morale which permeates the service under your command.

Please convey to your command my heartfelt appreciation of their work. I am proud of you all.

Sincerely yours,
John J. Pershing.

5. In all your work remember the arduous duties of the troops on the ground. When you are freezing in the air, they are wading over the battlefields deep in mud and debris; when you are getting the enemy's tracer bullets and anti-aircraft fire through your planes, they are going through the artillery and machine gun fire below you. Their losses correspond to yours. You must protect them and show them the way forward. Work closely with

them, because only by the combined work of all arms will our full power be developed.

6. Our low-flying system attack in echelon, massing of bombardment on the field of battle, and night pursuit operations, are new and efficient departures in air tactics on the western front. With the resourcefulness and ability of our personnel, much more will be accomplished.

7. Now is the time to put forward our greatest efforts, each officer entrusted with a unit must actually command it in every sense of the word and by his action and deportment be an example and inspiration to all under him. Prompt and efficient decision is the result of knowledge of what to do when the emergency arises. Officers who know their business will lead you. Get punch into everything you do. Trust your chiefs, support your comrades, and fight the enemy.

Wm. Mitchell,
Brig. Gen'l, A.S., U.S.A.

Organization commanders will see that the above order is published throughout their units.

I now felt that my task of providing the American armies with a good Air Service had been accomplished. It remained for us to assemble a great force of bombardment and pursuit planes with which to attack the interior of Germany. I was sure that if the war lasted, air power would decide it.

33

The Great War Is Over

November 1918

Our air attacks against the German airdromes, supply points and communications had begun to have a decided effect. The German citizens had been complaining to their government and becoming more insistent that they be given protection.

On November 4th, I had published a translation of a captured document on this subject, part of which read as follows:

AIR SERVICE INTELLIGENCE BULLETIN
No. 7

November 4, 1918.

GERMAN TRANSOCEANIC PRESS SERVICE:

Contrary to assertion of German cruelty towards prisoners which even English Government is now making, reference must be made to numerous declarations of prisoners themselves who indeed must know how they are treated. From long series of letters which could be produced, some typical examples may be cited. Stanley Ayte writes to his mother at Merrington, County Purham: "Have no anxiety, I am treated here better than we are by the British. We have plenty to eat, cigars and a good bed,

games and books and we are all very well. We have found out
so far that all Germans are from head to foot gentlemen. When
I was taken prisoner, I begged a German officer for a drink of
water and he gave me a bottle of brandy. Somewhat later we received bread and marmalade and then soup and warm coffee."
War Prisoner MacManar of 2nd Rifle Brigade writes on July
23rd, 1918, to his wife at Dublin: "Our being taken prisoner
was not so bad. I was not seized by terror thanks to friendliness
of German officers and men, who are without doubt fine fellows.
We are now hundreds of miles distant from the battlefield and in
the hands of friendly and polite enemy with whom we ought not
to stand on war footing."

A day or so afterward, I received some very interesting information given by Harold Willis, an American, formerly in the
Lafayette Squadron, who was captured in August and escaped
in October. The information he gave is as follows:

AIR SERVICE INTELLIGENCE BULLETIN
No. 9

November 6, 1918.

1. GENERAL INFORMATION—

INFORMATION FOR CAPTURED ALLIED AVIATORS,
FURNISHED BY SGT. HAROLD WILLIS, LAFAYETTE
ESCADRILLE, CAPTURED AUG. 18th, 1917, ESCAPED
OCTOBER 13th, 1918.

Aviators landing in enemy infantry or artillery lines are generally very roughly handled and their valuables, shoes, belts, and
other articles of clothing are stolen. Several American aviators
report having been shot at after surrendering. Aviators taken by
officers of hostile aviation receive much better treatment and
sometimes are not even searched at this point. An attempt is
made to induce officers to give information by kind treatment.

In the first concentration prison or pen, in the zone of the
Armies, one is nearly always approached by English, French or
Americans in the employ of the German Intelligence. An in-
stance of this is a Frenchman reported by nearly all officers pass-

ing through the prison of Montmedy. This man speaks with a strong accent of Southern France and speaks English brokenly, appears to be 22 years of age, 5 feet 10 inches in height, blue eyes too close together, and a very uncleanly appearance, retroussé nose, pimply complexion. A year ago he was wearing the uniform of a French soldier with the insignia of Under-Lieutenant and called Demela. He lived in a special room by himself and had special privileges. It is suggested that any person not known by other persons in the concentration camp should be suspected. I believe that officers possessing a small file can easily make their way out of the Fortress of Montmedy by filing a barred window of prison, escaping into street of citadel, and sliding into the moat at west of citadel, by means of rope of bed linen, and out of moat by breaks in masonry. The difficulty of this escape will be of course the passing through the enemy's lines, which has been successfully accomplished however.

One is taken from the concentration camp in the Zone of Armies to Germany in a small detachment which is not very carefully guarded for officers are generally too tired to attempt to escape. If one had a small luminous compass and map of the Rhine Valley and West Schwarz Wald region and jumped from the window or door of the train while crossing the floor of the Rhine Valley, one would have an excellent opportunity for success. These compasses should be as thin and as small as possible. Might be worn under the epaulet of coat, in thickness of collar, heel of shoe, etc. One's belt is always stolen sooner or later and for that reason cannot serve as a hiding place. The compass should be removed as soon as possible and placed in the middle of a piece of cheese, bread, soap or carried in the mouth or rectum. If the map does not crinkle when handled it is fairly safe in the lining of clothing. When jumping, one should try to avoid landing on the other railroad track because the steel rails are likely to cause severe injuries. If the officer escaping can swim well, he should make his way down the east side of the floor of the Rhine Valley near the foot of the mountains. Even without compass or map, by keeping the heights of the Schwarz Wald on one's left hand, one can direct himself with precision.

A sudden unexpected act always startles the German soldier to precious seconds of stupor and inaction. Many American aviators have jumped from express trains in motion, but none have ever failed on account of being stopped in the act. The toilet room windows are a favorite port of exit. One may always escape from the camp, located in the city of Rostatt itself. The bars of one of the windows can be removed by hand. One slides down a rope of sheets when the sentinel at that point is around the corner. Although several Americans have gotten clear here, the German authorities have never found the place. The other prisoner officers at this camp will give full information concerning this hole. The wire pens of Rostatt and the hotel and camp of Karlsruhe are practically impregnable. One should note that the hotel of Karlsruhe is lavishly equipped with electric microphones, two of which were found and destroyed by Lieutenant Savage of French aviation during my stay there. Nearly all aviators are taken from Karlsruhe to Landshut and Bavaria. They will be much more closely watched on this trip. The best place to jump would be somewhere between Stuttgart and Ulm. If one can swim well, head for west end of Lake Constance, and swim the Rhine, otherwise cross the Austrian Frontier at a point 12 kilometers from the lake, continue south up the Rhine Valley at foot of mountains and into small semi-neutral state of Liechtenstein near Felskirch and across the Rhine (which one can wade at most times of the year) into Switzerland. Four or five groups of Americans have succeeded in escaping from Landshut though they are very carefully guarded. None have succeeded in reaching the frontier on account of the long distance. American aviators are frequently obliged to travel in stocking feet going to and from Landshut on account of the frequent "dishonorable behavior."

One always finds all Allied officers eager to give all their food and clothing to one who seriously wishes to escape. Once in a permanent camp, one's chances are very much worse because all possible means of getting out of the camp have been tried many times. One is able to always find maps and compasses in any permanent camp if one is seen to be in earnest. The German soldier is always willing to accept a bribe if approached alone although sometimes they have not the nerve to help one much. Nearly all Russian soldiers and officers should be mistrusted. In every case where a proposed attempt to escape has become generally known among the Russians, the German authorities have also found out. One's chances are greatly improved if one can keep secret all preparations for escape as things leak out in a very mysterious way.

In traveling through the country, one should cross through no villages, never employ any kind of a bridge. Avoid main highways, and if using road, walk on side of road so as to hear others coming before they hear you. Start at 10:30 in the evening and commence to look for cover an hour before dawn. In thickly populated regions take a compass course across country. We found 100 grams of biscuit, 62½ grams of sweet chocolate, and 75 grams of sausage per day ample for a week's trip with the cabbages, apples, turnips, carrots, etc., which we stole. The sweet chocolate was the most warming and nourishing food we had. Further than 20 kilometers from the frontier one may direct himself by signs at cross roads. Small evergreen thickets or fields of grain are the best places to lie up in, in the daytime. One may throw off dogs by putting pepper on one's trail. An electric pocket light with its light reduced by means of placing a card with a pin hole between light and lens is very useful.

With the exception of the Holland frontier, none of the frontiers should be dangerous if one goes carefully. Sgt. Buckley, Lieut. Hitchcock, Lieut. Furyeor, Lieut. Isaacs and myself crossed the Swiss frontier through the Austria, Schauffhausen, Waldshutt and Laufenberg regions. None of us found barbed or electric wire or were bothered by dogs. One should try to make within a mile of the frontier the last day to survey the terrain, then do the last stages on hands and knees taking plenty of time, keeping off skylines, locating sentries by the slight movement of their feet which they invariably make or at the moment of the change of guard. Schauffhausen is the most dangerous as it is the only land frontier on the German Swiss border. Waldshutt is also well guarded on account of the presence of an English camp.

For a good swimmer, I should suggest the Rhine between Sackingen and Wallbach or between Klein Laufenberg and Ludengen, at other points the Rhine Bank is generally a high cliff. Lieut. Isaacs and I gained the bank by working down the bed of the brook at Emienstein. One passes under bridges with sentinels on them, but with care one can go noiselessly. The Rhine is 200 meters wide, extremely swift and cold. One is well treated by everyone in Switzerland.

We were able to use two sympathetic inks without detection.

A. Writing of saliva, developed by dashing a film of ink across paper, allowing it to stand a few seconds and then throwing a cup full of water across paper. Paper must not be rubbed during process.

B. Writing with a solution of crystallized shaving alum developed by baking paper to a point of browning. Arrange code words for these with your friends.

On November 7th, I was delighted to receive the Distinguished Service Cross, with the following citation:

> For repeated acts of extraordinary heroism in action at Noyon, France, 26 March, 1918, near the Marne River, France, during July 1918, and in the St. Mihiel salient, France, 12–16 September, 1918.
>
> For displaying bravery far beyond that required by his position as Chief of Air Service, 1st Army, American Expeditionary Forces, setting a personal example to the United States Aviation by piloting his airplane over the battle lines since the entry of the United States into the war. Some instances being a flight in a monoplane over the battle of Noyon on March 26, 1918, and the back areas, seeing and reporting upon the action of both air and ground troops, which led to a change in our aviation's tactical methods. A flight in a monoplane over the bridges which the Germans had laid across the Marne during July, 1918, which led to the first definite reports of the location of these bridges and the subsequent attack upon the German troops by our air forces. Daily reconnaissances over the lines during the battle of St. Mihiel salient, September 12th to 16th, securing valuable information of the enemy troops in the air and on the ground, which led to the excellent combined action by the Allied air services and ground troops particularly in this battle.

On November 10th, a communication of a German aviator gave us valuable information, which is related in the following:

AIR SERVICE INFORMATION BULLETIN
November 10, 1918.

1. *GENERAL INFORMATION*

(1) EXAMINATION OF GERMAN AVIATOR, CAP-
TURED NOVEMBER 10, 1918.

This pilot, together with an observer, Lieutenant Grafonmetch,
belonged to the 46th Bavarian Reconnaissance Flight at Briey
and was flying a 200 H.P. Rumpler Maybach. He states that he
was flying at 7000 meters and side slipped. As he was spinning
down his observer fell out. He pulled the machine up at 3500
meters when artillery fire forced his decision to jump from the
plane with his parachute. The plane landed in a field southwest
of Fontenay, as did the pilot and observer. He states that his
Flight made only deep reconnaissance for the Army "C" Detachment. They have been expecting the signing of the armistice for
some days, and this morning his squadron commander told him
that he did not want anyone to fly but those who wanted to take
a voluntary "joy ride" might do so, as there would be a republic
in Bavaria soon. He knew nothing about the withdrawal of German troops in the sector and set out to fly over the Tour-Nancy
sector to observe circulation. He thinks that there are Austrians
still in Metz. . . .

(2) CROSSING OF THE MEUSE BY AMERICAN
TROOPS

Two men of the 56th Machine Gun Sharpshooter Detachment, captured November 4 on Hill 260, N.E. of Liny, give an
account of the crossing of the Meuse by American troops.

This independent unit came from Lorraine on October 21st as
reinforcement of the 5th Bavarian Reserve Division and was
placed in position E. of the Meuse with orders to prevent passage
of the Meuse in case of an attack.

"Our ten machine guns were in position on the heights overlooking the river, with a view to preventing the Americans'
crossing. On the morning of the 3rd, we had our first glimpse of
them on the heights, opposite us. They came up over the crest
of the hill, first by twos and threes. The regimental commander of
the neighboring 7th Bavarian Reserve Regiment called our attention to them and ordered us to pick them off as they came

over. We could see them very plainly against the horizon. Our company commander, however, had ordered us to shoot only when it was absolutely necessary. We, therefore, did not shoot. We saw them coming over the crest of the hill in close squad formation, despite a heavy artillery fire from our side of the river. This was about 10 o'clock in the morning. Towards 4 o'clock we learned that they had already crossed the river higher up around a bend where we had not seen them. American artillery fire, which covered our hill apparently in search of batteries in a cut behind, had kept our outposts under cover. When we first saw the Americans, they were already across and were opening a path on this side.

The alarm was now given. But only one or two of our machine guns opened fire. That night we lay ready for action and the Americans on their side dug themselves in on the banks of the river. During the night the enemy pushed over many troops and built a bridge over the canal. Some of our guns were turned on this point to hinder their utilizing the bridge.

Our machine gun crews were relieved. About six o'clock a battalion commander of the 7th Bavarian Reserve Regiment ordered our guns to begin firing from the heights further up the river, in order to bring the entire bridge under our fire. On those instructions, some of our guns began firing. Our resistance, however, was relatively weak. The Americans had rapidly pushed on our flanks and cut us off from the rear. Only two of our gun crews with their guns managed to escape. The remainder were taken prisoners.

The commander of the 2nd Company declared that he could have inflicted heavy punishment on the Americans prior to and during their crossing the river had he not felt that this would have been needless bloodshed and would have served no particular purpose. It was evident from your rapid advance that we would have been cut off from one side or the other."

Information Section
Air Service, First Army.

Winter was now facing us, but with its coming we heard that the Germans were weakening and that the interior of Germany was becoming more and more a prey to the revolutionary movement.

As the time for the armistice approached and we finally realized that the war was ending, the nervous tension to which all had been subjected began to let up. Certain German pilots, who were known individually by the markings on their planes and who in turn recognized our men who had many victories to their credit, went out for one last fight. Very much as the knights used to do in days gone by, they challenged the opposing aviators to individual combat by flying around the hostile airdromes. I believe that the last German shot down by an American aviator was the one over which Major Maxwell Kirby gained a victory on the morning of the 11th of November.

No people knew better than those in the Air Service what a continuation of the war meant. We had all preparations complete to carry the war into the heart of Germany in the spring of 1919. The air weapons that would have been used would have caused untold sufferings. Chemical weapons most certainly would have been brought into play; gases for destroying cattle and sheep, and incendiary projectiles for burning the crops and forests.

Jokes of all sorts were played on different men in different organizations. A humorous summary of intelligence was published by the Second Section of the General Staff of the First Army, which was an excellent take-off on the daily summary of intelligence which had been put out for study during our whole participation in the war. It read as follows:

CONFIDENTIAL & SECRET   Hindquarters, 1st Army, Aef
For *Distribution by aeroplane*   Second Section, General Stuff

BULL No. 50.   November 10, 1918.

SUMMARY OF UNINTELLIGENCE
PART 1.

I. *GENERAL DEPRESSIONS OF THE DAY*

The enemy reacted violently all over the sector. Strong attacks west of the Meuse were thrown back easily by us. Small local attacks by our troops succeeded in driving the enemy from his positions. During the afternoon, violent counterattacks appear to have caused us to readjust our lines slightly to a depth of ten kilometers.

The day was quiet. Otherwise, there was nothing to report.

The enemy appears to place his main reliance on machine guns, infantry, artillery and aeroplanes to resist our attack. This is taken as an indication of something very significant, namely, the tremendous shortage among the enemy of all other branches. Otherwise there is nothing to report.

Two men were seen entering a ravine near (CHRILELY?). This confirms prisoners' statements of a general withdrawal to the Drideg-Stellung.

On the right, the enemy are extremely nervous. They showed their nervousness by raiding our trenches and throwing hand grenades at us.

II. ENEMY FRONT LINE

The enemy line follows ours in a general way, except in one or two places where it runs south of it. East of the MEUSE, it runs in an easterly direction to the left (inclusive). W. of the MEUSE, it runs in the opposite direction (exclusive). Thence it runs in a N.E. direction (inclusive) turning due N. for 200 M. Thence due S. for 200 M. From here on, there is no change. This has not been confirmed. . . .

XI. OUR AERIAL ACTIVITY

The dampness made the day impossible for flying. In spite of this, our planes were up in great numbers destroying numerous enemy planes and taking dozens of photographs in spite of the dense fog which rendered visibility impossible.

Our scout patrol of three planes met 20 Fokkers. The Fokkers immediately burst into flames and crashed.

The ceiling was so low that at times our planes were forced to run along the ground. In spite of this, we penetrated deeply into the enemy's territory bringing back invaluable information as to the location of towns, rivers and roads behind his lines.

Lt. Cholmondelay Brown destroyed three enemy balloons in their beds by descending upon them so suddenly that they became tangled in the bed clothes and were unable to escape.

Lt. Dunwiddy brought down a balloon at dawn. Owing to the darkness, Lt. Dunwiddy brought down one of our own balloons. Luckily it was an old one. The observer jumped but was not seen to land. Confirmation is requested.

XII. *ORDER OF BATTLE CONFIRMED*

Note. Be sure to get our next number "The War Number."

HEADQUARTERS PREMIERE ARMEE
OFFICE OF G-WHIZ

Europe, 11 November, 1918.

From 11 H. Nov. 11, 1918 to 11:11 H. Nov. 11, 1918.

1. HOSTILE SITUATION AT BEGINNING OF THE DAY:

Artillery and infantry belonging to the enemy are running very rapidly across the German border, pursued by Yanks and British tanks, who joined the rush of dashing Franks. Huns ran in great disorder.

2. INFORMATION RECEIVED OF ENEMY DURING THE DAY:

Interrogated prisoners say they might come back another day and start again their little fray, because they weren't frightened. But information late tonight (not from G-2, for this is right), shows that although they say they might, we know damn well they mightn't.

3. HOSTILE MOVEMENTS, CHANGES AND CONDUCT DURING THE DAY:

Boche infantry across the Meuse, artillerymen, machine gun crews got so mixed up they could not choose to tarry any longer. They couldn't see relief ahead, for if they stayed they'd all be dead, and so they went straight home to bed, where they knew they'd be stronger.

4. MAPS ILLUSTRATING ABOVE:

Look it up. . . .

On November 10th at 8:45 P.M. we received the following information as to the conditions of the Armistice.

CONDITIONS OF ARMISTICE

1. Armistice to be effective six (6) hours after signature.

2. Immediate evacuation of Belgium, France, and Alsace-Lorraine, with a delay of fourteen (14) days. The troops which remain after this period will be interned.

3. 5000 cannons of large caliber, 30,000 machine guns, 3000 minenwerfers, 2000 airplanes to be turned over to the Allies.

4. Evacuation of the left bank of the RHINE.

5. KOBLENZ, COLOGNE AND MAINZ occupied with a radius of 30 kilometers. The constitution of a neutral zone on the right bank of the RHINE. Depth of 20 to 30 kilometers. The evacuation in 11 days.

6. No material to be removed from the left bank of the RHINE. All factories, railroads, etc. to remain intact.

7. 5000 locomotives, 150,000 cars, 10,000 motor trucks, to be handed over to the Allies.

8. Germany to maintain the army of occupation.

9. In the Orient, all troops will be withdrawn behind the line as of August 1, 1914. No time limit stated.

10. Renunciation of the treaties of Brest-Litovsk and Bucharest.

11. Unconditional capitulation in East Africa.

12. Restoration of sums of money taken from the banks of Belgium, and of the gold taken from ROUMANIA and RUSSIA.

13. Return of all prisoners of war without reciprocity.

14. Handing over of 100 submarines, 8 light cruisers, 6 dreadnoughts. All other battleships to be dismantled and guarded by the Allies in neutral or allied ports.

15. Free Passage across CATEGAT. All mines to be removed. Occupation of all ports and batteries which could hinder free passage.

16. The blockade to continue. German ships can still be seized.

17. All limitations on navigation concerning neutrals by Germany are annulled.

18. The armistice will last thirty (30) days.

DISTRIBUTION: Chief of Staff, General Conner, Hq. Air Service Army Group, G-2 (2 copies), Map Room, Reports Section.

When an order of this kind comes to a fighting army, it is received with mingled feelings. Some think the campaign ought to be pushed to the limit and a complete victory obtained. Others think the loss of lives should be stopped as soon as possible, providing sufficient advantages are gained to insure that the desires of the victorious country shall be met.

During a war of this kind, one's nerves, passions and whole physical and mental make-up are tremendously overwrought and one's outlook is somewhat different than it would be ordinarily. During the last six months of the war, I doubt if I actually slept more than three hours a day. This was because the reports of the day's activities along our front did not reach my headquarters until about ten o'clock at night. They would then be arranged by the appropriate staff sections and I would begin their complete perusal somewhere around midnight. I would then dictate the orders for the following day and carefully check their proper sending to every unit. It would be two o'clock by that time and I would be up at five so as to watch the action of our forces that took the air before daylight.

When the order came to cease hostilities I realized that I was pretty tired and that everyone around me felt very much the same way. I was glad to see the terrific loss of life being stopped. With our green and untrained troops we were losing a great many more men than were our Allies.

On the evening of November 10th, I went to Toul, where I found the Staff of the Second Army preparing an attack for the following day. This, it seemed to me, was a rather foolish proceeding as it would lead to no benefit to us and would kill a great many men because the Germans would certainly resist them. The Division to be used was the 92nd, composed of colored troops who had had very little experience on the front. This attack was actually carried out the following morning with disastrous results.

As I went back to my headquarters late at night I could see ammunition dumps exploding on the German side, rockets being fired in the air and rejoicing going on wherever it was possible on the French side. Some could hardly understand that peace was at hand. A few of the peasants I talked to were very skeptical; the poor things had been at it for over four years and their minds had become so fixed with the idea of war that it would take some time to unfix them.

The morning of November 11th, I visited the commanding officers of the Air Service of both armies that were under me and congratulated them on the great work they had done. This was the first time in the world's history that great bodies of air troops had been brought together and fought as a single organization. We Americans had developed the best system of air fighting that the world had ever seen. We had entered into full combat with the splendid air troops that the Germans had trained for over three years of war before we joined. We not only held our own but greatly excelled in it. We could look with absolute confidence to the future if our system were maintained and our men who were trained in actual combat were given charge of the development to make America absolutely safe from hostile invasion.

The day has passed when armies on the ground or navies on the sea can be the arbiters of a nation's destiny in war. The main power of defense and the power of initiative against an enemy has passed to the air.

My reports on the morning of November 11, 1918, showed that we had present on the front, in the hands of American units, 740 airplanes. Of these, 528 were of French manufacture, 16 were of British manufacture and 196 were of American manufacture. One year and eight months after entering the war, the United States had only been able to put 196 airplanes on the front. We did practically all our fighting with foreign machines, the airplanes manufactured in America being inferior. There was no excuse for this.

My figure showed that from the time American air units entered into combat (March 1918) to the 11th of November, 1918, our men shot down and received official confirmation for 927 enemy airplanes or balloons, and during the same time we lost, due to operations of the enemy, 316 of our airplanes or balloons. This ratio of three to one was remarkable and much greater in proportion than the victories achieved by any of our Allies. The reason for it was that we had remarkable pilots and our tactics and strategy were superior to any employed elsewhere.

Everyone was rejoicing. After giving the necessary instructions to have every organization write up its war experiences, I decided to take a trip into Paris to see what was going on in the French capital. I took my largest automobile and gathered up some of my friends, who had been so kind to us during the war, and proceeded to the capital. Everyone who could was trying to get to Paris, and the roads were choked with automobiles.

We reached there quite late in the evening and found the Champs-Élysées in a great uproar. Men and women were pulling the captured German cannons, which had lined the street, up and down the pavements. Girls, dressed in soldiers caps and blouses, were going through the drill around the guns that the artillerymen were taught on the front. Everyone was singing, shaking hands, kissing each other, dancing, screaming and yelling—the most spectacular outburst of feeling that I have ever seen.

The people had been almost sure that they would be defeated in some way or other before the war was over and now they had actually obtained victory! How great it was, no one could tell; but they were victorious and their joy knew no bounds. They were very open in what they said about the Americans that night. Everywhere that an American soldier was seen he was hailed as a hero and a deliverer. And it was funny how quickly a French soldier could tell whether he had been serving on the front or in the interior.

We got a little supper, then started down in my automobile to the boulevards. Everywhere people were jumping on the running boards and embracing the chauffeur and mechanic who were driving the car. The streets surged with the populace and none but military cars were allowed to proceed. When we arrived, it was nearly midnight and a never-to-be-forgotten sight presented itself. People in all sorts of costumes, singing, shouting, yelling, crying, some of them fighting, and acting all sorts of ways, were there. A cordon of police closed the boulevards to all vehicles; but as a gendarme was telling my chauffeur that the street was closed, we were recognized by a crowd of pilots of the French Air Division, who had served under me at the attack of St. Mihiel and in the Argonne. They screamed, "Vive notre General Americaine!" and throwing the gendarme to one side, they almost picked up the automobile and carried it right down the boulevards.

I counted eighteen of them sitting on the roof, on the radiator, on the mud guards and all over the back. Men and women formed a ring, hand in hand around the car, singing the "Marseillaise" and "Madelon" and some of the aviators' songs, and carried us literally from one end of the boulevards to the other. Ours was the only automobile, I believe, that was on the boulevards that night.

The following day I worked in the Paris office and saw General McAndrew, our Chief of Staff, also Harbord and Dunwoody. On November 14th I went to Chaumont and had a good talk with General Pershing. He told me he wanted me to take the Air Service up to the Rhine with the 3rd American Army, which was being organized to occupy the territory up there in accordance with the treaty.

Only the oldest units in the Air Service were to go. They were to be filled up to their full strength with pilots, mechanics and men. Likewise the ground troops were to have the oldest and best organizations; General J. T. Dickman was to command the army. He had distinguished himself in all the fighting. He was of German extraction and spoke German with great fluency. It seemed strange how many Germans we had who distinguished themselves in our service, and what efficient officers and patriotic Americans they were. Of course it was not really strange, because we are made up of the nations of northern Europe, and all of the countries in northern Europe contain a great Germanic element, even the French.

On the 14th, an order was issued placing me in command of the air troops to go to the Rhine. All the other troops were given a schedule of training which would keep them busy until they could be sent back to the United States. We began to liquidate all our establishments and to turn in, store or sell all our property, keeping, of course, a sufficient amount ready in case there was any interference with the Armistice.

On November 17th, I went with our leading troops to Longuyon, which had formerly been on the German side. The enemy began to withdraw from our front immediately, leaving a great deal of artillery and many other things along the roads. The country however looked very well policed and very clean. General von Gallwitz, in command of the group of German armies on our front, was given only a week to withdraw his forces to the Rhine, a difficult thing to do under the conditions, because the whole organization of German territory had broken down behind him.

We gradually moved up to what had been the Zone of Armies. As we went north, we heard more and more of the effects of our airplane bombardment, particularly at Longuyon and Longwy. At Longuyon, there was great evidence of our aerial bombardment around the station and the round house, which had been hit squarely by a bomb thrown by a pilot in our 1st Bombardment Group.

I heard from the French Air Division that Metz was to be occupied on November 19th, and that General Pétain would review the troops when they entered. Colonel De Vaulgrenant and I decided to go. Also, I had one of my aides take some of our

French friends who were so anxious to be there and who had looked after our men well during the war. I arrived there rather early in the morning. The Germans had only recently fallen back and the French occupied a few advanced positions. The municipal authorities were in charge and kept pretty good order, although there had been some rioting, pulling down statues and other demonstrations.

I inquired whether any American prisoners who were wounded were in the city and soon met some of our men who showed me where the hospital was, so I went up there. There were about four hundred very seriously wounded men in the hospital. There were no anaesthetics, no morphine, no linen bandages—only paper—left in the hospital. The German Hospital Corps' men and nurses had left and turned over the care of these wounded to some Sisters of Mercy, who knew nothing whatever about taking care of wounded and who probably had never seen a man before. They were scared to death; about all they could do was to give the men a little food and water. In one dark room there was a First Lieutenant, shot through the abdomen; he was in terrible pain. He explained to me that while the Germans were there, they had looked after them well, but since there was no morphine nor any anaesthetics to alleviate his suffering, it was more than he could stand. This was the case with others and if these men had wanted to commit suicide, the Sisters could not have stopped them.

It was something that needed attention at once. As I left the hospital, thinking I would have to send clear back to our lines for assistance, I saw a French ambulance coming up the road. An ambulance in the French service is really a field hospital, not what we call an ambulance, which is merely a vehicle for transportation of the wounded. The French ambulance had all its doctors, nurses and equipment with it. I went up to the head of the column and was astonished to see sitting in the front ambulance a woman whom I recognized as Countess Benoit d'Azy. I had known her for many years, as her husband had formerly been a French naval attaché in Washington before the war. She was in charge of the nurses and ambulance. I explained to her what I wanted and what the conditions were, and without a word she turned the head of the ambulance around and proceeded to the hospital.

I returned a couple of hours later to see what was going on. Of course in a place like that the stench was terrible, one could smell the hospital for two blocks. These women, under Countess d'Azy, pitched right into the place. When I went into the wards, they were there working with their sleeves rolled up and covered with blood, but the place was cleaned out, the beds made, every man given anaesthetics and proper food, and everyone was smiling.

It is remarkable what these French women do; of course they have followed their men to war from time immemorial. I had never seen the Countess before except in a ballroom or at some social function. Here she was, a big strong woman, nearly six feet tall, with her hair cropped short, capable of doing as much work as any two or three people. She told me that as soon as they fixed up this hospital, they had to work all that night and the next day on two or three others. She wanted some sugar, as that was the only thing short, and I obtained a considerable supply for her. The Germans had always had a lot of beet sugar available during the war, even when the Allies were short of it.

The time now came for the grand entrance of the troops into Metz. The population was cowed but not at all cordial, being very pro-German. They had been prosperous under the Germans and thought that under the French the balance of trade would not come their way as it had in the past.

Just before the leading troops were to start on their march past, General Pétain took his place opposite the principal square with his staff around him. He wore a long gray coat without decorations and was mounted on a white horse of distinctly Arabian characteristics. His flags were carried by officers on each side of him. It was an absolute and perfect copy of Napoleon and his staff at the Battle of Marengo. The long gray coat without decorations was there and even the horse on which Pétain was mounted was almost a counterpart of the Arab charger that

Napoleon rode at that time. It seemed strange to me that a man of Pétain's strong characteristics and personality would copy anyone else, even as great a man as Napoleon, but the Bonaparte is so deeply imbedded in every French soldier's make-up that he is like the Divinity Himself.

Just before the column passed, General Charles Mangin fell off his horse on his head and nearly killed himself. This was taken as a very bad omen. Countess DeFenelon and my aide, Captain Shawhan, with two or three others, took him to the hospital and looked after him. Shortly after this, one of Colonel De Vaulgrenant's pilots who was demonstrating over Metz, flew down so low that he hit a telephone wire over the square just behind where we were standing, crashed into the middle of the square, killing several people and wounding others. This was also a bad omen for the entrance.

At last the great review was finished and Metz passed into French hands. We had dinner at the principal restaurant, which was run by a German family, and were served with excellent food. I think the upper classes in Germany always had enough to eat but they were very short of lard and fats of various kinds, and of course rubber, which they had not had for a long time. Children four or five years old were astonished at our rubber automobile tires, as they could not remember having seen any. They would come out and feel the tires and crawl all over the automobiles. One day when a lot of little German boys were climbing over the back of a newly painted automobile, I asked my chauffeur why he did not keep them off. He said it was almost impossible; he had tried to keep them off for a couple of hours but they acted like the boys did in the United States, and were not as obedient and quiet as French boys were. The people did not look unwell, but the children had very little milk.

I have never seen better behaved men than ours were in their march toward the Rhine. There was little straggling, no marauding and no robbing. The men had practically the spirit of Crusaders and everywhere made an excellent impression on the populace.

For the next few days I visited the German airdromes and

Richthofen's old group, whose ships had their noses painted red. When the pilots had left these airdromes, they had started the airplane engines and then turned the airplanes loose on the ground. They had run into anything that stood in their way and wrecked themselves. Not a single airplane on a pursuit airdrome was in condition to be used. The bombardment airdromes contained large twin-engine Gothas, only twelve of which could be used, although the wrecks of many others were about. Those that were serviceable had the magnetos removed from the engines, so we could not use them. All the airdromes showed the effect of our bombardment. The Germans told us they never felt safe whenever they lighted up at night for landing their planes, for fear we would immediately shoot up their airdrome. I was glad to get these proofs of what our efforts had amounted to.

On another airdrome there were about a dozen Junkers—all-metal armored planes—which had just come up to the front. The pilot's and observer's places and the engine parts were covered by armor, which would protect them from the fire of small arms. They intended to attack the reserves on the road with these. We had heard of these ships and I was ready for them, having worked out the tactics we should use against them when they came. We were going to attack them with our pursuit aviation with .45-caliber machine guns; also, I had some airplanes coming up with 37-mm. cannon. These Junkers were rather heavy and unwieldy and I think we would have shot them down quickly. However, the idea of having an armored plane to attack troops on the ground was a pretty good one.

On November 24th, I took Colonel Harold Fowler and started for Strasbourg, by way of Toul and Lunéville. In addition to our large closed Winton, I had an open Cadillac follow us, full of gasoline and oil, as I was afraid we might not be able to get any gasoline after we left the area of the American armies. On every road there were Frenchmen trying to get to Strasbourg or die in the attempt, and everywhere were broken-down cars, cars without gasoline, cars without tires, and cars that had fallen to pieces.

As we crossed the hill at Saverne, sleet began to fall and soon the roads were covered with ice. Fortunately we had chains for our cars but those who had none could make no progress and slid off the road from one side to the other, and all the way down some of the hills. We came to one automobile which had hit a tree and been quite demolished. Hearing a familiar call from one of the occupants, I looked over and found the car was full of French flying officers from the Air Division, nine of them in fact. I took a couple in our car and had the rest of them get in the Cadillac that was following.

As we entered Strasbourg, we were greeted with enthusiasm everywhere; it was quite different from the entry into Metz. The people were genuinely glad to see the soldiers enter, I think. The women were wearing their national costume, with great ribbons protruding on each side of the head. They were all smiling, and with their bright blue eyes, light hair and gay colors, were in marked contrast to what we had seen in the last year and a half in France.

The French troops who were to make the entry into Strasbourg came from the Fourth Army that had fought so hard in the Champagne, under the great General Gouraud. Again, Marshal Pétain, commanding the French armies, reviewed the entry. This time he was not mounted on a white horse à la Napoleon, but stood on the front steps of the City Hall with his staff, while those of us who were invited took our places alongside. Presently General Gouraud arrived in an automobile and dismounted directly in front of Marshal Pétain and saluted with his one arm. Pétain walked forward to meet him amidst tremendous enthusiasm by the people.

Just at this time I heard that some of my pilots who had been shot down and taken prisoners wanted to see me and I told them to come right up and watch the review. They were in pretty good shape, although some of them were wounded. We helped them out as best we could.

I went into a bookstore to purchase some publications and gave the proprietor a twenty-franc note in payment. The old gentleman went to a section of the wall behind the counter, scraped off some plaster, pulled out a brick, put his hand in the hole and gave me change in French money of Napoleon the Third's time. He had put it in there when Alsace was taken by the Germans, vowing to keep it there until the country was recaptured by the French. He had lived to see this and was delighted that I was the first one to present a French note in payment for goods at his store. He gave me a very interesting description of the German occupation. We talked for nearly an hour.

Many Alsatian soldiers were returning to the town in their German uniforms as Alsace had been subject to conscription along with the rest of Germany. They celebrated along with everybody else, mingling with the people in the streets.

In the evening, we had dinner at the principal restaurant which before had been known as the Kaiser's Restaurant. That sign was now painted out and a new one hung in its place which read "Café de la République." We had a great dinner, and the band played any tune we desired. Generals, Lieutenants, Alsatians and everybody mingled together without restraint. In our party was a French doctor who had been with the French Air Division; he had a long black beard and a remarkably deep bass voice. Whenever there was a lull in the proceedings, we would call on him to sing, and he would get up in his chair and make the whole place resound with his extremely laughable songs about the war. After dinner, there was a street fête in which everybody took part, officers of all ranks of the French service being in the crowd. This delighted the Alsatians but puzzled them as well, as the Germans, especially the officers of high rank, had been very severe and stood aloof from the people. With all the festivities, there was practically no disorder and I observed very little drunkenness, although liquor of all kinds could be procured anywhere.

The following day, after looking around the old and new towns, I started back to Longuyon by way of Metz, but found there that I could not go straight through as no roads had been opened up through no-man's land except by way of Nancy. So down to Nancy we went, and stopped at the Y.M.C.A. Hotel, the large hotel of the city which had been taken over by the Y.M.C.A. and was being run by an old friend of mine, Mrs. Jeannette Dixon from Milwaukee, Wisconsin. The next day we went on to Longuyon.

Our 94th Squadron was then occupying the former German bombardment airdrome just outside Longuyon, and Rickenbacker, Douglas Campbell, Meissner and several others had come up on a rubbernecking expedition, called a tour of observation. I do not think they had any passes, but I was glad they were able to get the Cadillac and get away with it. We had a wonderful dinner with all the officers, in the old German barracks. Around the walls were painted absurd scenes of the Germans bombing the French cities, and the British, French and American aviation opposite them. Major Kirby was present and was made to tell of how he had shot down the last German, and each one made a speech, sang a song or did his bit to entertain the rest.

As I left, I thought that this was practically the last of our pursuit aviation, and that, as we had no real air force such as other nations possessed, it would soon fade into oblivion, and probably never be resuscitated until the time came for another war. Then we would start out again by making terrible mistakes and perhaps be defeated before we began. This will certainly be the case if the Air Service is left under the army and not made entirely independent of it.

34

We Move into Germany

December 1918

On December 5th, taking Colonel Paegelow with me, I went to
Treves and looked over the airdrome. There was a large Zeppelin hangar at this place and in it the Germans had left one
hundred and twenty-one airplanes of all kinds. The German air
officers were still there in command and I arranged with them
about sending our own officers up to take over the equipment.
Colonel Paegelow spoke German. I was driving my own machine, a German Mercedes racing car, and had the chauffeur in
a little rumble seat behind. The German officers were very interested in this arrangement and asked if all the American generals drove their own cars. Paegelow told them that they did not,
but as we only had one general in the Air Service, he had to get
around very fast from place to place and, therefore, drove himself in order to do so.

From Treves I went to Koblenz. The last German troops
had left. The crossing of the Rhine by these veterans was a
serious occasion. They formed in the streets of Koblenz with
banners flying, arms burnished, and the muzzles of their rifles
and mouths of their cannon decorated with flowers by the populace. They marched across the Rhine to the strains of their great

national hymn "Die Wacht am Rhein" while the people wept.

This marked an epoch in the development of the German people. Not for over a century has a hostile foot touched the soil of Germany north of the Rhine. During that time the German people have grown from a lot of little kingdoms and principalities into one of the mightiest nations that the world has ever seen.

One cannot help but think that Germany threw up the sponge rather quickly during this war, compared to what she had done in the past. During the Thirty Years' War, her people were reduced to nothing, they ate rats and anything they could get. During the last thirty or forty years, the Germans have grown fat, rich, opulent and pleasure-loving, and it looks as though their moral fiber has been impaired to some extent by luxury and ease. The war had not yet been brought home to the masses of the German people except, to a small extent, through the air. Of course they knew it was coming but they hesitated to carry the war to a finish. Our President's Fourteen Points may have had a good deal to do with the way the German people acted. I think they had a great deal to do with the Kaiser fleeing from Germany, because he believed that if he stayed there, good terms in the Treaty of Peace could not possibly be obtained.

My old friend, Colonel Jim Rhea, was at Koblenz as the head of our Bridge Head Commission, and would take over the bridges from the Germans. On the German side, Major von Sigel is in charge. He formerly commanded the Hanover Military Riding School and I had known him before in that capacity. Recently he was Chief of Staff of the 76th German Reserve Division. He had with him his assistant, Lieutenant Schultze of the 76th. Schultze was for many years a resident of Seattle, Washington, but being a reserve officer, when Germany entered the war he immediately went home to serve with the colors. Schultze was the information officer of this division when they were opposite the 77th New York Division, when Whittlesey's battalion was lost. It was under Schultze's direction that the Germans put out the panels on the ground that were mistaken by our aviators for those of the lost battalion, where we dropped so much food, chocolate and cigarettes, which the Germans took and converted to their own uses. Schultze told me how he had captured the runners sent out by Whittlesey and had them examined. Our infantry men had acted in a splendid manner, he said, particularly one great big sergeant whom he had observed making his way by creeping along a creek bank. They knew he would have to cross it at its narrowest place to get over to the American lines, and Schultze put two or three men there to catch him when he slid down the bank. They overpowered him and took him to the rear, gave him a meal and then Schultze questioned him. The man stood squarely at attention, looked at Schultze and said, "You are attempting to extract information from me about my own troops; you may kill me or do anything else to me, but I will not say a word." And he never did. I do not remember the man's name.

Both these officers expressed themselves as being very highly impressed with the character of our American troops, not their fighting ability particularly, on account of their inexperience. They knew, however, when their attack at Château-Thierry was unsuccessful, that the whole power of ending the war lay in the hands of the Americans. Up to that time they had been sure that they would win the war, but the coming of our countless thousands of men and the ever increasing number of aircraft and artillery on the front, made them certain that unless the great losses suffered by our armies would cause us to pull our troops out of Europe, that the Germans were surely gone.

These officers thought that the war had been brought on by England. Had there been no war, they said, the extension of German commerce and their merchant marine would have driven England off the face of the earth as a commercial nation within twenty years. In order to hold her own, therefore, England had to fight or become a second-class power.

General Pershing had established advanced headquarters of the A.E.F. at Treves. This was done in case anything happened in Germany.

One would think that a commander of a victorious army such

as this would naturally be the candidate of one party or the other for the Presidency. I doubt, however, if General Pershing ever is. He has never been very close to the men; that is, he has never endeared himself to the private soldier in a way that would bring about a great public demand for a high political office. I do not know that he wants one. The Commander of the American Expeditionary Force is as high a position as any individual should ever desire.

The average man who has participated in the war thinks of the professional regular army man, particularly a graduate of West Point, as being a "hard-boiled," heartless and relentless disciplinarian and practically nothing else. There is a good deal to this, because the average regular army officer knows very little about the psychology of the masses, how the great body of his fellow men think and feel. He has been brought up in a more or less narrow machine-like atmosphere, which does not lead to the confidence of a great citizen army.

General Pershing had established advanced headquarters of the A.E.F. at Treves. This was done in case anything happened in Germany which required the presence of the Commanding General, and also as a means of having a representative of General Headquarters in that area to look after the line of communications of the Third American Army on the Rhine.

My office in Koblenz was in one of the municipal buildings, and its windows looked out over the Rhine toward the castle of Ehrenbreitstein on the other side. Opposite my desk was a bust of Julius Caesar. It was only a little way below here, near Weissenturm, that he crossed the Rhine, and I spent many hours translating his account of how he placed the bridge and whipped the Germans. I selected a place for an airdrome near the spot where he crossed. Koblenz is a nice city, there are good shops and a very good gun store here. The Germans are excellent gun- and rifle-makers and I ordered a couple of guns.

My staff were all busy writing up their views of various phases of aeronautical activities and I was giving them every opportunity to enjoy themselves and relax from their strenuous labors. We visited the armies adjoining us, from time to time.

We also carefully worked out our plans of operation, in case of a resumption of hostilities. No matter what happens, the Germans cannot possibly have an air service, as we have taken all of their airplanes. The treaty provides that their new airplanes be delivered to the French, English and ourselves, and I was accepting several hundred of them at Koblenz. We required certain ones in each lot to be flown by the German pilots representing their Air Service, who came down to Koblenz. Among them was Sergeant Donhauser, who is said to be credited with shooting down Lieutenant Quentin Roosevelt during the Château-Thierry operations. He was a little bit of a fellow, and had to be lifted into his ship by the mechanics. He was an excellent pilot, though. While trying out one of the airplanes, he flattened out too soon, hit a hangar and had a very bad crash. We sent him to the hospital and I told Paegelow to look after him.

The German airplanes were in very good condition. The Fokkers impressed us all greatly. They could be shipped on the train with their wings off, which were laid back against the sides of the fuselage. The gas tank remained full of fuel, and the engine was ready to start. They could be wheeled off the flat cars, the wings put on in about fifteen minutes, the engine cranked up and then they were ready for combat. Even their ammunition belts were full of ammunition. There was no airplane on the Allied side which could be handled in this way. The Fokkers had fuselages of steel tubing, called gas pipes by our men, which anybody could fix, even an ordinary plumber. There was nothing at all complicated about these splendid planes.

Everybody was preparing for Christmas, which of course is a great day in Germany; in fact, we get most of our Christmas customs from the Teutonic people. We had a little Christmas tree in my quarters and asked many of our friends in to partake of cheer of various kinds. Captain Miller had seen to it that everything the country produced was provided.

The two Red Cross workers assigned to the Air Service, Mrs. Schenck of Baltimore and Miss Watrous of New York, had brought up turkeys from Paris for our men. As turkeys were so scarce, they had to guard them carefully night and day. Due to their efforts, our men were among the few who had turkey on Christmas Day. We had a fine one at my quarters. Elmer Hazlett, who had been shot down in enemy territory near the Argonne and taken prisoner, had now rejoined us. He came in as thin as a hungry wolf. He had tried to escape three times, and the last time, when he was climbing under the wire fence, the German sentinel saw him and called on him to halt. When he refused to do so and tried to wriggle through the fence quickly, he stuck him with his bayonet where Hazlett sits down. He could not sit down for a while after that. Now when anybody asks Hazlett where he was wounded, he hesitates to tell them. I told him I would appoint him my aide at some future day. I heard that Alan Winslow had come back; we thought he was killed at Château-Thierry. I shall appoint him as my other aide. Winslow is minus a left arm, which had to be amputated due to the wound he received when he was shot down at Château-Thierry on July 31st.

Christmas week of 1918 was a happy one with us on the Rhine. The troops were all well quartered, well supplied and given every privilege possible commensurate with good discipline. It must be said that the discipline of the American troops cannot be surpassed. There was a great deal of fraternizing with the Germans—many of our men speak German. There were a good many orders published that our men should not associate with the Germans, but this did little good. As a matter of fact, these orders were only intended to apply where too flagrant violations occurred. The English fraternized with the Germans even more than we did.

January 1919

Shortly after the New Year, General Dickman told me that the Prince of Wales had been invited to visit our army on the Rhine and he wanted me to have him as my guest during his stay. I was rather reluctant to do this, as it is a good deal of a responsibility having the heir of any throne on one's hands—particularly that of such a powerful country as Great Britain. I told the General how I felt about it, but he insisted that I have the Prince, so I acquiesced. We did not know who the Prince would bring with him but I made elastic arrangements so that no matter how many came, they would be looked after. I also provided for the necessary guards because there is always the possibility that zealots or fanatics may take a shot or throw a bomb at a personage of this importance.

A couple of days later, the Prince arrived, driving his own car, a Rolls Royce, accompanied by one aide, Claude Hamilton, and a sergeant as orderly. Both the Prince and his aide were dressed in the uniform of an infantry Captain. I put the Prince in the suite opposite mine on the second floor of the little house and gave Claude Hamilton the suite on the ground floor.

It took only a few minutes of conversation for us all to be delighted with the personality of the Prince. He seemed just a nice big overgrown boy with all the instincts of a healthy young fellow. He was interested in everything, particularly the Air Service, and was exceptionally well versed in the history of this locality and what had been going on. During the latter part of the campaign in France, he was sent to Italy and he felt very badly about it. He is the most democratic young man belonging to the crown families of Europe that I have ever met.

We had several entertainments for him and he enjoyed dancing very much. It was Miss Watrous of the Red Cross who really taught him the modern steps.

Of course, many members of the German nobility were relations of his, whom he had known or visited in times past. Many of their photographs were around the walls of my house, and it was interesting to listen to the Prince's comments on the various ones and what he thought of them.

On the second day of his visit, the Prince asked me if I would take him in the air with me. I asked his aide, Claude Hamilton, what he thought about it. "Well," he said, "I have nothing to say as the prince is running the trip and it would not do any good for me to offer an opinion," so I told the Prince I would take him. I made the necessary arrangements at the airdrome, and we took the air in my two-seater Spad. He was very much at home in the back seat, read the map correctly and made comments about everything we saw and everywhere we went.

After taking off from the top of the hill back of Koblenz, I laid a course up the Valley of the Moselle. It was a lovely day in early January with the sun shining through holes in the clouds; the clouds were well up over ten thousand feet, at which altitude I flew. The vineyards on the terraced side of the precipitous hills of the Moselle Valley sparkled in the light, while the old cities with castles on the hills looking down at them formed the framework of the picture. The Prince knew the history of nearly all of them and told me about them while we flew. After going as far as Cochem, I turned to the left and laid a course for the Lorelei on the Rhine. This sharp cliff jutting into the river forms the legendary abode of a beautiful maiden who lured the boats of the Rhine to destruction at her feet. We approached the great river, passing over the Drachenfels, and could see the great statue of Germania on our right, overlooking the valley of the Rhine near Mainz. As we crossed, the sun shone directly on the Lorelei rock, turning its sides, covered with mosses and lichens, into an iridescent green. The Prince leaned over, tapped me on the back and said, "I think I can see her!"

We proceeded around our bridgehead, which is a semicircle about twenty miles away from Koblenz, and came back gradually by way of the town of Neuwied. This is the abode of the princes of Wied, one of whom was made King of Albania, but he did not stay there long as the people did not seem to like him particularly. The old Princess of Wied lives there in her castle, in a part of which some of our troops are quartered. She frequently walks around in her garden with a large white bulldog, her constant attendant. When we flew over Neuwied, there she was in her garden with the big white dog. I wondered if she knew that the Prince of Wales was flying over and saw her at that time.

From Neuwied we went up the Rhine until we came into full view of the mouth of the Moselle River, with the great statue of old Kaiser Wilhelm at the point. Above the statue, on the right bank of the Moselle, we could see very distinctly the old Roman buildings that still remain as markers of their centuries of occupation. With one turn over the city of Koblenz, I landed on the airdrome after one of the most enjoyable air trips I have ever taken.

The Prince was enthusiastic over it, as were all of our pilots. I think the Prince met and became acquainted with not only all the pilots on the airdrome but all the mechanics as well. There was not a man there who would not have done anything in his power to make the stay of the Prince of Wales as pleasant as possible.

After several delightful days, the Prince decided to leave, just as I received the following telegram from our army headquarters:

Jan. 6, 1919.

Brigadier General Wm. Mitchell,
Hqrs, Third Army,
Koblenz.

T 10100 period The President of the French Republic has conferred the Legion of Honor upon you period You will report at these Headquarters January 13th for ceremony of presentation by Marshal Pétain on morning of January 14th period Acknowledge period

DAVIS 1520

This was to be the first presentation of the Legion of Honor to any Americans, except that to General Pershing. Eight of us were to receive the grade of Commander and ten or twelve others were to receive the grade of Officer and Chevalier.

At about the same time, I received notice that I had been asked for from the United States to return there to be Director of Military Aviation. Accordingly, I closed up my affairs on the Rhine and proceeded to Chaumont, where Marshal Pétain decorated us with the Legion of Honor. He also presented some of us with an additional war cross, the Croix de guerre, for duty performed against the enemy.

I decided to run up along the British front, then to Belgium to see what had happened there from the beginning of the war to its close, then to England where I would take ship for the United States. On this trip I took with me Colonel Milling, my old Chief of Staff and later the Commander of the First Army Air Service, and my two aides, Elmer Hazlett and Alan Winslow; also Captain Laurence W. Miller, my Equipment Officer, who had been with me during the whole war. He supervised and kept all the records and correspondence, and went directly from Paris to England. The rest of us started north from Paris in two automobiles, after saying good-bye to our friends there.

I not only looked up members of our own service but also made my *adieus* to those of other countries who had helped us. Old Mr. James Gorden Bennett was dead, but another patriarch, Mr. Deutsch de la Meurthe, was still there. He was one of the great benefactors of flying, from its beginning and even at his advanced age of more than eighty years. When I went to see him this time, there was a group of men at his house organizing a society for furthering the development of anything driven by an air propeller, whether boats on the water, dirigible airships, airplanes or helicopters.

We went on toward Brussels. The British army was rapidly withdrawing from its area. The cities that marked the old front in some places were nothing but masses of ruins, and, in the case of Ypres, could hardly be distinguished from the surrounding country. Although the destruction was greater in northern France, the depth of the destroyed area did not extend more than twenty or thirty miles in most places. While in that area everything was level with the ground, still the total destruction does not compare with what occurred in our own country during the Civil War, when not only the area around the fighting armies was destroyed but very nearly the whole South was laid waste before the contest was ended.

I wondered how soon we should have to come back to Europe in arms again—never, I hope. It is not our place unless we intend to take charge of the destinies of the world, which at this time seems a little premature.

The great adventure was over and it remains for us to reap the benefits for our country, if this great world catastrophe is to leave any in its wake. I feel that I have done my duty to my country in every way possible, physically or mentally. I am proud of what has been accomplished, what my men have done and above all, proud to be an American citizen. We have the greatest country on this planet and it rests with us, who have fought its battles, who are familiar with the other countries of the world and who know what lies ahead of us, to keep it so.

Brigadier-General William "Billy" Mitchell was born of American parents in 1879 at Nice, France. When he was eighteen he joined the United States Army and served as a private during the Spanish-American War. Later he went to the Philippines, where he saw action fighting Aguinaldo's insurgents. In 1901, as a first lieutenant, Mitchell went to Alaska, where he was instrumental in setting up a primitive telegraph system. Later he went to San Francisco to help restore communications after the great fire.

By 1909 Captain Mitchell's interest in new ideas and activities had already set him apart from the regular Signal Corps officer. He asked leave to go to the Far East and make a thorough study of the area, which he did. Upon his return, he was appointed to the General Staff of the army, a remarkable honor for an officer only thirty-two years of age.

As a General Staff officer, Mitchell had the opportunity to study intelligence reports from all over the world. As he saw what other countries were doing with aviation his own interest began to grow, and in 1916 he learned how to fly. Six months later he went overseas to study first-hand the Great War. When America entered the conflict, he was already on the scene, and the story he tells in his *Memoirs* leaves no doubt as to his energies or abilities.

After the war, General Mitchell devoted his full time to advancing the then controversial idea of air power. In 1921 he proved that his bombers could sink a battleship, much to the discomfort of the navy. Of course, much of what he said and did met with angry opposition. When, in 1925, the dirigible *Shenandoah* was lost in a storm, he could contain himself no longer and accused the navy and war departments of "criminal negligence and almost treasonable administration."

For his outspoken actions, Billy Mitchell was court-martialed, demoted and taken off active duty for a year. He resigned rather than remain inactive in the service. He died in 1936.